Too Soon to Tell

Press Operating Committee

IEEE Computer Society Publications

The world-renowned IEEE Computer Society publishes, promotes, and distributes a wide variety of authoritative computer science and engineering texts. These books are available from most retail outlets. Visit the CS Store at *http://computer.org/cspress* for a list of products.

IEEE Computer Society / Wiley Partnership

The IEEE Computer Society and Wiley partnership allows the CS Press authored book program to produce a number of exciting new titles in areas of computer science, computing and networking with a special focus on software engineering. IEEE Computer Society members continue to receive a 15% discount on these titles when purchased through Wiley or at wiley.com/ieeecs

To submit questions about the program or send proposals please e-mail kguillemette@computer.org or write to Books, IEEE Computer Society, 10662 Los Vaqueros Circle, Los Alamitos, CA 90720-1314. Telephone +1-714-816-2169.

Additional information regarding the Computer Society authored book program can also be accessed from our web site at *http://computer.org/cspress*.

Too Soon to Tell

Essays for the End of the Computer Revolution

David Alan Grier

WILEY

A John Wiley & Sons, Inc., Publication

Published by John Wiley & Sons, Inc., Hoboken, New Jersey.
Published simultaneously in Canada.

For general information on our other products and services or for technical support, please contact our
Customer Care Department within the United States at (800) 762-2974, outside the United States at
(317) 572-3993 or fax (317) 572-4002.

Wiley also publishes its books in a variety of electronic formats. Some content that appears in print
may not be available in electronic formats. For more information about Wiley products, visit our web
site at www.wiley.com.

Library of Congress Cataloging-in-Publication Data is available.

ISBN: 978-0-470-08035-1

Printed in the United States of America.

10 9 8 7 6 5 4 3 2 1

This is a book for Dad

and if it is for him, it is also for Mom,

for Dad could not have played his role without her
just as I could not have written these words
without Jean
to whom this work is truly dedicated.

Contents

Preface

To Have Been Young in that Hour

REVOLUTIONS ALWAYS END WITH A PRESS STATEMENT. They may have started with slogans and protests and rioters in the street but they end with a single piece of paper that is marked "For Immediate Release." The words vary from case to case. Sometimes they suggest heroic action by selfless revolutionaries. Sometimes they state quietly but powerfully that order is restored and that the citizenry can return to their normal activities. In more than a few situations, they conceal with twisted and awkward prose the fact that the revolutionaries are not fully in control.

The computer revolution began in the heat of a global war, when the world's industrialized nations were devoting their energy and treasure to the manufacture of weaponry to be used against each other. In that hour, a small cadre of engineers and mathematicians tried to exploit the benefits of industrialized computation, of using machinery to do error-free calculation, hour after hour. Their new weapons demanded such computations. They needed numbers to aim guns, to navigate aircraft, to spy on the enemy over the horizon, and to warn friends of danger.

Until the last year of the war, the computer revolutionaries lived and worked in isolated clusters and were only vaguely aware of each other's existence. Their numbers included a lone German inventor who was toiling in isolation beyond the western front, an irascible physics professor who had an epiphany in an Illinois bar, the corporate researcher who built a test machine on his kitchen table, a staff of code breakers working on the grounds of an English estate, the young professor at a woman's college who joined the effort when she was called to war, and the committee of five which caught a vision in a moment and then forever squabbled over who had seen it first.

The partisans of automatic calculation—the term "computer" had yet to be applied to the new machines—held their first conclave in the months that followed the cessation of hostilities. They gathered in the city of Cambridge, Massachusetts, to share their experiences, talk of battles won and lost, and to prepare for the future. "During the recent war there was tremendous development of certain types of computing devices," recorded one member of this group. "Electronic devices have been constructed or are under development, which promise astronomical speeds for numerical processes."

Beyond a small cadre of workers, few people were moved by the prospect of "astronomical speed" and fewer still by "numerical processes." If the promise of their work was to be fulfilled, these few would need to convince others of the benefits that might be found in automatic calculation. In the months to come, their movement would need to recruit more leaders, more laborers, offices, and laboratories. They would have to find funds to support their work and institutions to decide how those funds should be spent.

At best, those early computer revolutionaries had only a few resources beyond their grand vision for electronic computation. National governments had funded the technology during the conflict, but with the end of the war, they were reducing their support for research and development. Yet, from this position, the revolutionaries would create a movement that would march around the world in six decades. Its progress was not always uniform, but its true setbacks were few. One generation of leaders passed away only to be replaced by another, fortunes rose and fell, new ideas were embraced in one season only to be cast away in the next. So the story ran until the computer had found its way into every corner of modern life and had left nothing new under the sun.

No revolution likes to admit that its days are past, that its influence is waning. The aged Bolsheviks cling to the notion that they are important to the world and that their ideas are relevant to the state of the world even when they are presented with evidence to the contrary. They emphasize the work that remains to be done even as they place the original revolutionaries in the little niches of the movement's pantheon. Yet, from time to time, some branch of the revolution will release a notice to the press with a confession that the days of glory are past.

Such an announcement can be found in the summer of 2005, the year before the computer industry was preparing to celebrate the 60th anniversary of their revolution. In that summer, a small trade association, one of minor consequence in this digital age, quietly reprinted a press release, stating that the residents of the earth possessed 820 million operating personal computers and that that number was "projected to top 1 billion in 2007."

With this simple announcement, the computer revolution came to an end. A technology that is in the hands of one out of every seven residents of the planet can no longer be considered new, or novel, or revolutionary. Personal computers have permeated almost every aspect of modern life. They are used to monitor, control, and govern much of the world's economic and social activity. In six short decades, they have fulfilled the hopes of those men and women who met after the second world war to plot the path of their revolution.

IN THAT FALL OF 1945, the world could claim no more than twelve operational computers, though few of these would meet the modern definition that includes a processor, memory, and stored program of instructions. The largest concentration of these machines was to be found on the eastern shore of the United States, but examples could also be found in England and even in Germany. The number of revolutionaries was also small. Perhaps a hundred people could claim to have worked with one of the new calculators. They were found not in the streets and garrets of the country but in the centers of political, economic, and educational power. Military centers. Ivy League laboratories. Wall Street offices.

Beyond those few technological centers could be found the men and women who would bring life to the computer revolution. The engineer in Burma. The philosopher in Brussels. The clerk in London. They would design the first commercial machines, expand the market for computers, write the first large-scale programs.

Among that group of future revolutionaries was my father, Thomas Stewart Grier, who was serving as a map clerk for the armies that had landed at Normandy and marched across France. Like most of the soldiers in Europe and the Pacific theatres, he was looking towards the future but he wanted no radical change in society. In common with so many in the war, he had witnessed the hardships of the Great Depression and the violence of the war. He wanted nothing more than a time of peace, a good job, and a quiet place to raise a family. He had an engineering degree to finish and he hoped that he might find a place in the field that had inspired him to pursue a technical career: the aircraft industry.

A decade would pass before my father stood in an aircraft factory and when that day came, the factory no longer made airplanes. Located in St. Paul, Minnesota, it held the offices of the Univac division of the Sperry Rand Corporation, one of the early computer manufacturers. Dad entered that building with seventeen other new Univac employees. Most were veterans of the war. One was a woman. All were pleased with their prospects.

Dad had learned about computers slowly. "I read about computers in the newspaper," he used to say. "Sometime after the war, I learned about a machine that some people called an 'electronic brain,' and I thought that it might be a good tool for business." He eventually became intrigued with the idea of working in a new industry, a field that was still not fully developed. Drawing on his childhood in the American West, he would occasionally compare the state of the early computer industry to the experience of the first pioneers to Colorado, Nebraska and Wyoming. "It was a new frontier," he said, "and I thought it might have a place for me."

The frontier, the idea of beginning one's life again in a new place, exerts a strong influence over the American imagination. "American social development has been continually beginning over again on the frontier," wrote the historian Frederick Jackson Turner. This "fluidity of American life," he observed, "this expansion westward—with its few opportunities, its continuous touch with the simplicity of primitive society, furnish the forces dominating American character."

In common with his ancestors who had moved to Wyoming, Dad wanted to join the computer industry in order to find new opportunity. At the time, no one quite knew how these machines could be used in businesses, in government offices, in schools, or in the home. But just as the settlers of the West had adapted existing civic and business institutions to the new area, the pioneers of the computer age would also rebuild institutions to take advantage of the new technology. Business would have to become more flexible, governments more far reaching, schools more comprehensive.

My father not only found a place in the computer industry but he was one of those dedicated workers who helped bring that technology to the world. At the time of his retirement, the tools of electronic computation were barely four decades old. My father, and those who served with him, could look back on steady and sustained accomplishments but most of them sensed that the community that they had created, the early community that surrounded the computer, had become fragile and was in danger of slipping away. They lived in the culture of the mainframe, the central system that was attended by a technical staff. They were about to enter the world of the personal computer. The more insightful among them saw another change in the gloaming light, the rise of high-speed digital communications.

In retirement, he watched the expansion of Silicon Valley, the growth of the industry in East Asia, and the rise of the small personal computers. From time to time, he would claim that the new computers were not the same as the ones that he had helped develop, especially when he was having trouble with the software that he was using to edit pictures of his grandsons, but he always felt that the entrepreneurs of the 1990s were merely relearning the lessons that he and his peers had learned. "There is nothing new under the sun," wrote the prophet. "Is there any thing whereof it may be said, See, this is new?"

The computer has been new to each generation that has encountered it. Year after year, young men and women attend training classes to learn the nature of this technology. They discover that the idea of the stored program can be patently simple and maddeningly complex, that the computer can be highly flexible at one moment and rigid at the next, and that a computer firm can be profitable in one quarter and vanish at the end of the fiscal year. These experiences do not always take the form of those encountered by that original group of revolutionaries but they often follow the patterns established by that generation. These patterns, once radical and new, have been reproduced, with some modifications, by the minicomputer generation of the 1970s, the personal computer users of the 1980s, and the Internet pioneers of the 1990s. Each decade has brought its own contributions to the digital age and each has had to build upon the years that preceded it.

"The wind whirleth about continually, and returneth again according to his circuits." Now that the cycles of revolution have brought nearly a billion personal computers upon this earth, it is perhaps time to acknowledge that these machines are no longer new and bold but have become part of the common cycles of life. It is time to offer the final statement of the revolutionaries to the public press.

This book is a collection of essays about the computer age that began in that fall of 1945. It takes its title from the old joke about the discussion between two radicals in those years that following 1945, the period that began the Cold War. One of them asks the other "What do you think will be the impact of the French Revolution, an event that occurred nearly 200 years before, on world history?" "It is too soon to tell," replies the other.

— — — — — — — — — —

This book is an effort to gauge the impact of a revolution that is "too soon to tell," too recent to give us enough perspective. Its purpose is not to give a history of the computer revolution that occurred over the past sixty years. Others have written comprehensive works on the development of computing technology and the comput-ing industry. Instead, this book is an attempt to explore the human patterns that the last half of the twentieth century bestowed upon us. Though the essays seem to cycle through the period in a chronological manner, they are actually looking at ideas that are both contemporary and timeless. They attempt to understand the relation between machines and human institutions, the connections between fathers and sons, the impact of rapid technological change upon one family, and the revolutionary nature of the computer—a technology that has tried to spin the world around a new axis.

The Computer Era (1946–1973)

The desire to economize time and mental effort in arithmetical computation, and to eliminate human liability in error, is probably as old as the science of arithmetic itself.

Aiken and Hopper, 1946

Out of Position

ON FEBRUARY 16, 1946, my father was caught out of position, unaware of the event that would define his career. On that day, the United States Army held a press conference to announce that it had built an electronic computing machine called the ENIAC. "One of the war's top secrets," reported the *New York Times* is "an amazing machine which applied electronic speeds for the first time to mathematical tasks too difficult and cumbersome for solution."

The ENIAC was the largest of the major computing machines that had been built during the war and was the foundation stone on which the computer age was built. The ENIAC was not a computer, as we now use the term. It did not have the basic elements we find in a modern computer and, originally, it could not be programmed electronically. However, by building the ENIAC, the University of Pennsylvania engineers grasped the design for the modern computer and recognized the importance of that design. "The old era is going," wrote the senior engineer, "the new one of electronic speed is on the way, when we can begin all over again to tackle scientific problems with new understanding."

Dad was in the Army at the time but far from the University of Pennsylvania. He was in southern France, serving as a teaching assistant at Biarritz American University, a temporary college established by the military. Had he begun his service with his high school friends, he would have been back in the United States. He would have served with Patton in the desert or fought at Anzio or landed at Omaha Beach with Eisenhower. However, he had been a late addition to the war, having been drafted in the middle of the fall term of 1943, and did not have the combat experience that would give him a berth on the first troop ships to leave France for New York.

Dad was part of the Western brain drain, one of the young men from western states who saw opportunity in education and prosperity in the large cites of the Atlantic and Pacific coasts. During the 1930s and 1940s, the high school graduates of Carey, Idaho; Great Bend, Kansas; Burlington, Iowa; and Huron, South Dakota, took leave of their birthplaces, took engineering degrees at the Midwest universities, and then went in search of jobs in Philadelphia or New Jersey or Boston or San Francisco.

Too Soon to Tell: Essays for the End of the Computer Revolution, by David Alan Grier
Copyright © 2009 IEEE Computer Society

He had been raised in Cheyenne, the first son of a lumberyard owner and retired school teacher. Their home sat under the glide path of the city airport, which was then a refueling and repair stop for United Airlines. Fascinated by the flying machines that passed overhead, Dad had learned to build model planes, fragile constructions of paper and wood that were powered by miniature gasoline engines. He hoped to be a pilot, the romantic male figure of the 1930s, or at least a designer of aircraft.

He had graduated from high school during the first year of the European war. His father, who spent a weekend each month as a cavalry officer in the Wyoming National Guard, had already been called into service. My Dad, however, was destined to study aeronautical engineering at the school where his mother had taken a degree, the University of Michigan. The university went into an accelerated war schedule shortly after his arrival, pushing the young men through their course work as fast as they could. Dad remained in school through the middle of his junior year. "We were all waiting for the call," he would say. "I received the news right after a midterm exam in thermodynamics."

Dad began boot camp in January 1944. He thought that he might become a navigator or some other member of an aircraft crew but his eyeglasses kept him away from airplanes. After three weeks of Basic Training, he was assigned to the Engineering Corps and ordered to repeat the experience with a new unit. His departure was further delayed by a final five-day leave, which allowed him to see his father, who was commanding a prisoner of war camp in Alabama, and his brother, who was a sniper in the infantry.

When he arrived in Europe, Dad was assigned to the staff of a mobile map depot. He spent the winter and spring of 1945 following the D-Day armies as they marched through Europe, delivering maps to the commanders on the front lines. The work was risky but it was not sufficiently dangerous to gain him an early return after the German surrender. My grandfather tried to hasten Dad's release from the Army, citing his own six years of service and the death of Dad's brother in the final weeks of the conflict. These claims carried no weight, as such hardships had been shared by many.

Anticipating that he would remain in Europe for at least a year, Dad applied to Biarritz American University. The school promised to combine the advantages of a French beachfront resort with the resources of an American college town. Only collegiate football would be missing. The town hall served as a library for a collection of books from American universities. Local buildings were commandeered for classrooms. Teachers came from the United States to teach courses that ranged from theatrical literature to advanced physics.

When he arrived at Biarritz in August 1945, Dad was assigned to a room in the Hotel de la Maison, which had a view of the ocean. His roommate, who came from the same army unit, labeled Dad as was one of the "studious types," because he enrolled in the analytic geometry course that fall. Studious or not, he had a grand time at Biarritz, a time that pushed aside the horror and sadness of the prior two years. With the other students, he spent his mornings by the ocean and his evenings in town. With a pair of binoculars that he had scavenged from the retreating German army, he and his buddies would scan the beach for women. On weekends, they would commandeer a jeep and travel into the Basque country.

"They are probably the most contented G.I.s in Europe," wrote the novelist John Dos Passos, who visited the school that fall. The professors were drawn from American universities, the secretaries were "British girls," the waiters were French civilians, and "the janitors [were] German prisoners of war." The American scientific societies kept careful watch on the curriculum to make sure that course credits would transfer to schools in the United States. The Mathematical Association of America generally approved the courses in its domain, but complained about "a disconcerting tendency" for the soldier-students "to prefer refresher courses" rather than the advanced seminars.

In November, after completing his analytic geometry course, Dad was offered the chance to remain at Biarritz. Only 80 men were given this opportunity. The rest were rotated back to their units or, in many cases, sent home. During this second term, Dad served as the teaching assistant for Thermodynamics, the course that he had been forced to abandon two years before in Ann Arbor. When he was given the chance to remain for a third term, he again accepted the offer, even though it might delay his return to the United States. He left Biarritz only when the university closed its doors in March.

Dad's decision to extend his time in France may have been one of those stars on which the fate of men is hung. However, such things are hard to verify. Had he chosen to return in January he might have seen a clear path to his original career in aeronautical engineering. By the spring of 1946, no path was obvious. He had fallen behind the mass of veterans who were re-entering civilian life. "It was clear that the airplane industry was contracting," he remembered, "and that there would be few new jobs for aeronautical engineers in the immediate future." As he shed one dream from his childhood, he reached for another. The boy who had once built airplanes from wood and tissue had also played in the front office of his father's lumberyard. After finishing his engineering degree, Dad enrolled in business school and completed an MBA with a concentration in accounting.

"By the time that I graduated from business school in 1948, I had heard about the ENIAC and had read articles in the business press about computers," he recalled, "but I didn't know of any jobs with computers." By then, returning soldiers had flooded the job market, making good jobs scarce. My grandfather urged him to return to Cheyenne and help run the family business, but small town Wyoming had little appeal to the man who had delivered maps to the commanders in Germany and had studied on a beach in France. After a summer's search, Dad found a job in Chicago. He would manage petroleum production for Pure Oil, a company that owned the mineral rights to the oil fields of southern Illinois and Indiana. He was not in the kind of position that he had envisioned when he had left Cheyenne, but he was not badly situated and he was free to move to any career that might appear more promising.

Seymour Cray's Cat

THE PHOTOGRAPH, EVEN THOUGH IT LONG AGO FADED to that aqua tint of 1950s snapshots, is far more vivid than any memory I have of St. Paul. The picture captures me as a toddler. I am wearing a north country snowsuit and holding a large gray cat. I am clearly enjoying myself. The same cannot be said for the cat, though she does seem to be a patient animal. For most of my life, this picture was nothing more than a record of our brief time in Minnesota. Then, one day, Dad mentioned that "the cat once belonged to Seymour Cray."

Cray was the most famous resident of the "Glider Factory," the former aircraft plant that served as offices first for Engineering Research Associates and later for the Univac division of the Sperry Rand Corporation. He had been identified as a highly talented engineer at both organizations. For Univac, he had worked on the 1103, the company's scientific machine. In the years to come, he would establish three more companies, two of which would bear his name.

Dad was offered a job in the Glider Factory in the fall of 1957. When he arrived in St. Paul, he knew little about computer engineering and less about computer software but he understood the oil industry, a business that the company had identified as a promising market. In particular, he was familiar with a new management tool, which was starting to spread through the industry, a tool called linear programming.

Linear programming, like electronic computers, was a technology that matured in the last months of the Second World War. It had been developed by the Army Air Corps as a means to help manage the deployment of aircraft with all of their spare parts, fuel, ammunition, and personnel. In studying these problems, researchers found that they were similar, in a mathematical sense, to an example that had been described in the economics literature, an example that was known as "the diet problem." The goal of the diet problem was to identify the least expensive meal that provides a minimum number of calories and fulfills certain other nutritional standards. In its canonical form, it considered 88 different foods, starting with beefsteak and ending with strawberry shortcake. Each of these foods had its own set of nutrients and each had its own cost.

The Army Air Corps developed several incomplete solutions to the linear programming problem before they found a practical way to approach the issue. This

Too Soon to Tell: Essays for the End of the Computer Revolution, by David Alan Grier
Copyright © 2009 IEEE Computer Society

final solution, called the simplex method, was created by George Dantzig, a recent mathematics graduate from the University of California. Dantzig's solution was clever but computationally intensive. Right after the war Dantzig had attempted to solve the diet problem with the aid of twenty-five clerks. These clerks had required four weeks to do their calculations. According to the computer designer John von Neumann, who reviewed Danzig's work, linear programming, the ENIAC could have solved the problem in slightly less than an hour.

von Neumann, who had worked both on the ENIAC and the Manhattan Project, actively promoted linear programming to American industry. He argued that it could not only solve operational problems for the Air Force, but could also be used to address similar issues for manufacturers. Companies could use it to minimize the cost of raw materials or the cost of warehousing. The petroleum industry had taken an early interest in the method. In the fall of 1953, Esso Petroleum had asked von Neumann to apply linear programming to a standard refining problem. "The problem as set up for solution at this time," they explained, "involves the blending of fourteen components into finished Esso and Esso Extra grades in order to maximize the gross refinery [production]."

At this point in his career, von Neumann was much in demand as an advisor to the government. He offered advice on the design of atomic weapons, the construction of electronic computers, and the development of military strategy. On a few occasions, he would work for private firms that could pay hefty consulting fees. "He only went to the major producers and refiners like Esso," Dad recalled, "He never visited a small company like Pure Oil."

After Dad arrived at the Glider Factory, he began to work on a computer code for the Univac that could do linear programming. He quickly started to make friends among the other employees but soon found that the company was divided into a pair of distinct camps. The first contained loyal Univac employees. The second consisted of a group of engineers who were planning to leave the company and form a new enterprise, Control Data Corporation. "It was all very secretive," Dad said. "If you walked into a clutch of employees when they were talking about Control Data, they would all go silent. To hide their plans, they held organizational meetings in bars that were located in some of the rougher parts of town."

When Control Data Corporation opened its doors later in the fall, many Univac employees resigned their jobs and moved to the new organization. Cray remained at the Glider Factory but only for a short period of time. He had promised Univac that he would not leave before he completed a contract that the company had made with the Navy. He finished that work in the early spring and departed as soon as it was over. "Many Univac people were looking to join Cray at CDC," Dad recalled, "but I had no choice. I had been in the computer business for less than 5 months. I had one small boy to feed and a second on the way. I could not take that risk."

Though he did not follow Seymour Cray, Dad did not long remain in St. Paul. The early years of the computer industry was a period of constant motion. Families shifted from one city to another and then back again with barely enough opportunity between the two moves to select a favorite restaurant or take responsibility for an overdue library book. "We came to St. Paul thinking that we would spend our life there," Dad said, "but we were gone before nine months had past." Univac assigned him to an office in Dallas, which was closer to the heart of the oil industry.

Dad was one of many people who moved through the Glider Factory during those years. Dozens of engineers, sales personnel, mathematicians, and managers spent a few months before transferring to another Univac facility or finding a job with some other company. These men and women saw the same sights and smelled the same smells but they had little or no contact with each other. In later years, some would meet and be surprised at their common heritage.

Because Dad and Cray shared only a few short months at the Glider Factory, they probably did not know each other. A novice employee would have had little opportunity to meet a senior engineer who had already announced his departure. It is entirely plausible that I had a closer connection to the great computer designer through my friendship with his cat.

But of course, the story of Seymour Cray's cat may be a myth, a snippet of a sky blue story faded to turquoise by the cycling years. Instead of being the Cray's pet, my favorite cat may have belonged to Cray's secretary, or to another Univac family, or to a kindly neighbor who took an interest in a curious toddler. At best, my friendship with this cat and my opportunity to be part of Cray's social circle was brief. Before a year had passed, I had abandoned my snowsuit and acquired a tiny cowboy hat with matching boots. The cat allegedly belonging to Seymour Cray had been forgotten and replaced with my newest best friends, a pair of bull terriers. It is plausible, I suppose, that these dogs belonged to H. Ross Perot or Jack Kilby or some other member of the Texas high technology community. To me, they were just dogs in the summer sun.

Songs of Comfort and Joy

CHRISTMAS IN TEXAS IS NOT WHITE LIKE WINTERS OF ST. PAUL but brown, the bleached dead grass that shines in the low-hanging sun of December. The days are short and the nights have cold fingers. The harvest is over, the summer is past, and the time of reckoning is at hand.

The staff of the Univac office in North Dallas did not quite know how to mark December in 1958. They were new to the region, refugees of northern cities that had staked their fortune to the computer industry. It was a new land for them, a place with strange foods and customs. It was a city far from family and friends. At times, it seemed to be a place far from God.

Their office, which was located on the campus of Southern Methodist University, was an experiment by Univac's parent company, Sperry Rand. Sperry had created the office in order to sell scientific computing services to the oil industry, services that that industry was not sure that it needed. The office's primary product was a refinery management service, which was based on the technology of linear programming. Univac claimed that this product would help oil executives maximize their profits of their refining operation. The oil company would provide a few key pieces of data, such as the stock of oil on hand and their refining capacity. With that information, the linear programming software would create a production plan based on the market prices. This plan would state how much gasoline should be produced, how much kerosene, how much light lubricant, and how much revenue.

The office had been operating for two years and had yet to show a profit. A few of the smaller refineries had tried the service and had generally been pleased with the results, but the large firms had stayed away. The production engineers of Esso may have rushed to meet with John von Neumann, but their counterparts in Dallas showed limited interest in the company's machine, a Univac 1103 that stood gleaming in its glass-encased computer room.

A few of the Univac staff had spent the summer at the company's Philadelphia offices learning new services that they might offer to the Texas business community. They learned about databases and general ledgers and accounts receivable. They returned to Dallas with a burst of energy but no real direction. Days with no customers stretched into weeks. Enthusiasm slid into frustration, which, in its turn, dropped into cynicism and collapsed into boredom.

Too Soon to Tell: Essays for the End of the Computer Revolution, by David Alan Grier
Copyright © 2009 IEEE Computer Society

The remedy for their restlessness was the Univac itself. When the computer was not being used by a customer, the technical staff was free to explore new ideas on the machine. They practiced their coding skills, experimented with new ways of sorting data, and tested different aspects of the device.

Perhaps the most intriguing feature of the machine was the audio output circuit. "Each computer console had a small amplifier and loudspeaker connected into a data path within the computer," explained one Univac engineer. This hardware had been added to the computer as a troubleshooting device. "When certain test programs were run to check the operation of the computer circuits, the loudspeaker would put out a distinctive series of tones."

The Dallas programmers were not the first to be attracted to the audio circuitry. An engineer at the Univac headquarters office in Philadelphia had created a program that would produce musical tones on the standard western scale. Dubbed the "Melody Maker" by its creator, this program had played a passable version of the Beer Barrel Polka for a Univac publicity event. Having read about this program, the Dallas programmers decided that they would create their own musical software, a program that would play Christmas carols.

The programming effort was led by John Kamena, a tall, quiet man who had been trained in mathematics. He did not know much about music. He enjoyed the big band tunes of his youth but the popular music heard in Dallas had little appeal to him. However, he loved to program and knew how to break complicated tasks into simple steps. After a day or two of experimentation, he created a little program that would generate sound at the pitch of middle C. It was "a beautiful rhythmic tone," wrote one observer, "not unlike an oboe."

Moving methodically through the problem, Kamena created a program that could produce all twelve notes in the standard musical scale and developed a simple scheme that would represent melodies by a series of numbers. His colleagues helped by translating piano music into code. First came "Jingle Bells," then "O Come All Ye Faithful," and finally, "O Holy Night." The music coming from the machine "sounds like and is Christmas carols," wrote a slightly astonished reporter for the *Dallas Times Herald.*

The reporter arrived on December 23 and was immediately smitten by what he saw. "Univac Scientific is the hit of the season at SMU," he wrote, "it plays Christmas carols." Kamena was both pleased and frustrated with the publicity. He was grateful that someone acknowledged the office's technical prowess but he also wanted to see the group succeed in its primary mission, the mission of providing scientific computing services. "Do you think you could, sort of, write something, too, about how Univac is generally used in education," he pleaded.

Kamena had great faith in digital technology. He knew that, each year, computers were getting smaller and less expensive, though perhaps he did not quite see the day when a machine far more powerful than his electronic oboe, the two-and-half-ton Univac, would be no bigger than a deck of cards. Yet he, like so many others of his time, saw the future of the computer in serious problems: in scientific work and in business data processing. Entertainment computing was too frivolous, too risky. To build a machine that would entertain people, one would have to solve not only technical problems but also adapt that technology to a complicated business, one that had to follow changes in public taste, offer innovative products, and yet minimize the uncertainties of the market.

THE MARKET OF 1958 WAS NOT READY FOR THE INNOVATIONS of digital music. The newest music technologies were two different formats of phonograph records. Both had been created a decade before as possible replacement to the old shellac 78 rpm records. Most audiophiles felt that the most promising technology was the 12-inch "Long Playing" (LP) record that had been introduced by Columbia Records in 1948. This disk could hold almost an hour of music, eight to ten times the capacity of the 78's. By the mid-1950s, this format was the preferred form of the New York record companies. The three best-selling LPs of December 1958 were all soundtracks of musicals that were playing on Broadway: *South Pacific, The Music Man*, and *Gigi*.

The competing technology was, of course, the 7-inch 45-rpm record of RCA, the "45" or the "single." It had been patented in 1949, the year after Columbia had patented its disk, and it had roughly the same capacity as the old 78, three minutes of music per side. Because 7-inch records were cheaper to produce than the 12-inch LPs, the RCA 45 was the preferred technology of the small regional record companies: Sun Records of Memphis, Chess of Chicago, and Motown of Detroit, a company that would release its first records in January of the new year. The 45 captured the 1958 classics of rock 'n roll, Jerry Lee Lewis' "Great Balls of Fire" and Chuck Berry's "Johnny B. Goode," as well as the unfortunate curiosities of the year: Bobby Darin's "Splish Splash" and David Seville's "Chipmunk Song."

Long before 1958, the music business could be divided into three major sectors: production, marketing, and retailing. Music production was handled by the record companies. The United States had three major record companies in New York (Columbia, Decca, and Victor), one in Los Angeles (Capitol), and a growing number of small regional companies like Sun, Chess, Stax and Motown. The retailing sector was in the hands of local merchants: department stores, appliance stores, and a new class of retail outlet, the record store. Music marketing was done by radio stations, which had evolved into a number of different formats, each promoting a different kind of music: classical, adult, country, R&B, and the new top 40.

If those Dallas programmers had decided that their future lay in the music business, they would have discovered that the path to commercial success was no more obvious than their own plans for the computer industry. Over the next two decades, music companies struggled to identify the technologies that promised the best fidelity, the greatest control, and the widest portability. Sometimes they chose well and sometimes they chose badly. Cassette tapes succeeded where eight-track cartridges floundered. Quadraphonic sound stalled but the compact digital disc replaced the LP.

While the music business was adopting these technologies, it was also developing strategies to stay abreast of public opinion while doing the things that good businesses have to do: expand markets, limit production expenses, and reduce the costs of distribution and inventory. The 1970s and 1980s saw a steady conglomeration in all three sectors of the music business. Music labels were combined into single gigantic firms. Radio stations were purchased by national networks. Family-owned record stores were supplanted by large chain stories. By the early 1990s, the music business had little room for a small, regional business. Such a firm simply could not accumulate the capital to compete with the large companies. The child of the 1990s who expressed a desire to own a record store or perhaps a radio station was gently guided towards a more plausible career, such as ballet dancer, firefighter, or astronaut.

We should not be surprised that, in 1958, a small group of computer programmers could not see how they might transform their two million dollar computer into a viable music business. Such an idea was far beyond their vision. However, we should be surprised that, thirty years later, the music industry would resist the digital distribution of music, even though this technology would reduce three major classes of business expense: warehousing expense, shipping expense, and the expense of collecting consumer information.

The opportunity missed by the major players of the music industry is even more surprising when we recall that modern digital music technology was created in full view of them and the public. The now ubiquitous MP3 file format was created by a committee of the International Organization on Standards, the Moving Picture Expert Group, between 1987 and 1991. The Internet, then promoted under the name "Information Superhighway," was well established in public consciousness by 1992. The music industry even promoted the digital distribution of a 1994 Rolling Stones concert from the Dallas Cotton Bowl.

There are, of course, many reasons that businesses fail to capitalize on a business opportunity. Sometimes they fail to appreciate a new opportunity. Sometimes they are trying to protect existing capital investment and revenue streams. Sometimes they are faced with a conceptual problem that they cannot solve. All three seem to have played a role in the music industry during the 1990s. The early attempts to distribute music on the Internet, those that began between 1992 and 1995, were generally limited to small groups of individuals. At the same time, the major record labels were making a substantial profit from their investment in compact disc technologies. Finally, none of the companies had a workable proposal for protecting their products and limiting unauthorized distribution of recorded music.

When the record companies did not embrace the digital distribution of music over the network, others took their place. By 1998, so many people were illicitly sharing music that compact disc sales were starting to fall. A year later, the practice of file sharing was institutionalized by Napster software. By the time that the record companies and recording artists reacted to these changes, they were too late. Large parts of their popular music catalog were in free circulation on the Internet, a circulation that materially damaged the music's value.

After a slow start, the major players in the popular music have moved forcefully to protect their assets. They shut down Napster and its variants, moved to limit open music sharing among a prime market segment—American college students—and created their own network outlets. Their story is a brutal reminder that entire industries can fail to see shifts in the market.

IN THAT DISTANT DECEMBER OF 1958, the small staff of that Dallas Univac office was torn between the hope that they cherished for their young industry and the concerns that they felt about the business prospects of the market for the scientific computing. Daily, they saw evidence that Sperry had misread the market for computing services. The office had a few regular customers. Perhaps the most loyal was an elderly oil baron, who came to the building once a week with his data in a brown leather folder and sat patiently until the computer had completed his production plan. Such business was not enough to keep their office open. A few of the staff were quietly looking at other job possibilities. John Kamena was preparing to leave the field of scientific computation and take a data processing position in San Francisco.

On December 24, they ended the day with a party that gathered around a small Christmas tree in the machine room. The *Dallas Times Herald* article was passed from hand to hand as the Univac played its full repertoire of carols. As they listened to the machine play the songs, the staff added their voices to the chorus. In that dark night, they stood on Jordan's distant shore and sang songs from their hearts. They sang for themselves and they sang for their business; they sang for their women at home and their babies tucked safely in bed. They sang, blissfully unaware that scientific computing would soon be reduced to a tiny fraction of the market and that eventually, less than fifty years from 1958, the best-selling consumer computer would do nothing but play music. That night they sang with pride in their hearts and the hope that they might have a better year. They sang into the dark the songs of comfort and joy. That night, they sang songs of comfort and joy.

Life on the Frontier

DAD HAD A SAFETY NET, the offer from my grandfather to return home and run the family business. Grandfather had gone through some difficult times after the Second World War. He had returned from his service to discover that his partner, who actually owned the majority stake in the business called Grier Lumber, was forcing him out of the company. After a couple months of searching for a new opportunity, he had purchased an old mercantile store at 16th and Capital, a retail establishment that offered the community household goods, furniture, and the services of an undertaker.

When Grandfather announced that he was purchasing a store, my grandmother asked him "What do you know about furniture or undertaking?"

"Nothing," was my grandfather's reply, "but I know something about business and I know how I can learn."

Unlike my grandmother, who had a bachelor's degree in Latin from the University of Michigan, Grandfather had never gone to college. In common with other men of his generation, he had learned the lessons of business through a series of apprenticeships, lower level jobs that had given him the opportunity to observe the art of commerce. This education had allowed him to rise, step by step, through the ranks of local businessmen and had allowed him to manage a successful retail lumber business.

Grandfather had learned some of his most valuable lessons by serving in the Wyoming National Guard. The guard was a cavalry unit, complete with horses, feed wagons, ammunition trains, and weapons depots. Each summer, the unit would assemble for two weeks of drill in some corner of the state. Working with the other officers, Grandfather would practice managing the large, and often ungainly, organization in a mock attack on an unnamed invasion force.

Through the 1930s, the Wyoming Guard had met once a month to drill the members' horses, practice a few maneuvers, and play a chukker or two of polo. In September of 1939, with war starting in Europe, the unit was called into active service. In quick succession, the senior officers resigned their commissions. One had a farm and could not answer the call. Another had an ailing wife. When the resignations ended, Grandfather found himself in command of the entire Guard.

Too Soon to Tell: Essays for the End of the Computer Revolution, by David Alan Grier
Copyright © 2009 IEEE Computer Society

After a lengthy train trip to the West Coast, the unit was stripped of its horses and was given assignments that had been vacated by regular army officers: the management of recruitment centers, training camps, and relocation facilities. After the shooting began, Grandfather found himself running prisoner of war camps in the American South, organizations far bigger and far more complex than he would have ever seen in Cheyenne.

After the war, Grandfather retired from the Guard and established a new command in the coffee shop of the Hitching Post Hotel. The Hitching Post was in the center of Cheyenne and was the natural gathering point for the local business-men. The president of the local bank would come. So would the editor of the *Wyoming Eagle*, the owner of Western Ranchman Outfitters, and the manager of the Union Pacific rail yards. They would start arriving at 9:30 and spend an hour or so drinking coffee, swapping lies, complaining about the government, and discussing their businesses.

As individuals, all of the regulars at the Hitching Post had more skill than they could employ. They could invest only so much of their energy in Western Ranchman or the Cheyenne National Bank and Trust before the law of diminishing returns mocked their efforts. The economy of southern Wyoming was small and offered few rewards to those who wanted to expand their businesses beyond its natural boundaries. As a group, the Hitching Post regulars looked for opportunities to pool their labor and work for the good of all. The focus of their effort was a local festival, an annual rodeo held at the end of July.

The rodeo was both a means of expanding the regional economy and a way of strengthening the local business expertise. The organizing committee was far more complex and managed a far bigger budget than most of the local businesses. It dealt with suppliers from Nashville and Los Angeles and New York. It had a contract with the Ogallala Sioux Nation of South Dakota. It had to deal with the competing problems of demanding entertainers, bad weather, and runaway horses. The rodeo committee provided an education in business that was available in no other way to the residents of Cheyenne. "This is what you should expect," the experienced members would counsel. "This is how we handled it last year." "This is what we would like to have done."

IN THOSE FIRST DECADES THAT FOLLOWED THE END OF THE WAR, the computer industry was not that different from the retail economy of Cheyenne. The first generation of programmers found that it needed a coffee shop where they could meet to swap lies and a local festival that would develop expertise. The programmers of the IBM 704 were the first to create such a common forum. In August 1955, rep-resentatives of all seventeen 704 installations created an organization that they called SHARE. This group pledged "to coordinate activities in the initial programming of machine methods," to develop software standards, and, more importantly, to share code.

At first, SHARE was given a tepid response by the officers of IBM, who saw the new organization as a threat to their position in the computer market. A strong volunteer organization might be able to compete with some of the services offered by IBM. However, the firm soon came to appreciate that SHARE was a means of expanding the computer market by creating and disseminating expertise. By 1957, the company was supporting the organization financially and providing a central repository for programs created by SHARE members. Within two years, this repository was distributing a million cards of programs each month.

SHARE was an early example of what came to be known as a "user group." Such groups proliferated through the 1960s. RCA, Univac, General Electric, and Honeywell all developed user groups similar to SHARE. In 1962, Dad moved from Univac to Burroughs and took the job of organizing the Burroughs group, an organization called CUBE, for Cooperating Users of Burroughs Equipment. That spring, eighty-four members gathered in Los Angeles to form the group. Unlike the founders of SHARE, who all came from scientific laboratories, the first members of CUBE represented a fairly diverse collection of businesses: banks and utilities, manufacturers and universities.

For the members of CUBE, the big civic festival was not an annual rodeo but a conference held twice during the year, in April and October. The conference would include technical tutorials, classes on advanced programming techniques, a rousing speech by a Burroughs vice-president, and an entertainer who appealed to an audience of middle-aged male programmers (a Broadway singer, a standup comic, a mariachi band). "Without CUBE," Dad would say, "these men are nothing but isolated programmers with no colleagues and no way to improve their skills. With CUBE, they are part of a community that gives them an outlet for their expertise and teaches them new ideas."

IN 1962, GRANDFATHER WAS COMPLETING SIXTEEN YEARS of successful service on the Frontier Days rodeo committee. He had spent two terms as chair of the night show committee ("Less important than the chair of the day show," he would joke, "but more important than the governor."). During the same period, he had modernized his mercantile business by restricting it to a single line of goods, a strategy that was not obvious to many small town merchants of his generation. He had sold the undertaking services to a funeral home, removed the general household products from his inventory, and started buying furniture from the Chicago Trade Market rather from Denver suppliers. He advertised the business as "Grier Furniture: Wyoming's Finest Furniture Store," a claim that had not an ounce of immodesty for it was also the only such store in the state.

Museum Pieces

ON OCTOBER 3, 1963, life ended for the Univac I, the first commercial computer, the Philadelphia cousin to the Univac 1103. The machine had been built by the leaders of the ENIAC team, J. Presper Eckert and John Mauchly, who had worked under the guidance of the National Bureau of Standards. It had been installed with much fanfare at the Bureau of the Census. Twelve years later, the machine was still operational but it could no longer keep pace with the new computers. Furthermore, it was scarred and tired. The control console, which had been built on a steel office desk, was worn and scratched. Cables were frayed and tubes dusty. All of the pieces were carefully packed into crates and shipped to the storage warehouse of the Smithsonian Institution.

"We do not think that when things come to the Smithsonian they are retiring," said the Institution's secretary when he announced the acquisition of the Univac. "We feel that they are starting a new career of usefulness." Yet, the Univac would never operate again. It was being moved into the mausoleum for innovative technology, the last resting place for the pioneering computers. Its warehouse already held the ENIAC, which had ceased operating in October 1955. The original twenty-eight boxes of the ENIAC filled a substantial corner of the building. Only a few of the original circuits had been lost to grave robbers.

From the day of its announcement in February 1946, the ENIAC had a strong claim on a place in the Smithsonian collection. It had been created during a popular war and captured the war's contribution to electronic engineering. Furthermore, it had done a decade of service in the central conflict of the twentieth century, the Cold War. Ten months after its Philadelphia debut, the machine had been disassembled and shipped to the Army's Aberdeen Ground in Maryland.

Shortly after its arrival at Aberdeen, the ENIAC was modified to make it programmable. The ENIAC programs fell far short of the modern program, but they were a substantial improvement over the original methods of controlling the machine. The "ENIAC was neither fish nor fowl," wrote two historians of the device. It was more than a simple adding machine but it was not quite a modern computer.

The revised ENIAC was almost continuously employed on weapons research. The work paused only for the short time required to install a second programming unit in 1948 and a new memory unit in 1953. The ENIAC was still doing production

Too Soon to Tell: Essays for the End of the Computer Revolution, by David Alan Grier
Copyright © 2009 IEEE Computer Society

work during its last weeks of life. Newer computers were far faster but the ENIAC was an old familiar friend to the researchers, a machine that still seemed naturally suited to ballistics work.

Three years after the ENIAC's demise, the Smithsonian accepted the remains of the computer that John von Neumann had built at the Institute for Advanced Study. They acquired the von Neumann machine for intellectual reasons, rather than for any service it may have offered to the United States. This machine was the model for a generation of computers, calculators that would be identified as "von Neumann machines." It had a programmable control unit, an arithmetic processor, and a memory unit. Its design had been copied by nearly a dozen different institutions. Researchers had visited the institute to see the original von Neumann machine, see it operate, and feel the heat of its vacuum tubes.

Compared to the ENIAC, von Neumann's machine was "quite small by the standards of the day." It occupied a single box, six feet long, eight feet tall, and two feet deep. While the ENIAC needed 18,000 tubes, von Neumann's machine had only 2,300. At the same time, the von Neumann machine could store far more numbers in its memory. The ENIAC could only manipulate twenty-two numbers. The von Neumann machine was capable of storing a little more than a thousand. The memory units looked like a row of twenty-four-ounce tin cans, jutting from one side of the machine.

The acquisition of the von Neumann computer was done in haste. The machine arrived at the Smithsonian warehouse with tubes broken and wires cut, even though the device had been fully operational only a few weeks before. It had been abandoned by the Institute for Advanced Studies following the death of von Neumann. The institute leadership had never felt that computer development was compatible with the organization's mandate. They ultimately converted the original machine development laboratory into a child care center.

Unlike von Neumann's computer or the ENIAC, the Univac I was a business machine. It had done no service in either the Second World War or the Cold War. Over its lifetime, the Univac had compiled statistics and sorted data. Its circuits were entirely unfamiliar with the mathematics of ballistics and the questions of weapons research.

Compared to its predecessors, the Univac I had been programmed by a relatively large number of individuals. Sperry had built forty-six copies of the Univac I and had installed them in government offices, private corporations, and three universities. When the console was placed on display, it attracted visitors who were thoroughly familiar with each button and knew the meaning of each warning light.

As the Smithsonian expanded its computer collection, it increased the number of people who had had direct contact with the historical artifacts. Dad never liked this aspect of the Smithsonian collection. "My career should not be placed in a museum until I've retired," he would say. Yet, by 1963, museums were the only place where many of the early entrants into the business could be found. Bendix, Raytheon, and ElectroData no longer had a place in the market. The surviving companies, including Univac, IBM, and even Burroughs itself, no more resembled the companies of 1946 than contemporary computers resembled the museum pieces of that era.

The Curve of Innovation

IT WAS A HOT DAY IN EARLY AUGUST. The large computer lab at our university had just re-opened after a six-week interlude that had allowed the staff to upgrade equipment. The old black processor towers had been replaced with small silver boxes. Instead of the bulky cathode ray tube displays, the tables were covered with light, slim flat panels. Standing in the midst of this equipment, I was attempting to explain the operation of the lab to a gaggle of new students. I had been hoping to demonstrate a new interactive wall display to the group but had been unable to get a key program to work. Never one to let to let a malfunctioning technology get in the way of a good presentation, a lesson that I had learned from my father, I was plugging ahead and trying to describe in words the things that I could not demonstrate in bits.

Standing at the back of the room was a senior undergraduate, her arms folded patiently across her chest. As I launched into the main channel of my speech, she walked quietly to the front. Leaning over the computer, she began to poke away at the keyboard. I couldn't see all that she did, as I had to focus on my audience, but I was able to catch sustained spurts of action followed by moments of contemplation. In a few minutes, she had stopped the system, downloaded a file, reconfigured the machine and brought the wall display to life in all its glory. As she started to move towards her position in the back, she flashed a quiet smile of confidence. "She has reached that brief moment of life," I thought, "when she is master of her world and believes that following the next release of software, she will be master still."

It was a moment to appreciate innocence, a moment to be grateful for someone who had not experienced the curve of innovation that has marked the world of the computer. We find that curve anytime a new product is announced. Every device is smaller, faster, more powerful than its predecessor. It starts on an arc of fanfare and acclaim that climbs through the marketplace only to return earthward in eighteen or twenty-four months, when an improved, expanded, and occasionally incompatible upgrade appears. This upgrade will serve its days on the curve and will be replaced in turn.

We step onto this curve the moment we sit in front of a computer and turn on the power. No matter how ignorant we may be of the internal workings of the

Too Soon to Tell: Essays for the End of the Computer Revolution, by David Alan Grier
Copyright © 2009 IEEE Computer Society

machine or how little we care about advancing the fields of human knowledge, we will find that we have cast our lot with these cycles of change and improvement. Soon we learn that we must spend a considerable effort to keep pace with change and, at some point, we all decide to step off the path. We conclude that we do not need to know all the details of the new release, that we do not need to run the computer in its optimal mode, that we can be satisfied with the old way of doing things, that we can give the lead to someone who is bright, energetic, and less familiar with the seasons of change.

Cycles of improvement pre-date the computer age. The annual cycle of agriculture sets aside days for clearing brush, expanding fences, and fertilizing the land. The season of improvement was marked by county fairs, where farmers learned best practices from their neighbors and bragged about their accomplishments in the previous year. In world of computer hardware, the county fair has been replaced by the trade show, and the cycle of improvement carries the name of Moore's Law.

GORDON MOORE FORMULATED HIS LAW IN 1965 when he was a young engineer with the Fairchild Semiconductor Company and when integrated circuits were still a new phenomenon. Less than eight years had passed since the first of these circuits had been etched on a single slab of silicon. Looking at the brief history of these circuits, Moore noted that the number of distinct elements in a typical integrated circuit had "increased at a rate of roughly a factor of two per year." In 1964, a sophisticated circuit might have contained 18 transistors, resistors, or capacitors. In 1965, the best circuits had 36. Looking ahead, Moore speculated that this growth would continue over "the longer term." He expected the circuits of 1966 to have 70 elements and those of 1967 to have nearly 150. He acknowledged that the exact "rate of increase is a bit more uncertain" but he asserted that "there is no reason to believe it will not remain nearly constant for at least 10 years."

Step by step, the computer industry followed the path that Moore had identified. Each year, computer chips became less expensive and more complex. After his allotted span of ten years, Moore revisited the idea and evaluated the decade of growth. He concluded that the complexity of an integrated circuit was still doubling but at a slightly slower pace. In this revision, he hypothesized that the number of elements would double every eighteen months instead of annually. No one seemed disturbed by the idea that the cycle of improvement had stretched to a year and a half. The revised Moore's Law was accepted as the governing principle of the semiconductor industry.

Over the last 40 years, we have come to view Moore's Law as a natural phenomenon, something akin to the law of gravity. We buy machines with the assumption that better, cheaper machines will be available in a year and a half. Programmers design new software for the computers projected by this law. Yet, as we probe the operation of the semiconductor industry, we quickly find that there is little natural about Moore's Law. The computer industry has been able to achieve the targets of Moore's Law only through careful, dedicated planning. Over the past fifteen years, the curve of innovation is plotted in a large, collaborative document known as a "roadmap."

If markets are the forum where computer firms compete, then roadmaps are the place where they cooperate. Roadmaps begin with conferences where chief technology officers and senior engineers from different firms check their corporate identities at the door and sit at a common table to describe how and where they will allocate their resources. These documents are not quite treaties and definitely not alliances yet they are agreements nonetheless. They are the common sense of "what technologies might be needed to continue down a historical progress/learning curve." They outline the needs for research, development, and investment.

As with many innovations, roadmaps were born in a time of perceived crisis. This crisis began in the early years of the 1980s and reached its climax at the end of the decade. Throughout these years, the complexity of integrated circuits was doubling every eighteen months but during each cycle, the American chip makers were losing two or three points of market share to their Japanese competitors. By the end of the decade, the American firms realized that they no longer had a competitive advantage in the global market. "Of the top ten merchant semiconductor companies in the world," reported the National Research Council, "six are based in Japan and three in the United States." Many observers believed that the American companies might never be able to regain a position of industry leadership. "If weaknesses in manufacturing and in the integration of research, development, and manufacturing are not corrected," remarked one commentator, "computer hardware manufacturers could find themselves serving only specialty markets."

Specialty markets were of no interest to anyone connected with the American semiconductor industry. Not to the engineers. Not to the entrepreneurs. Not to the nation's political leaders. In the last years of the decade, the United States Congress discussed the fate of the industry with voices of rising anxiety. Unsure of how to move, they created a National Advisory Committee on Semiconductors and appointed the president of Bell Laboratories as its chair. "The semiconductor industry in the United States is in serious trouble," the committee affirmed. "If this vital industry is allowed to wither away," they added "the Nation will pay a price measured in millions of jobs," it will forgo "technological leadership in many allied industries," and it will lose the "technical edge we depend on for national security."

The committee was filled with corporate executives and so offered recommendations that appealed to business leaders. It suggested that the United States needed to build a supportive business environment, promote capital formation, protect intellectual property, and reduce antitrust enforcement. "U.S. firms have acted independently," it observed and so "each company is burdened with the full costs of advancing every aspect of new technologies." To avoid this waste, the council suggested that American firms be allowed to cooperate in the "precompetitive environment."

From this recommendation came the idea of "roadmapping." In 1991, the Advisory Committee assembled a group of experts from the different industrial and research institutions to consider the problems of manufacturing computer memory. They asked the group to identify the steps that American companies would need to take if they wanted to produce a chip that could contain a billion bits of memory by 2001. The conference prepared a paper that identified the major problems that would need to be solved and the technologies that could address those problems.

A year later, the National Advisory Committee on Semiconductors repeated this process for a broader array of problems facing the industry. That meeting produced a paper that was known as the National Technology Roadmap for Semiconductors. Following this first roadmap, the committee has returned to this process every two or three years. These roadmaps have kept the industry focused on the goals identified by Gordon Moore in 1975. "In cases where more than one technology solution was being pursued," commented one observer, "time tables suggested when choices would be necessary to keep the industry on its historic productivity curve (in part, known as 'Moore's Law')."

With each roadmap, the semiconductor industry has renewed its commitment to Moore's Law. "Everyone in the industry recognizes that if [they] don't stay on essentially that curve," Moore has remarked, "they will fall behind." Staying on that curve is far from automatic. "The semiconductor industry's future success," argued the roadmap, "continues to depend upon new ideas," ideas that touch every aspect of chip design and manufacture. These ideas include lithography, the process of laying the circuit on the chip, as well as chip structure, testing methods, and packaging technology.

In four and a half years, three cycles of Moore's Law, the roadmap went through two iterations. Each cycle pulled the American semiconductor industry back towards the curve of innovation. Each roadmap acknowledged that the U.S. firms had regained a little footing, renewed some confidence, and recovered some lost market share. As the 1995 iteration began, the American planners felt that they were ready to make the roadmap an international document by inviting the participation of European and Asian firms. This act may have been motivated by generosity, by good engineering practice, or by the recognition that the resources of the entire industry were needed to keep the production of semiconductors in step with Moore's Law.

The International Roadmap of 1997 marked a unification of the industry. "It has become more and more expensive to develop the next technology," observed one industry leader. "It is hard to do that as an individual company. You have to leverage the technologies that are available around the world rather than develop them yourself." For a while, he talked about the work required to keep his firm part of that world-wide industry. By his own reckoning, he travels a couple hundred thousand miles a year, making regular contact with the airline business lounges of Geneva, Penang, Frankfurt, Tokyo, and San Francisco. It is a very competitive industry," he says, "If you don't link up, you die." But after a pause, he then adds, "but is linking up enough?"

For the past sixty years, we have been on a curve of innovation that has taken us from tubes to diodes to transistors to integrated circuits. For the past 40, we have called that curve "Moore's Law." We have kept to that curve not because of some relentless force behind the manufacture of semiconductors or because of random innovations across the industry but because that industry has mapped each step of the way and identified every problem that it must solve.

Ultimately, the pace of this innovation is determined by financial decisions. "We just will not be able to go as fast as we would like," Gordon Moore once commented, "because we cannot afford it, in spite of your best technical contributions." There will come a day when we step off the curve, when we will conclude that we do not want to follow that path that has guided our technological life over the last four decades. But for the moment, we still live at that point in the life of the electronic computer where innovation is normal and anticipated. Each day we believe that the world is different from the one in which we lived eighteen months ago and we expect that, eighteen months from now, the world will change again.

Public Image

FEW REVELATIONS ARE MORE EMBARRASSING than the discovery that you were once an example in your father's marketing speeches. For years, you live with the illusion that you were his darling and could do no wrong in his eyes. Then in a moment, you find an old packet of papers, turn a page, spy some added text in a familiar hand, and discover that your father not only knew your weaknesses better than you ever did, he was also willing to share them with an audience of complete strangers.

Through much of the 1960s and 1970s, Dad gave a standard speech on the future of computers as a business tool. He gave this speech to any audience that might include potential purchasers of new machines. He spoke to the Northwood Institute, the International Skilled Trades Convention, the International Association of Personnel Women, the Data Processors Management Association, the Illinois Business Education Conference, the AFL-CIO. He began the speech by reminding the audience that once there was only one computer in the world. A decade later there were 10,000. A decade after that there were 50,000. He resisted the temptation to predict the number of computers in 1976, the time when another decade of the computer era would have passed.

To give the story some life, Dad discussed some his personal experiences with the computer. He talked about accounting systems, airline reservations, and even a problem with a credit card bill. He was accidentally billed for a charge by someone who lived in the same city, shared the same last name, and had a credit card number that differed from his by only one digit. While many people would have taken this last incident as evidence that computers were creating more problems than they were solving, Dad saw a blessing in the experience. The bill was corrected in only three months' time and his credit rating was unaffected.

As he talked about the problem with the credit card, Dad began to discuss the public perception of the computer and how the public was starting to blame the computer for a variety of problems. As he progressed into this topic, he suddenly introduced me. "Even my 12-year old son has learned this," he said. "When report card time came around last spring, and he failed to bring one home, he explained that the computer had made a mistake and they were all late. It turned out to be another problem and he was only buying some time."

Too Soon to Tell: Essays for the End of the Computer Revolution, by David Alan Grier
Copyright © 2009 IEEE Computer Society

I have wondered if he paused at this point, interrupted by a gentle round of knowing laughter from the parents in the room. If they did and I had known about it, my humiliation would have been complete. I was suffering from those problems that only a child on the verge of the teenage years can appreciate: dislike of a new school, discomfort with a new group of peers, and frustration with academic work that had once been easy.

Fortunately for me, Dad did not end his speech with the story of my report card but moved to the main theme of his talk, which was the role of human leadership in the "intelligent, constructive and beneficial application of the computer technology to the many problems demanding solution." Though he could have easily talked about the many accomplishments of the computer in the two decades that had passed since the ENIAC press conference, he wanted his audience to look to the future and see the good that they could accomplish with computing technology.

In 1966, computers were still an industry of the future. The proponents of the new technology, like their predecessors a decade and a half before, promoted the potential of the computer rather than its achievements. More than a few followed the path that had been explored by the early pioneers in the field, who claimed that the computer would make us both rich and wise, reduce wars, and give us better weather.

My father, as the son of a small-town merchant, took a more modest approach to the future. He argued that the computer would improve the business environment, eliminate wasteful competition, and moderate economic cycles. It would allow ordinary businessmen to have better control over their inventories, easier access to distant markets, information to guide their decisions. Ultimately, he hoped that the new machine would eliminate depressions, such as the one that nearly bankrupted his father's lumberyard. When he talked about the future of the computer, it was not a future of boxes and wires, corner offices and technical papers. It was not even a future of leisure. It was a future that sprang from the world in which he lived, a future of families and small businesses and wayward 12-year-old sons.

The Enduring Myth
of Hardware

SOME TIME IN MY CHILDHOOD, I'M NOT EXACTLY SURE WHEN, I concluded that hardware is a myth. It doesn't exist. It is just a figment of our collective imaginations. Everything is software. Word processors? Software. Databases? Software. Ringtones? Software. Of course, something has to make the software work, but that entity itself is merely another form of software. A laptop, for example, is merely a condensed form of software. A portable electronic game is software packed so tightly, that like a black hole, it sucks the attention from anyone who dares to come near it.

Of course, I will concede hardware once existed. It roamed the land in vast herds that stretched from horizon to horizon. The earth shook when these herds began their annual migration from their breeding grounds in California to the great trade shows in Las Vegas. Sadly now, hardware is completely extinct. Its demise was caused by massive overpopulation and the degradation of prime desktop habitat.

My father never shared my ideas about hardware. If he had had his way, I would have begun my career as a hardware engineer. "They are the people who really understand computers," he would say. Dad, with his engineering education, was well versed in the concepts of computer hardware. During the early years of my childhood, he filled my days with games and toys that were designed to teach me how digital circuits operated. He bought me electronic kits, taught me about flip-flops, and explained the operation of core memory. We even spent a wonderful Saturday afternoon together deriving the logic circuit to do binary addition. It was interesting at the time, but it didn't stick.

I was more captivated by the idea of programming. Dad had given me a copy of a program on a dozen punched cards. This program would print a slogan on a Burroughs printer. The original version would print "Hello David" but I quickly learned how to modify it. Using a key punch machine, I would copy the cards up to a certain point. Then, I would type a new slogan. I produced "Happy Burthday

Too Soon to Tell: Essays for the End of the Computer Revolution, by David Alan Grier
Copyright © 2009 IEEE Computer Society

Peter" for my brother and "I Lov you Amy Sue" for my sister. (Spelling has never been my strongest.)

On one occasion, I was modifying the program but I either started the phrase at the wrong point or I typed something too long. When we loaded the program into the computer, it caused the printer to make a terrible noise and eject blank page after blank page. The operator saw the growing pile of green and white paper on the floor and panicked. Several minutes passed before he was able to bring the computer under control. Once things were again running normally, I was temporarily banned from the machine room. I know that I was slightly embarrassed by the mistake but I was exhilarated as well. "This is the exciting part of computing," I thought to myself. "This is what I want to learn."

So, instead of following my father's guidance, I shunned the study of circuit diagrams and voltage meters. Instead, I spent my time at Dad's office in front of the card punch with a programming manual on my lap. I tried to learn each statement of a programming language and determine what I might do with it. I had more failures than successes but I slowly progressed through the book. I will confess, though, that none of the successes was quite as dramatic as my initial encounter with the printer.

On one trip to Dad's office, he told me that IBM had recently announced that they were going to sell software. "They used to give it away for free," he said, "and now they want to sell it." I had not heard the term "software" before and did not know what it was. For some reason, I pictured a bin of nails, the kind that you would buy at a neighborhood hardware store, that were made of rubber. Dad explained that "software" was another word for "programs." "It will be interesting to see if they can make a real business out of it," he added.

On June 23, 1969, IBM announced that it would "unbundle" its software and sell it as a product. Most observers date the start of the software industry to that announcement, though they acknowledge that a few software firms operated in the late 1950s and early 1960s. "The industry was born," commented an early software entrepreneur, "almost literally like a rib out of IBM." During the late 1960s and early 1970s, IBM had a tremendous influence over the new software business, as users of IBM mainframes were the largest market for the new industry. Nonetheless, the company was no more able to shape that industry in its own likeness than my father was able to push my interests in the direction of hardware. The software business was shaped by a group of young entrepreneurs who had to define how their business operated, how it related to customers, and even how it identified the product of software.

IBM ORIGINALLY TRIED TO IDENTIFY THE NEW SOFTWARE FIRMS by the acronym ISV, which stood for Independent Software Vendor. The word "independent meant non-IBM," noted a leader of Software AG, one of the software firms to emerge in the early 1970s. The term was clearly meant to distinguish the new companies from IBM and carried a demeaning tone. It suggested that the new firms were not only independent from IBM but were also independent from new technologies, new developments, and even from each other. In the eyes of IBM, only one firm was worthy of the title of "Software Vendor," without the modifier of "independent." That firm was, of course, IBM itself.

The first challenge of the new industry was to erase that word "independent," to show that they represented a unified industry with common concepts, common ideas, and common ways of doing business. The first thing that these firms had to do was to define the nature of software as an item of exchange. Some suggested that it was a service. Others thought that it was a manufactured good. A third cohort argued that it was an entirely new kind of product.

This debate was far from academic for it determined how the companies could raise capital. If they could argue that the software was an asset or created assets, then they could use it to finance their company. If they could not make that argument, then these new companies were nothing more than a collection of independent programmers with only limited ways of accumulating capital.

The young CEO of a startup software company called Fortex Data Corporation recalled a banker who refused him credit by claiming "You don't have any assets here, nothing of value." Fortex had customers; it had contracts; it had a staff of able programmers. All of these had value but the bank was looking for something hard and valuable, something it could claim if the company failed. It took repeated visits to convince the bank that firm had assets. "Eventually, we had a $150,000 loan from the bank," reported the CEO, "and it was all secured by our accounts receivable. That was the only thing that they would loan against."

Commonly, new businesses define their field of endeavor by forming a trade association around their mutual interest. The National Society of Tax Professionals. The American Concrete Pavement Association. Such organizations define standard practices, recommend accounting methods, and advocate supportive legislation. In 1969, no one had formed such an organization for software developers, so the developers turned to an organization with similar interests, an organization called the Association of Data Processing Services Organizations, commonly known as ADAPSO.

ADAPSO had been formed in 1961 and it, too, had been a rib taken from the sleeping body of IBM. Through the early 1950s, IBM had operated a service bureau, an organization that provided data processing services to small companies that did not wish to lease computers or punched card equipment. IBM divested itself of this bureau in 1956 as part of a resolution of an anti-trust suit. The newly independent company, now called the Service Bureau Corporation, found that it was competing with a group of accounting firms, banks, and small companies that did the payroll, accounts receivable, and bookkeeping for small businesses. "It was such an entrepreneurial industry," recalled one observer, "All over the country, in every metropolitan area of any size, there was a little company springing up to provide this service."

Many of these service firms did not use computers. Some used punched card tabulators. Some had nothing more than accounting machines. Despite their different technologies, these firms had found common ground in the services that they provided. In 1970, this common bond began to attract the attention of the early software vendors. "Some of the software guys started showing up at ADAPSO meetings," remembered one participant, "because there were little bits of the program that were of interest to us."

The "little bits" of the ADAPSO program that were of interest to software vendors grew rapidly during the 1970s. By the middle of the decade, a substantial fraction of the group was engaged in creating and selling software. In 1977, the software vendors created a subcommittee on the image of their industry. The goal of the group was "to completely flip around" their relationship with IBM. They wanted software to be at the center of the data processing industry and IBM to be merely one of several independent suppliers of hardware.

One member of that subcommittee was the CEO of a service company called Comshare. At the ADAPSO meetings, he decided that he wanted to help expand the new software industry. "We designed a game plan," he recalled, "where we would set up regular and continuous appointments with the press." They started with *Business* Week, moved to *Fortune*, then to *Forbes* and *Barron's* and the *Wall Street Journal* and then started the cycle again. For three years, they offered topics that they thought were newsworthy but received only rejections in return. Finally, on September 1, 1980, their efforts were rewarded with a cover story in *Business Week*. "There was a picture of a computer box with the top opened up," he said, "and the title of it was 'The Empty Computer,' meaning that the computer was empty without software inside."

Nothing happens in a moment, no matter how dramatic that moment may be. The *Business Week* cover did not immediately change the public perception of the software business but it gave the industry important attention and "opened the way for many more articles." Step by step, these articles helped reshape the information industry. Software moved towards the center of this industry and hardware moved towards the periphery. Some of us believe that hardware has disappeared entirely.

SOFTWARE IS SUCH A FIXED PRESENCE IN OUR LIVES that it is hard to imagine a day when it no longer commands center stage, when it, too, becomes a myth. Yet, it seems to be traveling on the same path towards mythology that has already been trod by hardware. As developers embrace standards, precompetitive agreements, transparent functionality, the reality of software has started to fade. Soon a time may come when there is nothing left of it.

Recently, I heard a hint that the reality of software was slipping away. I was attending one of those publicity luncheons that occur with some regularity in Washington. A large firm was attempting to demonstrate its importance by hiring an expensive hall and offering a lavish catered lunch to the press and members of Congress. Between the wine course and the dessert, the senior officers of the company would make the case that their organization was good, that their cause was righteous, and that they were deserving of favorable treatment by the government. It exemplified a tiny piece of advice that was passed to me by my father. "Do not be surprised to find that people can be swayed by money," he would say. "In this world everyone has a price. You should be only surprised by how low that price can be and how frequently it equals the cost of an expensive lunch."

This luncheon was hosted by a large software firm that was trying to redeem itself from mistakes that it had made in marketing its products. The speakers were impressive, more impressive than the food, and promised that their company would be more transparent, more cooperative, more accountable, and nicer. In the middle of the talk, the speaker characterized his company's largest product, which is an operating system, as nearly invisible. It is, he said, "in and of itself, not very exciting. It's like a dinner table without the food—or a Broadway stage without the actors."

No one at my table noticed this statement. They were far more concerned with the mocha cake, which looked pretty on the plate but was decidedly mediocre on the tongue. They missed the fact that the company was still hoping to put its own cuisine on the bare table of its operating system and fill its empty Broadway stage with actors of its own choosing. The speaker even suggested that operating systems were "The Empty Programs" of our age and that government anti-trust regulators might want to look elsewhere to find the real value of the computer. It suggested that someday, software would be no more substantial than hardware. In the future, we may all be forced to explain an operating system to some uncomprehending child by saying "Once we had a thing called software. It was made by a large and wealthy industry and, most important, it was not a myth. It was real."

Choosing Our Way

I WAS NEVER MUCH OF A BASEBALL FAN, but in the late 1960s, one could not live in Detroit, the headquarters city of Burroughs Computer Corporation, and ignore the game that still claimed to be the national pasttime. At that time, baseball was one of the few good things about the city, which saw its manufacturing base shrink and felt the sharp sting of racial tension. In 1967, the local team, the Tigers, gave the city a dramatic summer of play and nearly became the American League champions. The following year, the Tigers won the World Series.

In such an environment, nothing was more important for a young man than the choice of your favorite player. The team offered many distinct options: the distinguished outfielder who deserved the championship, the recent recruit who brought victory in many a difficult game, the immensely talented pitcher who fell to the many temptations that press upon young athletes, the tall yet agile catcher who played game after game. From the team roster, my brother and I selected Earl Wilson, an African-American pitcher.

Wilson had many attributes that qualified him to be our favorite player. He was single-handedly responsible for some of the team's best games. For a pitcher, he was an excellent batter and regularly hit three or four home runs a season. He was also something of an outsider, a role that resonated with my brother and me. We didn't understand the full extent of his pioneering efforts but we could appreciate that he had a position that had been attained by few African-Americans.

Our interest in Wilson only increased when we learned that he was working at Burroughs during the off-season. It was an age when ballplayers had to work in the winter. They did not earn enough from the game to spend their free time lifting weights or visiting trendy restaurants. Those, like Wilson, who saw their career spiraling towards its end, were especially anxious to find a job that might lead to long-term employment.

At Burroughs, Wilson worked with the marketing department. He lent his presence to a number of events but also spent the time learning how the company managed and sold its products. My brother and I learned of Wilson's presence at the company when Dad presented us with a pair of autographs. Mine read "To David Alan Grier, my good friend. Hope to see you at the stadium next year, Earl Wilson."

Too Soon to Tell: Essays for the End of the Computer Revolution, by David Alan Grier
Copyright © 2009 IEEE Computer Society

My brother and I hoped to meet Wilson at Dad's office but Wilson left Burroughs before Dad could find time for such a meeting. I suggested that we might get a chance to meet him when he returned to Burroughs after the baseball season.

Dad demurred. "I don't think he'll be back next year," he said.

I immediately asked why Wilson would not return. It seemed to me that a job at Burroughs offered two unquestioned benefits. First, you'd get to work with my beloved father and, second, you'd have a career in the exciting world of high technology. Dad paused for a moment and then began a conversation with me on the choices that men must make.

The discussion was a little bit awkward because it touched on the subject of racism, a topic that was well known to every Detroiter at the time. Dad was quick to speculate that Wilson might not want to be a pioneering black executive at Burroughs, though he was quick to say that the company would welcome him back. However, the bulk of the discussion focused on how men think of their careers: their skills, their opportunities, their goals, and the uncertainty that dogs their path.

"I could have stayed with Univac," he said, "or joined a startup or moved to California. But I felt that this job was best for me and would be best for your mom and best for you kids." Having spent a little time with Earl Wilson, Dad believed that the baseball player was weighing the same kind of issues and would likely conclude that the computer industry was not his best choice.

Friend of the Band

DAD BOARDED A FLIGHT TO SAN FRANCISCO, settled into his seat, and pulled a book out of his briefcase. For its day, it was a long trip but such travel was a common part of his life. He had moved from the job of product specialist to the director of customer communications for Burroughs. Twice a year he hosted the large conventions for companies that leased or purchased Burroughs' computers. In most years, one of the conventions was held in California.

The conventions usually lasted four days and included a variety of activities. They would be framed by a pair of large plenary sessions that usually included talks from senior corporate officers and major figures from the world of computer science. Grace Hopper, who had served on the original COBOL programming language design committee, was a regular speaker. So were Alan Kay, Nicholas Wirth, and Don Knuth. Between the plenary sessions, Burroughs hosted small breakout groups to talk about specific products. The users themselves would reserve rooms and discuss their common interests. They would talk about solutions to problems, compare best practices for managing Burroughs computers, and demonstrate software that they had written for their businesses.

Initially, these biannual gatherings were collegial affairs. Only a couple hundred people attended. All the users had the same set of problems and everyone knew everyone else. However, by 1970 the numbers had grown close to 1,000 and the intimacy was gone. Some of the attendees were far more sophisticated than others. Some did not know much about programming and system management. Some knew little about dealing with computer vendors. In this new environment, a few of the users became frustrated by the meetings. They came to the conferences with a problem in mind and could find no solution that met their needs.

At the two meetings of the prior year, the plenary sessions had been interrupted. Programmers had stood on their chairs or rushed the podium. They had made speeches that detailed the problems that they had with the Burroughs machines or the software or the service and had demanded an answer then and there. Dad was able to talk with individuals who were disrupting the meeting and calm them down but the disruptions continued to escalate.

One attendee of these conferences claimed that he had the role of "loyal opposition," though his actions suggested that his loyalty was limited. He "kept three subgroup sessions stirred up simultaneously," Dad observed. "His technique involved asking a provocative question from the back of one session, immediately jumping to the session next door to repeat the performance and continuing on to the third." At one point, Dad had to call hotel security to remove him from a room of angry programmers.

On this trip to San Francisco, he was preparing for another meeting and was trying to address what seemed to be a growing rebellion. He was working on the plane for the meeting as the airliner sat at the gate waiting to depart. The scheduled departure time passed with no sign of final preparation for takeoff. After a half hour's delay, a flight attendant announced that the ground crew would need an extra thirty minutes to load a special shipment of luggage that included 168 boxes.

"Where is that coming from?" Dad said almost to himself.

"It's musical instruments," said a young man in the next seat. "It's equipment for a band."

Dad thanked the man, who had "long hair and a full beard" and went back to his work. Midway during the flight, when the attendants were serving a meal, he struck up a conversation with his neighbor.

"What is the band?" Dad asked. "Would I have heard of them?"

"They're called the Grateful Dead," was the reply. "They just finished a concert in Detroit and are returning home to San Francisco."

Dad asked if the young man was part of the band. "Yes, I am," was the reply.

Dad knew little about rock and roll but he loved music. Grand Opera was more his style. He would schedule his Saturdays around the weekly broadcast of the Metropolitan Opera. I grew up believing that most men had a natural and enduring of relationship with the opera. Men would time their trips to the hardware store so that they would not miss the Queen of the Night sing her arias in the *Magic Flute*. Men would stop their chores so that they could stand with the audience during the chorus of the Hebrew children in *Nabbuco*. Men were able to answer all the questions from the Opera Quiz, the standard intermission feature of the broadcast.

I was disabused of this belief only when I went away to college. During my first Saturday at school, I was shocked to find that not only had my roommate never listened to the opera broadcast but that he also had absolutely no interest in hearing the songs of a melodramatic tale sung by five loud voices, accompanied by a large orchestra. With little attempt at being gentle, he informed me that my Dad was an excessively devout opera supporter, a diehard opera fan, perhaps even an opera nut.

Dad and his seatmate began a conversation about music that lasted for the rest of the flight. Dad expressed his concerns about the limitations of the rock and roll beat and his neighbor countered that it was no more restrictive than the rhythms of swing jazz or even the common meters of German Lieder. The two talked of harmony and lyrics as the plane flew across Wyoming and Utah and Nevada. At the end of the trip, they shook hands, thanked each other for the pleasant conversation, and went on with their business.

When I heard about the trip, I wanted to think that Dad had sat next to Jerry Garcia, the lead guitarist of the Dead but that proved not to be the case. Dad was able to identify Garcia from a photo on a Grateful Dead album and state that Garcia had sat behind him on the plane. Dad's companion may have only been a minor member of the entourage, but, if that was so, he was quite knowledgeable about music. He was quite interested in Dad's work with computers and surprised to learn that Dad had once helped program a computer to play Christmas carols. The two of them spent most of their conversation discussing how computers might be used to create and store music.

"He was a very interesting person," Dad said in summary. "Nothing like the stories of rock and roll musicians that you read in the papers."

I suppose that Dad could have engaged his new found friend on the subject of customer relations and would have found that the Grateful Dead had plenty of practical experience with the issue. They had already developed a group of dedicated fans, called the "Deadheads," who followed the band from show to show. They were an especially loyal group of customers, if they may be called by that name, but they also felt that they had a privileged relationship with the band, a stake in what the band performed, how they approached their music, even in what they wore on stage. It might have been an interesting discussion, but it almost certainly would not have been a topic that would have occurred naturally to the two of them.

IN REALITY, THERE IS NO SIMPLE ROAD between the darkness and the dawn. Dad had to find his own way to satisfy his disruptive customers. He approached the problem as a good businessman and analyzed it from several points of view. He consulted with friends and colleagues. He tried to determine the best practices in the industry by talking with his counterpart at IBM, the director of the users' group SHARE. This individual told Dad that they often had contentious discussions at their meetings but he had never seen anything that had threatened to disrupt the gathering. With no other ideas to address his problem, Dad prayed about it. He was a man of faith and felt that business could benefit from divine inspiration as much as another human endeavor.

As the next users' conference approached, Dad began to grasp, at first darkly, the idea that the Grateful Dead had already learned about their customers: the notion that computer users felt that they had a special connection to the design and manufacture of the machine. They were a highly sophisticated group, far more sophisticated than the vast collection of automobile drivers or television owners. They knew a great deal about their machines and, because of that knowledge, they wanted to be taken seriously.

From that inspiration, Dad was able to make a simple plan to engage his customers in his biannual conference. He convinced the senior executives to hold office hours and allowed any customer to make an appointment with them. He brought the product managers to the meeting to talk about the future of their computers and to listen to the feedback from the users. Finally, he established a roundtable forum with the managers responsible for product support, so that they could listen to the issues facing the users and, if appropriate, adjust their plans for fixing problems.

"These changes stopped the disruptions like that," Dad would say, and then snap his fingers. He told this story several times, without varying a detail. I must admit that I never quite believed the description but suspected that he made these changes over a year or two. When you grow up believing that every male in the United States cries openly when listening to the final scene of *La Bohème* on a Saturday afternoon, you can get a little skeptical at times. Yet, when I found his records of the biannual customer meetings, I discovered that they supported his version of events. In the spring of 1971, the meeting almost ended in a riot. An angry customer had mounted the stage like a jealous lover determined to finish the comedy with revenge. At the next meeting, when Dad's strategy was in place, the meeting went smoothly and without a complaint. Dad had found a way to engage his customers. Like the Deadheads, I suppose. Or the fans of the Metropolitan Opera.

Family Portrait

MOM RARELY INVOLVED HERSELF IN THE COMPUTER BUSINESS. She would kiss Dad goodbye at the front door, making sure that his tie was straight and his shoes were polished, and then return to bed. She was a night person, one who found it easier to stay up late than to rise early.

Like Dad, she had studied at the University of Michigan and come of age during the Second World War. Though she did not serve in the military, she volunteered for a year away from home and family. She took a teaching job in Long Beach, California, where the school district had become swollen with the children of soldiers and sailors and shipyard workers. She shared an apartment with a college friend and lived the kind of life that you can when you are young and confident and free from parental oversight.

She returned to Michigan at the end of the war. "I had wanted to stay in California," she would say, "but then I would not have met your Dad." Apparently grandfather convinced her to come home. We have always believed that he promised Mom that she could study fashion design in Michigan, but we have no hard details about this event. All we know for certain is that she moved back to Michigan, married a young Army private and started a new household on the north side of Ann Arbor.

During those first years of marriage, that delicate time when a couple is learning to make decisions and present a common identity, Mom and Dad experimented with different roles. Mom worked, teaching first graders in a Detroit suburb. Dad cooked meals and cleaned the house, while taking courses by day. As they grew together, they stepped onto their own curve of innovation. Each cycle of the year, each life event, each new child required them to adapt to new challenges and new demands. As she moved along this path, Mom was willing to divide labor along a line that separated public tasks from private. She would provide a foundation for the family at home and rarely venture into Dad's public world. She would always find the computer a mystery but would be able to see her contributions to Dad's success.

DAD'S COMPANY HELD AN ANNUAL PARTY for employee families, an attempt to make spouses feel that they had a stake in the corporation that took so much attention from their husbands. The events often had the feel of a school

Too Soon to Tell: Essays for the End of the Computer Revolution, by David Alan Grier
Copyright © 2009 IEEE Computer Society

carnival with formal clothing. Children, wearing some version of their Sunday best, would be running up and down the hallway, hiding under desks, poking at computer keyboards and playing games that were supposed to teach them about Daddy's business. The wives often stood in an awkward clutch near the bar, trying to find a common subject of interest that was not their husband's career.

One year, the company made the mistake of asking the wives to select the color for a new line of computers. In the lobby, the product managers had placed three mockups of the new system. One was painted gray and red, the colors favored by the engineers. Another was blue and white, a combination that was similar to the colors of IBM machines and one that had been recommended by a marketing consultant. The last was bare metal. A poster invited the wives to select paint chips and choose their own combination.

The organizers of this event did not foresee how the women would approach the color selection. They probably assumed that the wives could not identify a color combination that would prove more popular than either the gray and red or the blue and white paint jobs. To their surprise, the women formed a committee of the whole, selected a chair, and systematically reviewed the different options. At the end of the day, they had rejected the pre-determined schemes and recommended their own combination, something that was closer to the popular colors of the day: sky blue and silver, perhaps, pink and purple, avocado and burnt yellow.

The men were surprised at the outcome and didn't know how to respond. They faced the prospect of ignoring the advice of their marketing team or admitting that they never intended to accept the decision of their wives. Knowing that company discipline required that they use the recommendation of the professionals, they tried to dismiss the women's conclusion, an act that was done awkwardly and that irritated all concerned. The party ended badly and became the cautionary tale for the next decade, a story of the problems that one could create on a family night.

MOM NEVER LIKED THE COMPANY FAMILY NIGHTS but she was willing to help Dad with one public role, the production of marketing photos. Dad often served as a model for the marketing photographs that are part of a genre known as "White Guy with Tie." These photos show one or two men in business clothes surrounded by a collection of computer equipment. The men, rarely professional models, look ill at ease, as if they had only worn a tie once in their life – at their wedding, perhaps, or the funeral of a close friend. They are doing something that is vaguely related to computer operations, such as reviewing some output from the printer or looking at a circuit board in the processor box. No matter how hard they try, they usually communicate with their body language exactly one idea: "I am very uncomfortable and want to get out of this photograph as quickly as I can."

Dad was one of the few who was comfortable in marketing photographs. Rather than pretend to do something technical, he would cross his arms, right over left, and look directly at the camera as if he were posing for a family portrait. His first photograph was for the B-5000, the first machine for which he developed the marketing campaign. Recognizing that the B-5000 was quite different from computers already on the market, he immersed himself in the technical details of the system. He mastered the ALGOL language, learned the details of "non-von Neumann architecture" and explored the elements of the Master Control Program.

The technical details gave him a confidence about the machine – he once gave a talk about "non-von Neumann machines" to an audience that included a collaborator of the great John von Neumann – but those details did little to shape the marketing campaign. As the date for the release of the B-5000 drew near, the computer project fell further and further behind schedule. The trade press suggested that the B-5000 might never reach the customers and might never actually work. Some in the company believed these reports. After visiting the company plant to assess the progress of the machine, Dad gave a report to an industry meeting that began with the phrase that would sell the new computer: "My name is Tom Grier, and I've touched a B-5000."

"I've touched a B-5000" on advertisements, flyers and even on little campaign buttons. The phrase became the caption for a photo, which showed Dad standing in front of an operating machine. Dad is staring into the camera, looking strong and confident but the picture itself is amateurish. It was taken at a trade show and displays the back of a few too many heads that are trying to see the machine. One of the heads seems to belong to George Romney, who was then Governor of Michigan and was attending the show as a means of promoting local business.

The B-5000 photograph was repeated for each new model of Burroughs computers. There is a photo for the B-5500, for the B-220 and for the B-6500. Each of these is more sophisticated, more polished than its predecessor. The last of these photographs is one for the B-2500. It was taken in a studio in downtown Detroit after Dad had finished his work for the day. Mom joined him at the session, driving through the rush hour traffic with my brother, my sister and myself.

The studio was swathed in a dull white paper in order to eliminate sharp shadows. The new computer stood in the middle of the room, carefully lit by overhead spot lights. Dad stood to one side, waiting for Mom. She brought a new selection of ties, a spare suit in case the one he wore did not photograph well and a bit of advice. "Clean the soles of your shoes so that you don't track dirt onto the paper." She adjusted his appearance, straightened his tie and sent him onto the studio floor.

Dad found his position, turned, crossed his arms and looked towards the camera. The photographer gave suggestions as shutters clicked and motors whirred. "Work with the camera." "Be strong." "Be friendly." "Think of your audience." The words may have had some practical effect but they were less important than the picture that he saw next to the camera. Mom had arranged the three of us so that we presented a reflection of what Dad was trying to project. In this one picture, Dad was not playing a computer technician pretending to do something interesting. He was a father, standing next to his wife and surrounded by his children. It had the touch of honesty because it was nothing more than a family portrait.

The Age of
Information
(1974–1987)

The process of preparing programs for a digital computer is especially
attractive, not only because it can be economically and scientifically
rewarding but also because it can be an aesthetic experience much like
composing poetry or music.

Knuth, 1973

Coming of Age

"ONCE I WAS YOUNG," THE TALE BEGINS, "and that machine was powerful." If you haunt the corridors of computer museums you will hear a certain kind story told again and again. The teller of such tales is usually an older man, though occasionally one finds a woman of equal years. He or she is standing in front of an old computer and is surrounded by a family ensemble. Not all of these family members are paying attention. A few are wondering how grandfather could possibly have been young. One or two may doubt the claims made for the computer, which bares to the public the scars of its final dismantling. Torn cables hang from the side of the machine and empty sockets, which had once held flashing lights, stare with an empty gaze.

These stories follow a common pattern and are repeated at every computer exhibit in the world. You hear them in Silicon Valley at the Computer History Museum and in Paderborn, Germany, at the MuseumsForum, and in Bozeman, Montana, at the eclectic exhibits of the American Computer Museum. They describe a new technology and an intriguing world. They build to a climax, a difficult problem that was mastered only through hard work and ingenuity.

If you listen carefully to these stories, you quickly learn that they are not about the machine but about the speaker. They are coming-of-age tales, a form of narrative that permeates our culture. They are part of a literature that includes David Copperfield and Elizabeth Bennett and Huck Finn. They tell how an individual put aside their childhood identity and became a full member of an adult community. "When I encountered this computer," the speaker will explain, "I learned the logic of programming." "I discovered how to create a business." "I began my life as an adult."

Coming-of-age tales are not merely stories about growing older. They speak of renewing a community, conquering fear and pushing back the darkness. We tend to tell them in a heroic mode, which places the leading character at the center of the action but they are better understood as a universal tale, an experience that is shared by an entire community and illustrates how that community grew and progressed.

Too Soon to Tell: Essays for the End of the Computer Revolution, by David Alan Grier
Copyright © 2009 IEEE Computer Society

MY OWN COMING-OF-AGE TALE involved not a machine but an application, word processing. It begins in 1974, when I was a student at college. The school had an underutilized DEC PDP-11 computer. I had time on my hands, a rudimentary knowledge of programming and the thought that I might write a word processor. I had seen a crude word processing program at my father's office, a two-part system that ran on a Burroughs B-6700. The first part of the system allowed you to edit the text. The second part formatted the material and printed it. With the exuberance of untested youth, I decided that I could replicate the idea on the PDP-11 machine.

I wrote my word processor while I was taking a course entitled "Dead English Poets." I saw that the course required seven essays in 14 weeks, if my memory serves me correctly, and I knew that such a work load would test me. I had written enough papers to know that I did not produce text in a straight linear fashion. I would make some notes, scribble across them, sketch an outline, throw it away, circle the room, curse the sky and repeat the process. Perhaps, I reasoned, a word processor would bring some structure to my efforts.

The seven essays paced my work. Chaucer provided the first test for my word processor. At this point, the system was barely operational. It would accept input text and print it on a dot matrix printer. The result was crude and difficult to read. My professor, who was then unaware of what I was doing, suggested that I needed to replace the ribbon on my typewriter. He also noted that the type font seemed strange.

Shakespeare nearly proved my undoing. I foolishly thought that he would be my "muse of fire that would ascend the brightest heaven of invention." I believed that I had a sufficient understanding of the Bard of Avon and could devote most of my time to my program. As the deadline approached, I began to perceive that I did not fully grasp the ideas behind the play in question and, at the same time, that I was misusing an important function in computer system library. As a result, I did not spend sufficient time on either writing or coding.

The final draft looked more like a free-form poem than a critical essay. My word processor spread the 2,000 words of text across three dozen pages in a formatting nightmare. It started and stopped paragraphs at random and printed only one word, "insight", on page 9. The instructor gave me a passing grade out of pity. "The best example of unintended irony ever produced," was his only comment.

I moved through Milton, Pope and Wordsworth before the word processor acquired a basic feature set. Chastened by my experience with Shakespeare, I began to plan my week in advance. I would identify the new things that I wanted to add to my system and make sure that I had enough time to test the code. I also learned to gather the necessary material and prepare an outline before starting to write. I remember working late into the night on my Wordsworth paper and walking home through the biting cold of the Vermont winter. "O pleasant exercise of hope and joy!" the poet wrote in his own coming-of-age tale. "For mighty were the auxiliaries which then stood upon our side, us who were strong in love!"

It was a time of love and a time of mastery. The accomplishments of a few months' work gave me a new identity. With my little program, I established myself as an expert on a new computing technology. Other students asked to use the system to prepare their papers. Professors wanted to see how it worked. A college vice president requested a demonstration even though he expressed doubt about the idea. "It will mean that every student will want access to the computer," he commented.

In a coming-of-age tale, the new adults must move forward. They must be ready to demonstrate their newfound skill in larger and larger worlds. At the same time, the community itself moves forward. Barely two years after my demonstrations of word processing, I faced a new landscape. In that world, I could not have made a mark with my simple program. "Widespread acceptance of computer word processing has begun," wrote a programmer at Rutgers University. "Word processing advertisements are even beginning to appear on television, an indication that manufacturers like IBM and Wang believe that the mass market is ready to accept the technology." Software companies were trying to turn the new personal computer into a word processing tool. Among these early firms was MicroPro, which sold a system called WordStar. "We actually shipped it in June 1979," recalled the company founder. "And then the jet took off!"

WORDSTAR WAS ONLY ONE OF THE STEPS that brought word processing to adulthood. A more important step came in 1980, when researchers at Xerox PARC began to work with one of the new laser printers. Though still quite expensive, these printers promised much to the fields of word processing and publishing, as they had the potential to reproduce any font or image. However, these printers were still far from being able to deliver on their promise, as they were easily overwhelmed by large flows of data. They "handled letters and simple images well," wrote one observer, "but for anything more detailed, [they returned] the message: 'Page Too Complex.'"

An easy solution would have been to wait through two or three or four cycles of Moore's Law, until the laser printers acquired enough memory and processor power to handle the problems of 1980 but that strategy would have merely made the field older, it would not have brought it to adulthood. Two researchers at Xerox PARC, John Warnock and Charles Geschke, decided to address this problem by looking at word processing as a form of programming, a way of organizing commands and data. They learned how to control the information sent to the laser printer by borrowing the ideas of object-oriented programming, a style that was developed by researchers trying to simulate the physical world on a computer.

The idea worked so well that it became obvious with hindsight. Each part of a printed page was represented by a programming object, a piece of a program that combined both commands and data. Text would be handled by one class of objects, pictures by a second class, and drawings by a third. "Their system could do simple things fast," commented one engineer. Yet at the same time, it was flexible enough to describe "full graphics and scanned images."

The story of Warnock and Geschke, which ultimately led to PDF files and the Adobe Corporation, is but the simplest form of a coming-of-age tale. It is a variation of the story of a young man who frees a village from the grips of foreign soldiers or bandits or dragons or any threat that preys upon the common good. A richer set of stories are those of exploration, the coming-of-age tales in which youth leaves the boundaries of a community and travels to an unknown world. In the field of text processing, such a story is best represented by that of Tim Berners-Lee and the World Wide Web.

The origins of the World Wide Web are often connected to Vannevar Bush's 1945 article "As We May Think," in which he described a machine which we have come to call the Memex. This link is misleading in that it only considers the birth of an idea and fails to consider the childhood that precedes the coming of age. Bush saw neither the structure nor the technology of the web. "The Bush [machine] is a powerful microfilm instrument," observed the scholar Ted Nelson, "but it is not suited to idiosyncratic personal uses, nor to evolutionary modification [of text]."

Nelson began to consider the problems of organizing text and data in the mid-1960s. "The original idea was to make a file for writers and scientists, much like the personal side of Bush's Memex," he wrote, "but there are so many possible specific functions that the mind reels." He compared Bush's machine to encyclopedias, the *Interpreter's Bible*, a Shakespeare compendium, legal reference works, PERT charts. In making these comparisons, he began to appreciate the role of cross references and the way that the modern computer could track such references. "Let me introduce the word 'hypertext'," he wrote, "to mean a body of written or pictorial material interconnected in such a complex way that it could not conveniently be presented on paper."

For the next two decades, hypertext was an awkward teenager. It promised much but had not found enough grace to be able to enter the adult world. "[R]ich returns can be expected from research on the most appropriate conceptual organization of vast amounts of information," proclaimed one pair of computer scientists in 1981. "[H]ypertext systems are the next generation of word processing," suggested another article. A substantial body of literature argued that hypertext would replace encyclopedias, training programs, note files, data bases, help systems, chalk boards, sticky pads and the backs of envelopes. A number of hypertext systems were developed through the 1980s and several were placed into public circulation but none of them proved to be a solid platform for further growth.

Hypertext had its coming of age in 1991, when Tim Berners-Lee decided to employ it in a system that would organize information on a computer network. Berners-Lee was a relatively new employee at the Centre European for Research Nucleaire (CERN) in Geneva when he began to think about the problems of dynamic information. After reviewing the kinds of information that circulated at CERN, he concluded that the organization was "a multiply-connected 'web' whose interconnections evolve with time." He saw this ever-changing human web as delicate and vulnerable. When people leave the organization, he noted, the "technical details of past projects are sometimes lost forever, or only recovered after a detective investigation in an emergency." He believed that he might be able to correct this weakness with a computer system that replaced human connections with computer linkages. "The aim would be to allow a place to be found for any information or reference which one felt was important, and a way of finding it afterwards."

In his proposed system, Berners-Lee combined the idea of hypertext with the concept of a markup language. Markup languages, now familiar to many in the

Hypertext Markup Language or HTML, were roughly 15 years old in 1991. They had been developed in the 1970s and 1980s as a means of managing documents and organizing complicated sets of information. One of the early markup languages, Generalized Markup Language, was created by IBM programmers in order to describe the structure of corporate documents, including manuals, memos and press releases. It used a system of tags that divided a text into smaller structures: chapters, paragraphs, title pages, indices and the like. The early versions used the symbols ":" and "e:" to indicate the beginning and end of sections. These tags foreshadowed the now familiar symbols of <> and </> that became, in 1986, part of an industry standard markup language, called appropriately the Standard Generalized Markup Language.

In less than two years of work, Berners-Lee and his colleagues at CERN created a new identity for the computer and for the rising technology of high-speed data communication. A generation would gain their first mastery of the computer by exploring the ideas that the CERN group had assembled. Many would point to their web, coded in native HTML, as the project that taught them the potential of the computer. Some of these pages would be silly, some would be personal, some would start new businesses, some would lead to new discoveries. Nonetheless, they helped HTML mature into a substantial computer language and also begat a family of linguistic tools for describing and manipulating text and data.

SOFTWARE, SUCH AS HTML OR PDF FILES, does not make for the best museum exhibits. Perhaps it does not gather physical dust, like old fossils or stuffed birds, but it also offers little that can be easily displayed to the public. You can display an old manual, or a picture of a screen display or a stack of punched cards, but these things are not the software. The problems of displaying software are being debated by museums and we trust that their good efforts will find a solution so that we can imagine a day, perhaps 30 or 40 years from now, when grandmothers and grandfathers will stand, with fidgety children in hand, before an exhibition on the history of the old World Wide Web. Unconcerned about the attention span of their charges, they will launch into a story of their accomplishments in the 1970s or 80s or 90s. Aware that technology has advanced over the years, they will emphasize the difficulties of HTML, how much they learned in the process and the wild ride of the Internet bubble. "That was an important time to me," they will say. "I learned a lot during those years. That is when I grew up. That is when I learned to be an adult in the world."

Riding with Bohannon

BOHANNON WOULD ARRIVE AT OUR HOUSE AT 6:30. If we left before 6:45, he could drive us to downtown Detroit in 30 minutes. If we waited until 7:00 before clearing 15 Mile Road, we would need a full hour. Bohannon knew every nuance of the route: the timing of the stoplights, the location of cops, the likely points of accidents.

Bohannon would flash his lights as he entered the driveway, a signal that was supposed to bring us to the door. If he believed that we were dawdling, he would tap his horn in a rising crescendo that moved from a gentle beep to a bone shaking honk in less than 60 seconds. "Bo," my Dad said after one particularly lengthy blast, "you'll disturb the neighbors."

"Maybe," Bohannon replied, "but it won't be me that they'll be mad at."

The morning commute was my introduction to the world of men. For 30 minutes, I would sit in the company of two old colleagues as we drove to the main office of Burroughs Corporation. The two of them would head to their offices in the product management section, where they would plan the marketing strategies for the next model of the company's computers. I was headed for the machine room, where I was working as an apprentice operator.

For the first minutes of the ride, we chatted about nothing of import: the morning news, recent sports results, a television show from the night before. Bohannon usually had a new dirty joke to tell, though most of them were really nothing more than off-color puns. "Did you hear the one about the motorcycle rider, who was following a repair van too closely and got hit by the truck's radio aerial," is how one story began. Dad didn't like these stories and would interrupt them by saying "Bo" and then would give a nod towards me.

"Hell," Bohannon would say, "you don't think the boy knows this already."

It was a generous sentiment but far from true. When he got to the punch line, a play on the word "venereal," I had no idea what he meant.

Bohannon had been a Navy pilot in the Second World War and shared Dad's love of aircraft. When the two began talking about airplanes, you would have concluded that they were the best and oldest of friends. Yet even after I saw this camaraderie, I felt that there was some kind of gap between the two men. Though Bohannon lived by himself only a few blocks from us, he rarely came to our house

Too Soon to Tell: Essays for the End of the Computer Revolution, by David Alan Grier
Copyright © 2009 IEEE Computer Society

for any reason other than the drive to work. "He has his own friends," Dad would say, "confirmed bachelors all."

By the midpoint of our commute, roughly at the point where we crossed 8 Mile Road and entered into Detroit proper, Dad and Bohannon would begin talking about business issues. Both of them dealt with communications problems, the task of explaining the benefits of computing technology to customers. Dad worked with the companies that had purchased Burroughs equipment. Bohannon dealt with the sales staff and potential customers. Together, they planned advertising campaigns, organized conferences, wrote speeches and designed brochures.

Ever year, Dad and Bohannon organized a sales contest that rewarded the top members of the staff with a trip to the Super Bowl. "It's surprising how hard someone will work to get a bad seat to a mediocre football game," Bohannon liked to say. Though both enjoyed sports, neither liked to go to the game. "It's fun to see the celebrities," Dad explained, "but the salesmen are always drunk, the game is often boring, and we have to take the least desirable seats."

On the day of the game, they would pack the salesmen into a bus and then retire to a hotel bar. They would claim a pair of comfortable chairs, order a beer for Bohannon, a cup of coffee for Dad, and would settle down to enjoy themselves. I never witnessed any of these events but I would guess that the two of them spent little time talking about the game and most of the afternoon discussing business.

In our shared commutes, I had to listen when the talk shifted to the computer industry. I was still a novice and could contribute little about activities that interested them. During their conversations, I would turn my gaze out the window and follow our progress through the tired streets of Detroit.

Our route took us past the old Ford plant in Hamtramck, the place where the modern assembly line had been invented and the Model T had been built. It had once been the center of the automobile industry and a desirable neighborhood, but the production had moved to other sites and the workers had moved out to the suburbs. As we got closer to the Burroughs offices, we passed through the Chicago neighborhood. This area had seen several cycles of rising and falling fortune. It had once been the address of 19th century industrialists before they had abandoned it for the suburbs. It had seen a resurgence as the home of the Motown musicians before they had left for Los Angeles. The central Burroughs office stood on the edge of this neighborhood. It had once been an industrial plant before the company had remodeled it into a corporate headquarters.

I would part ways with Dad and Bohannon at the front door. We'd flash our badges. They would go to the right and I would go to the left. Dad would wish me a good day and Bohannon would utter a colorful and inventive version of the phrase "Don't let the bastards get you down." It was his little welcome into the community of adults, the sign that I was entering into the world of business.

The Language of Bad Love

ONCE THERE WAS A TIME when computer manufacturers made house calls. Their employees would travel to customer sites in order to upgrade operating systems, fix software bugs, train personnel, and generally assist the customer's computer manager. It was, of course, a simpler age. The weather was temperate. Good could be distinguished from evil. Love reigned triumphant. It was an era when technical representatives, the common name for the employees who visited customer sites, had to carry a full set of computer manuals in the trunk of their cars and would communicate with their home offices through the pay phones commonly found at gas stations.

In my last years of college, I served an apprenticeship as a tech rep. Each morning, I would gather with the other reps in the company cafeteria to get my day's assignment. We would sit at long tables, dressed in that odd fashion combination favored by technical personnel of formal business clothes and crepe-soled shoes. It was our time to sip coffee and share gossip. We spent much of our days in isolation, traveling from site to site in our cars. Yet, we knew as much about our customers, our company and ourselves as if we had been connected by a high-speed data network.

My supervisors were Steve and Lisa, who were in their early 30s when I joined their team. Steve was an expert on operating systems and could diagnose problems without ever referring to the reference manuals that he had buried under layers of soda cans and wind surfing paraphernalia. Lisa was skilled at reading memory dumps, the snapshot of memory that spewed out of the printer at the moment the computer failed. She would approach the work with a set routine. Clutching a high-lighter in one hand and a pen in the other, she would work through the pages of symbols, annotating the job table, coloring the file headers and circling any bit of code that seemed out of place.

On most mornings, our list of customer problems was fairly routine. An auto parts distributor that had forgotten how to reboot its machine; a county courthouse that was having trouble with the sort package; a labor union that could not clear enough space on its hard disk. As we traveled from site to site, our conversation would usually slide towards Lisa's impending wedding, which was scheduled for the fall. She had known her fiancé for 10 or 11 years but was coming to doubt her

Too Soon to Tell: Essays for the End of the Computer Revolution, by David Alan Grier
Copyright © 2009 IEEE Computer Society

commitment to the marriage. "The more I learn about him," she complained to Steve, "the more I wonder what will be left for the marriage."

Though Lisa would freely share the details of her love life, she did not like to be questioned. Should Steve or I suggest that she might want to rethink her plans, she would immediately interrupt. "It will work out," she would say more to herself than to us. "I'm sure that it will work out. We will learn how to make it work." She would end the conversation with the unanswerable retort "You're guys. What do you know?"

In mid-summer, we were assigned a problem from a hospital on the edge of town. The facility had pretensions of becoming a major medical center, the Mayo Clinic of the area. It had built a modern complex modeled on some English college and renamed itself after a famous 19th century biologist who had explored the operation of the digestive system through a series of ethically questionable experiments.

"What is the problem?" I asked as we drove to the hospital's computer center.

"We made a promise in the heat of passion," replied Lisa, "and hoped that they would forget the commitment when the morning came."

The hospital was operating an early network, a set of small computers that were connected to a mainframe. Their technical staff claimed that the network was too slow. Our salesmen claimed that it operated as specified in the contract. Lacking any concrete evidence for either claim, all they could do was argue. For the better part of the morning, Steve and Lisa battled with the hospital managers. Each side talked around the problem, hoping to find a strategy that would catch the others off guard. When the end of the meeting approached and no agreement was in sight, all parties decided that we needed a program that would monitor network operations, that this program would be written by me, and that it would be written in COBOL.

"Why COBOL," I asked when we got into the car. "I don't know COBOL."

"They only had enough money to buy the engagement ring," said Lisa in her most strident of voices. "They never bought a full set of compilers."

"I will have to use the exponential function," I protested. "COBOL doesn't even have an exponential function." I wasn't certain of this last fact but I thought it was unlikely for a business language to have the full set of higher mathematical functions.

"Listen number boy," said a weary Steve from behind the wheel. "If we ever want to drive away from this hospital and never think of them again, they're going to have to show us theirs and we're going to have to show them ours." In case I hadn't understood, he added, "They're going to want to see how we gather the data and they don't know nothing but COBOL."

With that conversation, all debate was over. The time had come for me to start writing the program. The next morning, instead of going on the road with Steve and Lisa, I sat down at a computer terminal in the tech rep office, put the COBOL manual on my lap and started pecking away. I needed a couple of hours to write a simple program and more time than I am willing to admit to complete the code that gathered the network data. Oddly, I found that it was not that hard to compute an approximation to the exponential function using arithmetic that had been designed for dollars and cents. I just needed to remember that e^{-1} equaled 0.37 not \$.37.

Lisa reviewed the program after my second or third day of effort. "Did anyone tell you that you write COBOL like a PL/I programmer?" she asked.

"But I don't know PL/I," I protested.

"Even better," she said. "You write COBOL like an ignorant PL/I programmer."

Before I finished the code, I had received comments not only from Steve and Lisa but also from our boss and the regional manager. In our world, programming was far from a solitary activity. You did not write programs to please yourself. If you put an idea into signs and symbols, you had to be ready for comment and criticism.

EVEN AT THE TIME, COBOL, the *Co*mmon *B*usiness *O*riented *L*anguage, was hardly the most fashionable tool for exploring the operations of a computer. It was language for accounting systems and inventory databases. To write a network monitor in COBOL was roughly the equivalent of writing a modern newspaper story in Chaucerian English.

COBOL had its origins in the period when languages were tightly identified with a purpose. FORTRAN (1957) was the scientific language. ALGOL (1958/60) was for algorithms and systems. LISP (1959) was for research in artificial intelligence. COBOL (1959) was the language for business.

The oldest of these languages, FORTRAN, began its life as proprietary project of IBM. IBM assembled a team of a half dozen programmers and installed them in an office near the company's Manhattan headquarters. During its first years of operation, the FORTRAN group did not have much contact with anyone outside of IBM or even with other programmers in IBM. They were located on the 16th floor of a building and had to take an elevator to reach the computer room.

As the largest of the early language developments, the FORTRAN team did not have many models to follow. We "simply made up the language as we went along," recalled John Backus, the leader of the group. Also, they were not inclined to pay attention to other ideas about programming languages. "It was typical of the unscholarly attitude of most programmers then," wrote Backus, "that we did not bother to carefully review the sketchy translation of [other] proposals that we finally obtained" for language features. Only as they began to prepare for the first release of FORTRAN did Backus and the others accept suggestions of others. They showed an early release of the code to programmers at two large IBM sites: United Aircraft and General Electric.

The ALGOL project, which started shortly after the first release of FORTRAN, was a much more public activity. It was a more sophisticated process that involved researchers from two committees, one located in the United States and the other based in Switzerland. These committees were quite interested in the linguistics that underlay computer programming. They circulated proposals for the language syntax and solicited comments. Their second proposal, which was released in 1960, received a great deal of attention because it employed an algebraic structure to describe the language, a structure now known as the Backus-Naur Form. Researchers, occasionally identified as "ALGOL lawyers," spent hours studying descriptions of the language, identifying inconsistencies and arguing over ambiguities. One pair of critics claimed that they had found that some parts of the syntax were "so subtle that ALGOL translators cannot be trusted to handle them correctly."

From its inception, COBOL was a large, transparent project. Every aspect of its design drew comments from vendors, from users, and from academic computer scientists. The goals for the language were drafted at a conference, convened in May 1959, which was sponsored by the U.S. Department of Defense. These goals were published with a minority report that criticized almost every decision of the conference, including one that had seemed obvious to many in attendance: the idea of using English as the basis for the new programming language. The "English Language is not a panacea," argued the critics, "as it cannot be manipulated as algebraic expressions can."

The design for COBOL developed the following summer and was completed in the early months of the fall. Most of the syntax was debated in public meetings, where individuals were free to share their ideas. When the final specifications were published in November of that year, they received more comments—some harsh and pointed—from both users and vendors. One of the COBOL designers was among the critics and ultimately decided to remove his name from the report. He pointed to several aspects that were "major deficiencies which reduce its effectiveness as a common language."

A common language requires a common understanding. We get that common understanding for a new language by offering the design for public criticism and comment. Some 40 years after the release of FORTRAN, the designers of the new Java language were able to solicit comments from a large fraction of potential users by posting their design on the World Wide Web.

In March 1995, programmers at Sun Microsystems placed the source for Java on the Internet. Within two months, the compiler had drawn the attention of system developers, academic programmers and the merely curious. As the language began to find an audience, emails started flowing into the Sun offices. "At first it was maybe 20 e-mails a day," recalled one Java developer. Then it became hundreds and eventually thousands. Some were questions. Some identified bugs. Some made comment on the language design. At first the Java designers were able to answer each email but they soon fell behind the expanding pile of correspondence. By the start of the fall, they had written a system to send a common letter to every incoming letter from the growing community of Java users.

Soliciting comments is not the same thing as opening a design for modifications by any individuals. Java was based on a strong theoretical design and decades of experience with the languages C and C++. The Java designers were looking for relatively small modifications to their specifications. Did the syntax of Java make sense? Were the actions of the language consistent? They looked for information that the earliest language designers had desired to have. "[E]xperience with real users and real compliers is desperately needed before 'freezing' a set of language specifications," wrote one of the original COBOL designers. "Had we known from the beginning that COBOL would have such a long life, I think that many of us would have refused to operate under the time scale that was handed to us."

BY THE TIME THAT I FINISHED MY NETWORK ANALYZER, my work had been a public document for nearly a month. The hospital systems administrator had reviewed the code, section by section, checking ideas that he approved and making notes in the margin. To my relief, he had nothing to say about my approximation to the exponential function. When he had completed his review, we installed the program at the hospital and let it run for a week. I then collected the data summaries and prepared a simple report.

I presented my conclusions to a joint meeting of managers. The hospital staff sat on one side of the table. We were on the other. The discussion quickly became testy, because the report exposed the operation of the system for all to see. Our managers were generally pleased with the results, for it showed that all but two applications were performing as specified in the contract. Of the two programs, one generated no comments from either side, as it was not very important. However, the second program was the point of contention between the computer vendor and the customer as it was an important part of the hospital's data processing system.

The meeting lasted well into the afternoon. Every aspect of the troublesome application was debated. What was it doing? Why was it consuming so much memory? Had my program measured it correctly? In the end, the two sides reached a compromise that seemed acceptable to all. The hospital accepted the claim that the network generally met the standards outlined in the contract. Our company conceded the problems with the one application and agreed to address the issue by rewriting the program or by giving the hospital a little more memory or something like that.

With the hospital problem resolved, Steve, Lisa and I resumed our regular rounds of auto part distributors, county courthouses and union offices. For a time, we were the subject of much discussion at the morning meetings, as nothing else had been so contentious that summer. Then on one Monday morning, Lisa was late arriving at the cafeteria. She walked in the door with a firm stride and a tense jaw. Her eyes were protected with dark glasses and her voice had a grim determination, as if she merely wanted to get through the day.

"Is everything OK?" we asked.

She paused, debating what she might want to tell us.

"Yeah," she said.

"Do you want to talk about something?" we asked.

She paused again. The cafeteria was starting to get quiet for the morning meeting. Several pairs of eyes had shifted our way and an equal number of ears were tuning into our conversation. Lisa glanced around the room and reached a quick conclusion.

"I don't feel like listening to criticism from men today," she said, "Let's go to work."

For most of the summer, Lisa had indulged herself in the language of bad love, phrases that were smart, sassy and, ultimately, self-protecting. For reasons that we all could guess, that language had just failed her. It was not a form of expression that could stand public scrutiny in a difficult time.

Common Knowledge

DAD TRIED VERY HARD TO BE EVEN HANDED, but he occasionally found it difficult to balance his sense of business propriety with his desire to include me in his world. In public, he avoided all shows of preference. If I was going to have a career in the computer industry, I would get no favors from him. Even in private, he attempted to keep the scales evenly balanced by avoiding certain topics. He knew a great deal about his business, about our company and about the unit in which I worked. He was proud of what I was doing but he wanted me to make my own reputation and not borrow my accomplishments from him.

Occasionally, he slipped. He told me of a large sale before my boss received the news. He accidentally let me know that one of my supervisors was leaving for another job even though no one had agreed to the final details of the transfer. He guided me away from one salesman, who was well-known to be trouble. He also told me about Ro.

Ro shared an office with me. Her name was short for Rosemarie or Roxanne or Rosalind or some pretty and delicate label that didn't quite suit her. She was brash, funny, confident. She had also worked with Dad. The two had met a decade before, when she was a new employee and Dad was running the corporate training division. Ro had had been a student in some of the division's classes.

This division was located in a 1940s vintage office building in downtown Detroit. The neighborhood had once been a vibrant area, with families and children and tree-lined streets, but that era had passed. It was tired and old, dirty and a little dangerous. It held the clubs where the Motown musicians had gathered after their recording sessions to improvise into the night. The best music was found in basements with low ceilings, unlicensed alcohol and cocaine at market prices. These were not the kind of places that attracted promising computer professionals. Most students would eat dinner in the hotel and retire to their rooms for a couple rounds of drinks and television.

Ro had been in a training class where the evening events had gotten out of hand. Some men had gotten drunk. Voices were raised. Tempers broke. Fists were employed. Security guards were called. Little damage had been done, though an ego or two had been bruised and a couple of individuals had lost four of their five wits and all of their common sense.

Too Soon to Tell: Essays for the End of the Computer Revolution, by David Alan Grier
Copyright © 2009 IEEE Computer Society

During a phone conversation that ended one working day, Dad told me that Ro had been remarkably calm during the incident, "as if she knew how to deal with anger." He was clearly impressed by her strength and by her technical abilities. His fatherly love wanted to tell me more but his managerial training held him in check. "There might be …" he started and then halted. "It could be," he said next. There was another pause, as he tried to determine which of his thoughts came from the better angels and which did not.

"She could be a good colleague," he finally said, "but I would not want to see you pattern your lifestyle after hers."

He shifted the subject quickly and shared a little family news. Finally, clearly succumbing to the idea that he had to protect his son, he returned to the subject of Ro.

"She once worked in a Playboy club," he said. "She was a bunny."

That was it. Not illegal but perhaps slightly compromising. An association that he did not want for me.

I never raised the issue with Ro. Only once did she bring the topic to the conversation.

"You talk with your Dad regularly," she said.

"Most every day," I responded.

She paused and looked at me for a moment. "Do you know?" she asked with a bit of a grimace. "Do you know the story?"

"Yes," I replied, "he told me sometime back."

She took a breath. "It was between programming jobs," she said. "I had left a position when the manager told me that you had to be a man to be able to work with computers." She paused, clearly wondering what she wanted to tell me. "The hours were terrible, the costumes were uncomfortable and, no matter what you hear, the tips were awful."

Conflict-Free Memories

"SO, EXACTLY WHAT ARE YOU SAYING?" Ro asked.

I was standing at the front of a company conference room and was staring at my peers, all of whom were silently grateful that they had not been called to give the first trial marketing presentation for Ro. None of us were particularly pleased with this assignment but we knew that it was unavoidable. We were building a complicated computer and were hoping to sell them to a fairly sophisticated group of customers. It seemed unlikely that any of these customers would purchase one of the machines without talking with the people who were designing and constructing it.

Before I could answer her question, Ro restated her query. "What message are you trying to convey?"

Ro was the marketing expert on our staff. After she stopped programming, she had spent nearly a decade working in marketing units and understood the basic strategies of presentations far better than the rest of us.

"I'm trying to explain how the machine works," I replied. I had been pleased with my presentation. I had described the operation of the device's high-speed memory, one of the key features of the machine. It was called "multi-bank parallel access conflict-free memory," a name that was difficult to utter without scrambling the consonants.

"OK," she said, "How will that explanation make the potential customer want to buy the machine?"

"That's not my assignment," I countered. "The sales people are supposed to make them purchase the computer."

Ro giggled. It was an explosive giggle that was often the first sign of trouble. "No," she said, "We are all trying to sell the machine. How will your explanation make them want to sign a contract?"

"Well," I said, "my presentation will make them feel that we have designed a good machine and that we really know what we're doing."

The gratitude among my peers was no longer silent. They were smiling and whispering among themselves, pleased that I had drawn the short straw.

Ro stared at me for a moment, cocked her head and said, "So, they're going buy the machine because they think that you're so smart?"

Too Soon to Tell: Essays for the End of the Computer Revolution, by David Alan Grier
Copyright © 2009 IEEE Computer Society

"That's not exactly…" I started but Ro was not giving me a chance to respond.

"Because if that is what you think," she continued, "you will lose the sale the minute that you stumble over some design element and say something like confrict-flee memory."

I stood quietly in front of the group, a little impatient with Ro's sermon. I was trying to decide what I would do next when Ro stood up and looked beyond me. "Help him out," she said to the other programmers. "He's going to have to talk to a German customer in three weeks. If he isn't ready, one of you will have to go." She surveyed the group and then asked the question again. "Why should someone buy our machine?"

Someone quietly snickered "confrict-flee memory" but the phrase was overwhelmed by a response from the back of the room. "Because it's fast," someone said. The comment was quickly modified by another "Because we believe that it might be fast" and the room dissolved in laughter. A voice in the back added "Sell them a Cray," referring to our most successful competitor.

Ro laughed with the group but she looked around the room with an expression that was both stern and imposing. "Fast is a feature," she said. "The color is a feature. The name is a feature. The vectorizing complier is a feature. Even the conflict-free memory is a feature." Pausing for effect she then asked "What benefits will our machine bring to our customers?"

The room was quiet for a moment or two. Then someone offered "They can do their work more quickly?"

Someone muttered the word "feature" but Ro said "No, that is right."

"It will need fewer programmers," suggested one peer. "They will get top speed out of existing programs," said another. "It will be cheaper," responded one individual who added "we hope."

The group laughed but Ro continued. "These are the benefits of the machine. These are the main points of any marketing presentation." Turning to me, she said, "Now give your speech again but organize it around these ideas."

I was rattled from the experience and bumbled my way through the second trial. I got lost once, mispronounced the name of several features and even made a serious technical blunder. Still, I learned the lesson. I needed to make the customer understand why they should buy the machine rather than give then a tutorial on how the machine worked.

MARKETING COMPUTERS HAS ALWAYS BEEN A DIFFICULT TASK. While a small group of individuals or companies have always been willing to buy the newest or fanciest technologies, far more customers have needed to be convinced that computers will improve their lives, simplify their activities, or increase the profit of their business. This point was well understood by the founding president of IBM, Thomas G. Watson, who impressed upon his sales staff that they needed to present the benefits of IBM technology first and the features second, if at all. He pushed this message in sales training classes, summer meetings at IBM's plant in Endicott, New

York and even in a series of rousing company songs that were called the *IBM Songbook*.

Even though Watson emphasized presentations and sales skills, he recognized that his company's technology was a sophisticated tool that was best understood by actions rather than words. It was easier to understand the equipment if you watched it operate and saw how it supported a business or a laboratory than if you merely listened to a talk or read an article. So he decided to establish demonstration sites, real installations that would illustrate the benefits of IBM equipment.

Watson, who served as IBM's president from 1914 to 1956, was actually selling one of the key predecessors to the computer, the punched card tabulator. Yet, to the customer of his day, these tabulators were just as sophisticated as the modern computer is to current customers. Furthermore, Watson faced challenging economic problems. He had reorganized his company's product line at the start of the Great Depression and wanted to expand his sales at a time when the global economy was shrinking. Looking for a way to demonstrate the benefits of his machines, he decided to give some of his equipment to a select group of universities. Columbia University in New York, Iowa State College, the University of Michigan, the University of Texas, the University of Oregon, Vanderbilt College for Women, Fisk College for African-Americans.

The schools were given the machines for free or for greatly reduced rents and were allowed to use them as they pleased. Most used them for administrative work: accounting, recordkeeping, registration. Some allowed faculty to experiment with the machines in the evening hours. A few placed them in laboratories that were open to both researchers and students. Over a period of three or four years, each of these institutions developed their own expertise in using the equipment. In 1935, they were asked to share their experiences in an IBM-sponsored book, *Uses of the Punched Card Method*. The principal aim [of this book] "is to show *what* the Punched Card Method can do and *why* it can do it," wrote the editor, "with the *how* delegated to a secondary place."

Unmentioned was the fact that the project was intended to promote IBM. From these institutions came a generation of workers who were skilled with punched card equipment. These individuals would employ the equipment in the government data processing offices, corporate accounting offices and in scientific laboratories. This generation included Wallace Eckert, John Atanasoff, Harry Carver and Grace Hopper.

As punched card tabulators gave place to electronic computation, the computer companies followed the lead of IBM's example. They demonstrated the benefits of their machines at universities, in corporate offices and in specially constructed sales facilities. By the early 1960s, the preferred venue for such demonstrations had become the trade show, a gathering where vendors could display their wares and show potential customers the kind of things that their machines could do.

The 1963 Spring Joint Computer Conference was something of a watershed for computer demonstrations. It occurred just as the vendors were introducing third-generation computers, the machines that would set the standards for modern computers. "It was more than just another debut or show," wrote one contemporary. The show had 80 major exhibits and was held in what was then the world's largest exhibit space, Cobo Hall on the Detroit waterfront. The biggest vendors rented space for two weeks in order to prepare for the three-day show. For days, their machines sat in little isolated clumps as they were cabled together and tested by field engineers.

Many of these machines were introducing technical concepts that were still new to the computer world: operating systems, multiprocessing, hierarchical memory, disk storage. These features were the *how* of their era, the technical accomplishments. Many at the conference were interested in such features. Marketing representatives scheduled special talks on these new features to visiting engineers, local high school students and the technical staffs from their competitors.

In spite of the best efforts of the sales staffs, most people at the conference wanted to see the *why* and the *what* of these computers, the benefits of a more flexible and powerful computing tool. They learned how a computer staff could keep the machine in constant operation, disconnect one part while another part continued with its work, complete short jobs while bigger jobs continued to process. These traits demonstrated the real value of the new machines, the reason why someone would abandon their old computer, rewrite their programs and convert their data to a new format. "It was the greatest show we've had yet," remarked one salesman, "because we physically proved that [our machine] does what we said it would do."

AS I PRACTICED MY SPEECH FOR THE GERMANS, I found myself distressed that I could not speak about the design. I felt that it was more honest, more fair to place our technical contributions before the public than to speculate about vague commercial advantages. I was growing irritated with Ro, anxious about my job, and disgusted, in a self-righteous way, with the demands of marketing. I did not want to be a mere spokesman. Ro sensed that I was getting emotional and guided me to a graceful conclusion of the session. However, she could not entirely release me from the conflicting thoughts about marketing.

Later in the day, after we had returned to our regular duties, I called Dad to vent my frustrations with the trial presentations. He listened to me rant for a time but offered no word of sympathy. When I was done with my complaint, he responded with a short story.

About eight or nine years before, he held a meeting at a private club in Atlanta, Georgia. As he discussed the final arrangements with the staff, the club manager took him aside and told him, with a soft and gentle voice, that a couple of black customers would have to eat in the kitchen, as the club members would not accept them in the dining area. To Dad, a customer was a customer, and he insisted that the club abide by the letter of its contract. The manager refused, stating that he had to follow the will of the members. The two debated the issue for a couple of hours, well past the scheduled start of the event, until some combination of threats and rewards made the manager relent.

During the dinner, one of the waiters dropped a bowl of soup on the company president. To Dad, the act seemed deliberate, a bit of petty vengeance that might provoke the Burroughs leadership. He was concerned that the company president, who had reputation as a bully, would take offense and disrupt the evening by arguing with the club manager.

To his surprise, the president gave an impressive performance that night. Though the club manager did nothing to apologize, the president showed no emotion. He knew the stakes of the evening. He looked at Dad, smiled and went back to his food. "He didn't even flinch," Dad recalled.

Perhaps the best lessons are taught by contradictions. The bully who refused to be provoked. The former Playboy bunny who knew how to explain computing technology. As you begin to understand the import of such stories, you make the lessons your own. As I made my final preparations for the presentation, I was still uncomfortable with the idea of stressing benefits and avoiding technical details, but I did as I was told. I was certain that the customers were going to interrupt my talk and ask about parallel processors, high-speed buses and conflict-free memory but I was wrong. They asked how our machine might interact with the computers that they already owned but never began to probe the inner parts of our device. As I left the podium, one of the salesmen slapped me on the back. "Good job," he said. "You were confident. That is what they needed to see."

On the Right Side of the Road

WHEN YOU SPEND TIME IN THE WORLD of business and engineering, you learn the truth, almost universally acknowledged, that any group of men can find themselves a rich and engaging subject of conversation by uttering seven simple words: "So what are you driving these days?"

Beginning with this phrase, generations of men have found an unending source of interesting topics. By talking about automobiles, they can express thoughts they otherwise would never put into words. They talk about love and hope, their fears for this world, and their embarrassment at their own weaknesses. Cars provide men a way to talk about those subjects that they publicly dismiss as feminine: fashion, community and personal relationships.

Before starting my career in the computer industry, I briefly worked at an auto dealership. One of the salesmen took me aside and gave me a brief word of wisdom about automotive conversations. "Women like to hear men talk about cars," he confided, "because women believe that the way a man treats his car shows how he will treat his wife."

I've never been able to verify this claim nor have I really understood why automobiles have such a pull on the male mind. I have speculated that the Y chromosome might have some field devoted exclusively to the theory of the motor vehicle, that our education of boys instills a love of speed and motion, or that men have a fundamental character flaw, which has been ruthlessly exploited by advertising companies.

Embedded deeply in most discussions of cars are the twin themes of independence and control. Men can recall the days when they had mastery over their machines, when they could open the hood and adjust the performance of their car. They can talk about points and plugs, oil and filters, tires on blocks and grease beneath the finger nails. In our day, such works convey an unacknowledged nostalgia because the mechanisms of the modern car are no longer a topic of study for the contemporary man. Indeed, the modern car cannot be considered mechanical at all but is merely a multiprocessor that rolls on wheels and takes gasoline as its source of power. All the great minutia of automobile lore, the ideas that have so dominated male conversation for most of the 20th century, have vanished into that invisible mist of bits and bytes that we call software.

Too Soon to Tell: Essays for the End of the Computer Revolution, by David Alan Grier
Copyright © 2009 IEEE Computer Society

AMERICAN AUTOMAKERS ADAPTED COMPUTER CONTROLS in a single year, 1980, but the story of the automotive computer properly begins in September 1973. In that month, the car companies finished their most successful year in history and prepared for the new 1974 models. No one expected 1974 to be as good as its predecessor, but most observers believed that it would come close. Everyone in the industry was surprised when the first week of the model year witnessed a decline in sales. The dealers had lured customers to the showrooms with all the usual tricks: balloons and searchlights, free food and beer, silly contests and swimsuit models. The public had responded to the inducements but few were willing to buy. "Last year we sold a couple dozen cars on the first night," complained one salesman. "This year we sold two."

Some salesmen blamed the poor sales on new features in the 1974 models, features that made the cars heavy, complex, and more expensive. The new models were equipped with stiff bumpers to absorb shocks, electrical interlocks to guarantee that all seatbelts were fastened, antipollution systems to scrub noxious gases from the exhaust. The sales staff could have spent an entire year complaining about these burdens but their energies were redirected to a bigger problem in October. On the 11th of that month, the fate of the 1974 models was sealed by the news of the First Oil Embargo. The oil-producing nations of the Middle East had decided to reduce petroleum sales to the United States. They were angered that the United States was supporting Israel in the latest Middle East conflict, the Yom Kippur War.

In a matter of few days, the supply of gasoline could no longer meet the demand for fuel. Customers grew anxious. Lines formed at gas pumps. Service stations ran short of supplies. Many Americans felt a sense of crisis, a feeling that was compounded by one of the harsher winters in recent memory. From the perspective of history, this crisis was relatively short. The First Oil Embargo lasted barely six months. However, in that time it depressed the sales of 1974 cars and convinced many people that the country needed to reduce its dependence on imported oil. By the following fall, the American Congress was preparing to require fuel–efficiency standards for all cars sold in the U.S.

The automobile industry disliked the proposed standards and tried to thwart them. The automakers urged President Gerald Ford, formerly a congressman from the auto-producing state of Michigan, to veto the legislation.

"Why don't we outlaw cancer?" complained a Chrysler executive. "Then any doctor who doesn't cure cancer in five years should have his license picked up."

In other times, President Ford might have been willing to veto the bill, but he held a weak hand: He was an unelected president—he had just replaced the disgraced Richard Nixon—and he lacked strong national support. The best that Ford could do for the auto industry was to relax a few of the safety standards and then sign the bill. The new law gave the auto makers five years to improve the gas mileage of their cars by 40 percent.

In that bleak winter of 1974, the automakers already knew that computers would likely provide the technology to meet the efficiency standards. For three or four years, their engineers had been discussing the processor chips that were being used in pocket calculators. They speculated that these chips could be used in future automobiles as precision engine controllers that would improve fuel economy and simultaneously reduce pollution but they also believed that several decades might pass before such controllers became common.

At that time, the automakers used engine controls that differed little from the systems they had deployed in the 1940s. These systems were built from a combination of mechanical and electrical parts: the carburetor, distributor, and spark advance. Because these controllers were relatively crude, they rarely made the engines run in an optimal state. They would often provide slightly too much fuel to the cylinders or ignite the spark a little too late to make the best use of the gasoline. Still, they were simple to make and well understood by thousands of mechanics and car owners.

The first computer-controlled ignition system to reach the market was MISAR, a General Motors product that was installed on the 1977 Oldsmobile Tornado. The Tornado was a luxury vehicle, and the customers who purchased it were willing to pay the costs of a new technology. Furthermore, the car needed to be redeemed from a spate of bad publicity. The Tornado has been identified as one of the most wasteful cars on the road. A U.S. government report had estimated that it could travel only 8.6 miles on a gallon of gas.

The "MISAR system provides almost infinite [control] flexibility to meet the requirements for fuel economy, engine performance, and exhaust emissions," claimed a company report. Using electronic sensors, the system monitored factors that influenced engine operations: air/fuel ratio, intake air temperature, intake manifold air pressure, engine temperature, engine speed, throttle position, unburned fuel in the exhaust. The system converted this information into commands that controlled the engine's timing and the amount of fuel injected into the cylinders.

General Motors followed the MISAR project with a second, more sophisticated computer system and declared, perhaps a little prematurely, that computer-controlled automobiles were "on the threshold of ending all auto pollution." The Ford Motor Company, not far behind General Motors, introduced a digital system of its own. In the winter of 1978–1979, the big three automakers began retooling their manufacturing facilities to incorporate the new control systems. However, this activity was only part of the work that needed to be done before the companies could deploy digital engine controls. They also needed to develop new suppliers for electronic parts and retrain the nation's auto mechanics.

All of the American automakers had difficulty procuring enough chips for their engine control systems. Domestic firms, such as Intel, National Semiconductor and Texas Instruments, were unable to supply a sufficient number of components. "It's a worldwide supply situation," reported a General Motors engineer, "because the industry is really going to be saturated with orders." Both General Motors and Ford turned to foreign suppliers for their chips. General Motors purchased their parts from European manufacturers. Ford ordered their semiconductors from a Japanese firm, Toshiba. These orders substantially increased the size of the semiconductor market and allowed the foreign companies to expand their production.

The problems of procuring supplies of chips were relatively small compared to the demands of training a large maintenance staff. There "isn't any way you're going to go out and find 30,000 PhD electronics people to service cars at the dealerships," concluded a manager at General Motors. Ford's management concurred with this assessment. The "do-it-yourselfer is being closed out on such things as routine engine tune-ups and carburetor adjustments," said a Ford representative. He observed that "Changing and adjusting ignition points, for example, used to be ritual of auto maintenance. But this chore has vanished due to electronic ignition systems that are now used industry-wide."

While the assembly lines began to build the first of the new models, the maintenance departments wrote new manuals, retrained the company mechanics to use a new diagnostic system. This system utilized a small computer that read data from sensors or directly from the memory of the car's processors. The new equipment was in place by September 1979, the month that the 1980 cars reached the showroom floors. According to a General Motors engineer, the new automotive computers represented the "biggest technological advance since the 1950s" for the auto industry. "We would not have installed them without the government's mandate for better fuel economy and cleaner emissions," he declared.

Even though the 1980 cars were substantially different from the cars of the prior year, they were relatively simple computers. Most only had computerized engine controls. Only the luxury cars had computers for locks, breaks and air conditioning. Nonetheless, the auto industry had taken a big step and would soon expand the computer controls in its products. In the next decade, virtually every aspect of automobile operation was controlled by digital technology.

"DO YOU WANT TO SEE MY HUNDRED-DOLLAR SWITCHBLADE?" asked Chip.

I was a little surprised with the question, as I thought the two of us had been talking about cars. Chip, who worked as a truck driver, had just purchased a new van and was showing me every piece of digital technology it contained. It had a computer for its engine control, another for nonskid brakes, a third for headlight control, another for the cab heater, and the list continued with a digital radio and a navigation system. We had been happily discussing all these little computers when Chip unexpectedly asked me about seeing his switchblade.

Before I could answer, Chip reached into his pocket, extracted a black plastic rectangle and slapped it on the table. I picked it up, turned it over, and was a little surprised when something sprung from one side. I looked at it closely and saw that it was an auto key.

"It's a computer," he said. Chip then described how he had needed a spare key for the van and had ordered one from the factory for a cost of $100. When it arrived, he had asked the van dealer if the processor needed to be programmed. After assuring Chip that the key should be ready to go, the dealer followed him to his van, where Chip put the key in the ignition, and tried to start the vehicle.

Nothing happened. No clicks. No buzzes. Nothing.

Chip then took his old key from his pocket and tried to start the van. Again, nothing happened. At first, the two of them thought something might be wrong with the van, but they quickly realized that the security system had taken control of the vehicle. The system didn't find the right security code on the new key, so it refused to start the engine. After identifying one bad key, it would allow no one to start the engine, not even someone with the correct key.

The slightly embarrassed dealer quickly reset the security system and sent Chip on his way. Chip left with a new story to tell and a new appreciation for the place of digital technology in his truck. Not only did the chips control the vehicle, they also gathered and stored operational data. "It tracks the oil in the crankcase," he said. "If you use the wrong brand, it will know."

Our conversation felt familiar, as it focused on subjects that had been discussed by three or four generations of men. Yet, the story had changed. We were no longer talking about our mechanical ability but marveling at the sophistication of the vehicle, not discussing what we could do but what we could understand. We could still start a good conversation with the phrase "So what are you driving these days?" but the answer to that question suggested that we did not have the same kind of authority that our fathers and grandfathers might have had.

Fork in the Path

RECENTLY, WHILE I WAS GIVING A TALK to a local business group, I was interrupted by a question that was only loosely related to my presentation. Did I have an opinion, one member asked, on the suitability of women for scientific and technical careers? The issue had recently been raised by the president of a major research university, who had suggested that many women might be incapable of scientific work. In an instant, the room became quiet. I sensed that the issue had initiated a debate within the group and had drawn a battle line between two opposing camps.

"I am loyal to my grandmother," I began. I went on to explain that my mother's mother had been trained as a mathematician at the University of Michigan and had graduated in the class of 1921. That year, half of the mathematics students had been women. I added that I also knew, from much personal experience, that my grand-mother would have objected to the notion that women were not the equal of men.

"If she had been at dinner when that college president stated that many women were not suited to be scientists," I said, "she would have immediately sent him to his room without dessert." I added that I had felt the firm hand of my grandmother's correction on many an occasion and could testify that the president would have been denied all sweets "until he had written an individual letter of apology to everyone that he had possibly offended."

Everyone in the room laughed, though at least a few voices carried a nervous tone. "Not good enough," said one man at the back. "What do *you* think?"

"I think that I am the loyal grandson of a woman scientist," I repeated, "and believe that there is nothing more I need say."

Family relationships—father to son, mother to daughter, grandmother to grandchild—are the fundamental connections that we have in modern society. We learn the nature of these relationships as children and use them as models for the relationships that we have in the civic, commercial and educational worlds. Many a company has tried to portray itself as a happy family. The bosses are like fathers. Office managers take the role of mothers. Our fellow-workers, our peers, are the equivalent of brothers and sisters.

These comfortable family relationships have been expanded and tested by the computer industry. Bosses take to the road and become absent fathers. Co-workers are distributed around the globe with no sibling connection beyond an Internet link. None of them has been tested more than those for women: mother, daughter, sister. Over the past 30 years women have found that computer technology offers new opportunities, new positions, new roles. At the same time, that technology has shown how firmly our ideas about women are carved into the foundations of our society.

MY GUIDE TO THE ROLE OF GENDER in technology was Ro. Because of her connections to Dad, she and I settled into roles that resembled those of an older sister and a younger brother. She guided me though the lessons of a new employee. She taught me how to act in front of our boss, critiqued my presentations to the customers, and even suggested, at first gently but later with some force, that not all of my clothes were appropriate business attire. She even warned me that a secretary in another division of the company was on the prowl for a husband and had identified me as a likely candidate, a warning that was later confirmed by one of my male colleagues.

Perhaps the most important advice Ro gave me came at a key moment in one project. As we were finishing some important work for this task, one of the sales people suggested that we might want to replace the performance numbers with improved values. He suggested that this was appropriate because the company hoped that our computer would soon be much faster.

I became angry at this request. I felt that salesman was unethical and wanted to denounce him to my boss. I told Ro of my plans, undoubtedly adding a sheen of self-righteousness. I expected her to support me and was surprised to learn that she didn't. She pointed out that the salesman was quite senior to me, that he would probably deny that he asked me to falsify performance numbers and that he would probably claim that I was being uncooperative. She told me to do the task that the salesman requested but when I presented them to the boss, to call them "estimated performance numbers" and be ready to explain how I created those estimates.

As Ro had anticipated, our boss immediately wanted to know how the numbers had been calculated. I explained that the sales department had wanted to know how the next generation of the machine would perform. He dismissed this idea with some phrase such as "We have to sell the machine as it operates, not as we want it to operate." In a moment, the problem was resolved, no one was embarrassed and we moved on to other issues.

FROM TIME TO TIME, I ATTEMPTED TO PROVE THAT I was not the kid brother, the subservient sibling following in Ro's every step. Few of these episodes did me any good. Usually, they only confirmed the fact that Ro knew more about technology and the business world than did I. One day something caused me to give a lengthy speech on how the computer would change the world for women. Ro listened with a look of long-suffering patience on her face. As I was ending my little sermon, she gave a curt little laugh and started to tell me the story of the obscene operating system.

Some eight or ten years before, Ro had taken a course on the company's operating system class and was one of two women in the class. On the first day, the instructor had quickly introduced himself and had hurried through the preliminaries of the course. "He was clearly anxious from the start," Ro recalled. Rushing into the first lecture, the instructor started fumbling with his words and began speaking in vague generalities. As he tried to describe the basic structure of the operating system, he quickly revealed the source of his anxiety. He was uncomfortable teaching the women because the operating system in question was designed around a sexual metaphor.

The genesis of the sexual metaphor came from an obvious and somewhat silly pun. When the operating system started a new process, it employed a concept known as "forking," a series of steps that copied the data of an existing process and established the new process as a branch of the first. At some point in the design of this system, a programmer had noticed the similarities between the word "fork" and a common term for sexual intercourse. Once he had established that link, he began applying other sexual puns. The data structure that held requests to start new processes was known as the "fork-queue," an initialization procedure was called as the "mother-forker," the first step of starting a new process took the name "unlocking the frock." Once these items were in place, it was only a short step until the code was filled with sexual imagery, puns and double entendres.

Some people are able to discuss sexual imagery in front of a mixed audience without a shred of self-consciousness. Others can antidote the sting of such words with a careful apology or a well-crafted dismissal. Ro's instructor had no such skill. He was never able to summon enough composure either to move beyond his discomfort with the sexual ideas or to explain the operating system properly. The students, both men and women, left the class feeling that the instructor had failed them and that they did not fully understand the underlying technical ideas.

Ro and another member of the class complained about the metaphor and its impact upon the quality of the instruction. This complaint was passed through the company and produced a request to modify the names within the operating system. At first, the operating system department resisted the modifications. "The developers just didn't understand the issue," Ro recalled. "This was a time when customers were regularly entertained at topless bars." They apparently argued that the system worked well, that the metaphor was not visible to most customers and that any change would introduce errors into the code.

In the end, operating system developers lost the fight. According to one observer, they were forced to concede that the sexual metaphor made it difficult for some people to explain the operation of the system to others. In the next release of the program, they used a new metaphor that was vaguely related to the British colonization of North America. It wasn't a very interesting metaphor. At the same time, it never interfered with technical training or customer presentations.

THE STORY OF THE OBSCENE OPERATING SYSTEM suggests an obvious conclusion, the idea that men dominate the computer business, as they dominate other business sectors, and use their power to exclude women. While this conclusion has much truth, it fails to capture the full dynamic of the industry. The computer industry has needed more technical workers than it could find among the available group of men. In turning to women, it has had to make adjustments, though it has usually ceded to these adjustments on technical grounds.

In its early years, computing "was a relatively welcoming field for women," concludes Janet Abbate, a scholar of gender and computation, "it offered them a rare chance to put their technical abilities to work." The earliest computing projects, those of the Second World War, employed women in technical positions. Grace Hopper worked with Howard Aiken on the Harvard Mark I; Clara Froelich assisted George Stibitz at Bell Laboratories; Kathleen McNulty and a dozen other women were part of the ENIAC project. In the years that follow, we find Ida Rhodes and Margaret Fox at the National Bureau of Standards; Gertrude Blanch at the Air Force Research Laboratories; Mildred Koss at Univac; Jean Sammet and Ann Hardy at IBM; Mary Lee Berners-Lee (the mother of World Wide Web inventor Tim Berners-Lee) at Ferranti; and Dame Stephanie Shirley at the head of her own software firm.

Many of these women worked in software development, a field that was not well defined in their time. In the 1950s and 1960s, software development was a lump of soft clay, awaiting the print of the hand. It had no fixed categories of "programmer," "software developer," "systems analyst" or "software engineer." When these companies were unable to find enough men to write software, they opened their doors to women. When skilled women were reluctant to come, the companies offered them extra inducements. "Because experienced programmers were in high demand [during the 1950s]," recalled Mildred Koss, "I was able to work part time until my children were in school."

The unfulfilled demand for skilled programmers had also brought Ro into a career in computer science. In the late 1960s, she had started looking for a job after an injury had forced her to drop out of college. Because she knew FORTRAN and some assembly language, she came to the attention of a local office of General Electric, which was then marketing a computer. They offered her a job, but she did not stay long. "The building had no women's bathrooms," she explained, and after one frustrating day, she felt the need of telling her boss "exactly what it was like to be a woman."

A brief period of unemployment followed this exchange. Ro survived the time by taking the job at a Playboy Club. A second firm offered her an interview. At first, this company seemed to be no more promising than the first. The manager "was extremely uncomfortable," Ro recalled. "He clearly did not want to hire a woman but he had little choice. He kept repeating that he had never hired a girl for a technical job." Even with such a dubious introduction, she took the job, quickly gained the attention of the firm's senior managers and soon moved into a job with national responsibility.

When Ro shared an office with me, she was approaching the mid-point of her career and was starting to move into the company's leadership ranks. Her progress was neither as smooth nor as easy as it might have been for a man but she was still able to find parts of the firm that appreciated her technical skills. She ended her career overseeing one of the company's research divisions, something that resembled an in-house venture capital office. "I would get to hire bright off-the-wall young people with specialty skills that you have never heard of," she said, "I set up a little business incubator where I would try to leave these thinkers alone to develop their ideas."

Ro described this last job about a decade after she left the firm. As she talked about her position, she reviewed the basic models for the roles that women can follow in business. To the roles of mother, wife and sister, she added a fourth, mistress, which recalled the challenges of the operating system class. As she talked, she described how she worked with the young researchers. "I was the daughter in the fairy tale," she said, "who had to spin the straw into gold." Her young charges needed to be constantly reminded that they had to produce something in return for the money that they took from the company. She had to guide these researchers, protect them from other divisions of the company and champion their ideas. "I had to reconcile differences, stop fights, and nudge ideas into products."

"Was it really the role of daughter?" I asked, "or were you more of a mother? Or sister?" I didn't really want to go to her last category. Ro paused and laughed and said, "I was a woman in the computer business and that is all there is to say."

The Best Deal in Town

JACK WALKED OUT OF HIS OFFICE with a grin on his face and a letter in his hand. "If business gets any better," he announced, "I'm going to quit this dump and join the Foreign Legion." We were unsure how to interpret this announcement and decided that the best course was to stay at our desks and await an explanation. We knew that business had not been good and understood too well that Jack had an unusual way of expressing dismay. Only the week before, Jack had vented his frustrations by suggesting that we might try to market our new computer at the entrance to a subway station.

"We'll put up a big sign," he had said. "One minute of supercomputer time: $1. The best deal in town."

No one had laughed then and no one was prepared to laugh now. We had faced disappointment after disappointment as we worked to develop and market a high-speed scientific computer, one of a class of machines that had been termed "supercomputers." Delay had followed delay. A simple design had grown complicated. Marketing opportunities had appeared on the horizon, loomed large in our vision and passed before we were able to attack them.

Even the first demonstration of the machine had been a disappointment. On that morning, the newly born supercomputer had failed to respond for nearly two hours. The control lights flashed, the disk whirred, but nothing happened. When the machine finally accepted a program, it had limped through the calculations. Jack had retrieved the program output when it appeared at the printer, scanned it for a moment, and then solemnly addressed the assembled group of engineers and managers.

"Colleagues," he had said, "we have spent $25 million dollars to breed a champion race horse." He looked down at the numbers again and then stared at the crowd. "But we are no closer to that goal than if we had begun by cloning a white whale."

With such a history, Jack had little credibility as the bearer of good news. After the machine was operational, he had made at least three dozen marketing presentations and had yet to sell a single machine. Sensing the distrust among the assembled group, he paused. "What do I need to do?" he asked. "Should I run buck naked through the halls yelling 'Eureka'?"

Too Soon to Tell: Essays for the End of the Computer Revolution, by David Alan Grier
Copyright © 2009 IEEE Computer Society

The thought of the burly ex-chemist running unclothed through the building brought a smile from one corner of the room, a giggle from another, and a gentle sigh from Emily at the secretary's desk.

"We have victory in the Pacific," Jack announced. "We will sign the instruments of surrender tomorrow at noon. We have sold a supercomputer to Japan."

The room filled with the cry of voices, the slapping of hands, and the suggestion that business cease for the day so the staff could retire to the "Old Automaton," a cramped and decaying restaurant across the street.

The sale was a major accomplishment as the market for scientific computers was crowded with six companies. Each claimed to have the best machine, the quickest chips, the cleverest software, the fastest design. Each had invested millions of dollars in its supercomputer and each believed in the value of its investment.

IN THE ANCIENT DAYS, EVERY COMPUTER was a supercomputer. The ENIAC bore this title, even though it was the fastest computer by default. The Univac I, which was far from the fastest machine of its age, was once characterized as a "super-duper electronic brain, which can think in terms of a couple of quintillion mathematical problems at one time." For more than two decades the term was regularly applied by eager sales people to describe any innovative machine but by the 1970s, the word "supercomputer" had narrowed in scope so that it referred to scientific computers. The machines most commonly associated with supercomputing were those designed by the computer scientist with a dubious connection to my childhood, Seymour Cray.

In the years that had passed since I had lived among the engineers and cats of the Univac Corporation, Seymour Cray had become the leading designer of high-speed computers. His latest machine, the Cray-1, was nearly synonymous with the term "supercomputer." That machine, which had been released in 1976, was extraordinarily fast for its time. When all processors were fully operating, it would perform 80 million floating point operations per second. It also looked like a special machine. Shunning the traditional boxes of ordinary computers, Cray built a machine that looked like a cross between a prop from the first Star Wars movie and a couch from the lobby of a Parisian hotel. The central processor was a cylinder, about 6 feet tall, that sprouted brushed aluminum fins. Around it was wrapped a black vinyl bench that held the power supply.

The first Cray-1 had been purchased by the Los Alamos weapons laboratory. This laboratory had traditionally acquired the fastest computers in order to simulate the explosions of nuclear warheads. The lab's first machine, the MANIAC, had briefly claimed the title of "World's Fastest Computer." The organization's scientists were so anxious to take delivery of the Cray-1 that they were willing to take the machine without mature software. The computer arrived at the laboratories with only a simple operating system and an ordinary assembly language. It lacked the common tool of scientific work, a FORTRAN compiler.

FORTRAN was essential to the work at the laboratory, as most of the large scientific programs were coded in FORTRAN. It was doubly important to the researchers who wanted to use the Cray-1, as the new supercomputer was very difficult to program. The machine had two processors, a serial processor and a parallel processor. The parallel processor was much faster than the serial device but it was also more complex. It required programmers to produce code that repeated a small number of operations on large sets of data. Such programs were often awkward and ungainly, inverted versions of simple tasks. They would overwhelm an ordinary machine but, on a Cray-1, they would run with no common speed.

"Originally, Seymour Cray had set out just to build 'the fastest computer in the world'," observed the historians who chronicled the development of the Cray-1, "and let the users worry about software." Few of the early customers, beyond Los Alamos, liked this idea. In particular, the National Center for Atmospheric Research "decided not to buy the machine unless [Cray] supplied system software as well." Cray accepted this demand reluctantly. "I would rather use the corporate resources to explore and develop newer and more unique computing equipment," he wrote.

At first, Cray built four computers a year. He had no real competition and plenty of potential customers. He sold his machines to the government laboratories, large engineering firms, and weather agencies. Slowly, this success began to attract some competitors: Texas Instruments, Control Data Corporation. Burroughs was a late entry in the market. None of these firms worried Cray or his employees. "I always found that Cray salesmen were very friendly," Jack would later recall. "They didn't believe that any firm like ours could compete with them." In fact, the American firms proved to be poor competitors. Control Data was the most successful but it was only able to sell a handful of machines. Texas Instruments sold one.

By 1982, the supercomputer market would start to expand beyond the borders of the United States. Of the 61 functioning supercomputers of 1982, seven were located in England. Six were in Germany, four in France and two in Japan. Seymour Cray was pleased with these sales but other computer scientists viewed them with alarm. There "is the worry that American basic research and engineering science are going to fall behind," argued one scientist, "especially in light of the progressive national policies that Germany, France, Great Britain, and Japan have concerning the exploitation of the supercomputer's potential—including policies to make super-computers available to their university researchers."

Over the next six years, Cray began to feel real competition from other firms. Only half of the new supercomputers came from Cray. Some came from new American firms. A growing number came from three Japanese companies: Fujitsu, Hitachi, and NEC. All three had taken market share from Cray. By 1988, NEC machines were considered to be the fast computers in the world.

The rise of the Japanese supercomputer industry troubled the leaders of the American computer business. When a "group of leading computer science experts in the United States gathered to assess Japan's progress," reported one journalist, "they emerged envious and more than a little scared."

This was one more piece of bad news in a time of great anxiety for American firms. American companies had seen large parts of their computer hardware business move to Asia. Japanese firms had become the dominant makers of memory chips. Fujitsu was trying to purchase Fairchild Semiconductors, the company that supplied chips to Cray.

It isn't always easy to identify a trade war. You don't see troops massing on the frontier, weapons being stockpiled, or soldiers being trained. During the 1980s, the evidence that a trade war existed between the United States and Japan was indirect: complaints from sales personnel, observations of labor officials, questions posed by Chambers of Commerce. The field of supercomputers was one of the few examples of an open battle between the two countries. "It is a matter of national pride and national identity," wrote one commentator. "The United States took 20 years to build its supercomputer industry. Japan has built its industry in six."

THE AMERICAN GOVERNMENT held a defensive position in the growing conflict over supercomputers. From its tower, American leaders anxiously viewed the field of battle, unwilling to believe that Japanese firms were building competitive machines and unsure how to act. To many observers, including most of the Cray corporate management, the Japanese government seemed to be unfairly subsidizing supercomputer sales. These individuals claimed that Japanese firms were dumping machines, selling them to American institutions at a price that was substantially below the cost of development. Accepting these claims, the American government demanded that Japan restrict the export of its machines. Japan took a different point of view and rejected the American assertions.

For five years, the U.S. and Japan fought over supercomputers. After exchanging charges and counter charges, both countries concluded that they could not win the war and accepted a ceasefire. They signed an agreement restricting the supercomputer trade but few people thought that it would do any good. The head of Cray complained that the agreement only allowed the Japanese firms to "see all the contracts that we are excluded from."

The U.S.–Japan agreement on supercomputers brought neither peace in our time nor a world safe for big machines. Many of the companies in the supercomputer business struggled. Increasingly, the stock holders in these firms, as well as their employees, asked if they should commit more of their time and treasure in the business. After a decade in supercomputer sales, Jack weighed this question and decided that a better opportunity could be found in some other part of the computer industry. Over the years, he had sold only the one machine, and had collected only a paltry preliminary commission on the sale. He had to support a wife, a daughter, a horse, a country home. The income he desired could only come from selling a product with a larger market.

His departure was a subdued affair, a lunch that was more awkward than joyful. We were not sure if we should be wishing him success in his new job, which was with a Japanese firm, or if we should ask a blessing of him. He was not in a philosophical mood. "One day I had to ask if I had been conned," he said. "I needed to know if I should devote the rest of my life to supercomputers. I could not answer that question, and so I decided that I had to find a job that would better support my family."

Jack was not the only individual to question his support of the supercomputer industry. In the first years of the 1990s, both the United States and Japan began to doubt their need to support the development of high-speed computers. In the United

States, the change was driven by the end of the Cold War, the four-decade-long conflict with the Soviet Union. The country was no longer facing an aggressive enemy, and hence was able to reduce its support of military research, research that had sustained a number of supercomputer firms. In Japan, the doubts were fueled by a recession that undermined the economy. In a six-month period, the Japanese stock market lost 38 percent of its value. The country could no longer continue its support for high-speed computers that did not generate revenue.

The end of this era of supercomputers was marked by the decline of Cray's company. Its name was no longer synonymous with the supercomputer. In the spring of 1993, the company attempted to sell its top machines to seven different laboratories. Only one agreed to purchase a Cray.

DURING HIS CAREER SELLING SUPERCOMPUTERS, Jack had described high-speed machinery with many metaphors. As he left the company, he returned to a favorite. "They are like a Ferrari sports car," he said. "They are fast. They are beautiful. They cause men to go temporarily insane." His staff had heard the story before. "They cost a fortune and spend 90% of their life in the shop being adjusted."

"No one really wants to own a Ferrari," he concluded. "They want to have a wealthy uncle buy one and then lend it to them on weekends. That would be a great deal." For American supercomputers, the rich uncle proved to be Senator Albert Gore, who championed a bill to promote advanced computers. "Advances in computer science and technology are vital to the Nation's prosperity," Gore wrote. Understanding that such machines were as seductive as an expensive sports car, Gore argued that most of the country's researchers did not need such a machine. Instead the United States government should have a "high-capacity and high-speed national research and education computer network" to "provide researchers and educators with access to computer and information resources." He wanted to put a sign out on the sidewalk that read, "One minute of supercomputer time: $1." It would be the best deal in town.

Crossing the Divide

RECENTLY, I WAS SEDUCED INTO PURCHASING A NEW VERSION of a particular piece of graphics software. For months, I had held strong to the mast as the Upgrade Sirens sang their beautiful tunes across the waters. "The updated version is better," they called, "and it has more features." I held to my convictions until that soaring melody was joined to a dark refrain. "The old software," sang the chorus "will no longer be supported." With those words, I sent my credit card number on a voyage to the commercial side of cyberspace and waited for it to return with the promised upgrade.

The process took barely 30 minutes but when it finished, my word processing software no longer worked. Being dependent upon a good word processor for my livelihood, I immediately fired an email to the support staff of the firm that had sent me the upgrade. This email was answered almost immediately by a pleasant young man named Sanjay, who indicated his willingness to help.

From here, the story played out in a predictable way. Though Sanjay certainly had many admirable qualities, he was not much of an expert on software. All of his answers came from scripts that he barely understood. After three or four fruitless exchanges, he confessed that he could not identify the source of the problem. When I asked, in a tone gentle but firm, what I might do to restore my system, he offered a surprising reply. Rather than offer an apology, he suggested, without a hint of irony, that I should learn more about the computer and attempt to fix the problem myself.

His comment stung a bit, but set me on the course that ultimately resolved the problem. For about an hour, I stared at the list of processes as I tried to start and stop the program. Seeing a pattern, I did a little bit of Internet searching and found a little piece of code that put things right. This solution brought a mix of emotions. I was proud that I still had some technical skill, relieved that my computer worked again, and a little disoriented by the exchange with Sanjay.

In hindsight, I came to realize that Sanjay was not really a trouble shooter, a technician who knew enough of the scientific method to identify and isolate a problem. He was merely a guy who was paid to read the reference manual for others. He only knew how to work with standardized knowledge, with ideas that are

Too Soon to Tell: Essays for the End of the Computer Revolution, by David Alan Grier
Copyright © 2009 IEEE Computer Society

organized into fixed and narrow categories. His job was created by two parallel forces that marched through the second half of the 20th century. The first is obviously the rapid growth of the information technology industry, the industry that created the means to organize, process, and transmit data around the world. The second is the rise of the global trade.

THE AGE OF THE COMPUTER AND THE MODERN AGE of global trade can both be traced to February 1946. In that month, the University of Pennsylvania announced the ENIAC and the representatives of 18 countries began drafting a new set of rules to govern international trade. These rules, known as the General Agreement on Tariffs and Trade or GATT, initiated a tremendous expansion in world trade. "It was a time of recovery, development and growth in the world economy," recalled one participant in the talks. Firms found new markets for their goods and "[t]rade grew faster than production."

As the trading economy grew, it changed the basic nature of business operations. It forced business leaders to think in terms of global production and global markets. They would purchase raw materials in one country, operate production facilities in a second, and market the finished goods in a third. For the first two decades of this new era, economists struggled to find patterns in the new flows of goods and services. "Anyone who has sought to understand the shifts in international trade and international investment over the past twenty years," wrote the economist Raymond Vernon in 1966, "has chafed from time to time under an acute sense of the inadequacy of the available [economic concepts]."

From his observations of the emerging global trading system, Vernon created a simple model that has become the common way of describing how high-tech goods and services develop in the world economy. This model, which is often called the "Vernon cycle," has three distinct stages: development, maturation and standardization. In the development stage of this theory, a product can be made only in close proximity to the knowledge that created that product. In the second stage, maturation, the product can be made in any technically sophisticated economy. In the third stage, standardization, the product is so well understood that it can be made in the area that has the lowest manufacturing costs. The area that invented the product, which once exported it, now becomes an importer.

The Vernon-cycle is often illustrated with the example of magnetic core memory, a form of high-speed memory that was invented in the early 1950s and was relatively inexpensive for its time. Core memory consisted of a woven grid of fine wires, much like a coarse metallic cloth. At the points where wires crossed, they passed through tiny magnetizable cores, little ceramic units that were shaped like an "o". By applying current to the appropriate wires, the computer could magnetize a specific core, thereby storing a value in the memory. By applying current to a slightly different set of wires, the computer could read the contents of the memory.

Core memory was developed in at least two different computer laboratories: Howard Aiken's computing laboratory at Harvard and Jay Forrester's laboratory at MIT. These two facilities produced very different versions of core memory and both laboratories required highly skilled individuals to help build the devices. At Harvard, the computer engineer An Wang not only designed the memory, he also helped to build and test it.

Core memory remained in the development stage through the mid-1950s. It was spread through the young computer industry by projects such as the Air Force Sage system and the IBM Stretch project, but it remained firmly rooted in the major computer research centers. None of the manufacturers agreed on a common design for such memories and all of them kept their manufacturing facilities in the United States or Europe.

Between 1955 and 1964, core memory was in the maturation stage. It had become the memory of choice for most commercial machines. It had also evolved into a couple of commonly used designs. In roughly 1964, it moved into the final stage of the Vernon cycle, the period of standardization. At this point, the major computer manufacturers understood how to design core memories and were looking for ways to increase their production of such memory and decrease the cost of manufacture.

To increase memory production, computer companies were attempting to develop one or two common designs that could be manufactured by machine. IBM was particularly aggressive in this effort. It created vacuum forms to hold the cores and hollow needles to do the weaving. One IBM engineer decided to take another approach to the manufacture of these memories. "He took a few bags of cores, rolls of wire and some core frames to Japan," reported historian Emerson Pugh. "In ten days he returned with hand-wired core planes as good as those that had been wired by the automatic wire feeders in the [American IBM] plant."

Within a year, IBM was importing core memory units from Japan and gaining the benefits of lower production costs. Pugh reported that the Japanese memories were "a few dollars per plane cheaper" than those made by machine in the United States. Yet, in moving core memory production to Japan, IBM was influenced as much by its own engineering practice as by the cost of labor. Over a period of eight years, IBM engineers had developed detailed sets of rules and specifications for the core memory units themselves and for the manufacture of those units. As they did this engineering, they anticipated that core memory planes would be woven by machine but they found that their work also allowed hand weavers to do the work. If IBM had not done such a thorough job of engineering, they would not have been able to send memory production abroad.

THE VERNON CYCLE HAS BEEN REPEATED for other pieces of computer hardware including the memory chips, processor chips, motherboards and digital displays. In each of these cases, companies have been able to move their manufacturing to low-cost facilities because they have done the engineering that allows them to make use of such facilities. Over the last two decades, companies now consciously design their products to make use of low-cost facilities that are located at a distance. No longer do they make the step into Vernon's standardized stage of production without knowing the full ramifications.

In the last decade, we have had to consider the idea that the Vernon cycle also applies to services as well as products. Some services, such as call centers or the help desk that assisted me with my software, are clearly standardized activities. Such services sport regular management practices, systematized ways of storing information and rules for engaging customers. Hence, they have followed the Vernon model, and moved to countries with the cheapest labor.

At the moment, the computer science community is attempting to determine if software engineering is following the Vernon cycle and becoming a service that can move to the lowest cost site of production. The answer to this question is far from clear. Though software engineering has rules and standards, it cannot be easily compared to a standardized service, like a help desk, or to a standardized product, like core memories. At the same time, some of the larger software projects to move out of the United States seem to have a mechanical or rote nature. The work by Indian programmers on the Y2K Problem is a commonly cited example of this phenomenon. This work required some creativity and a fair amount of knowledge but it dealt with a narrow, technical problem.

WHILE WORKING FOR BURROUGHS, I had a brief exposure to the forces that move software engineering services to lower cost providers. I was given the task of adapting a large engineering system for our Burroughs' supercomputer. I found the work straightforward but overwhelming. The programs had several hundred thousand lines of code that needed to be adjusted. When I asked for help, my manager assigned me two assistants, Naveed and Vikram. Neither of them were Burroughs employees. Both worked for the Tata Group, an Indian company that provided temporary software services to Burroughs.

The three of us finished the project in about six weeks of brutally systematic work. I remember not a single lesson from the experience. No mastery of new language structure. No clever programming techniques. No creative solutions. For days on end, we poured over line after line of code. We altered variable names, simplified complex statements, adjusted variant syntax and checked the program output against results from a Control Data computer. It was miserable work.

My only pleasant recollections of that experience were the evenings, when Vikram, Naveed and I took to the town. We were three young men with time on our hands, money in our pockets and a city to explore. During these nights, my colleagues introduced me to the wonders of Indian food: to naan, to tandoori chicken, to rogan josh. In return, I offered ice cream, barbecued chicken and baked ziti at the Italian market.

Over these meals, we attempted to share the stories of our lives. We tried to talk about where we had gone to school, what our parents had been like, what games we had enjoyed as children, how we had become interested in computers. As the summer progressed, we found that we could not discuss the simplest things about ourselves without delving into our own cultures. How do you explain your affection for meals of aloo gobi without talking about your mother and her mother? How do you describe your love for popular music without explaining the culture that created that music? How can you even talk about political leaders in an interesting way without speaking about the historical forces that brought those leaders to power?

Eventually, our dinners became quiet affairs. We might attempt to explain the evening's meal or make simple references to the events of the day but we would usually say little until someone initiated a conversation about technology. Even then, we stuck to narrowly constrained subjects. We would never speculate on the future of Burroughs or the strategy of the Tata group. Instead, we would talk about the subjects that we had in common: the problems with the program code and potential solutions that we had found in the computer manuals.

SOME 30 OR 40 YEARS AGO, when computers started to establish themselves in business and government, they drew complaints from people who disliked the standardization that came with the new machines. "I am a person, not a number" was a common rallying cry for those who were resisting the new technology. In the last 15 years, global trade has produced a similar reaction for similar reasons.

Like the computer age, the era of global trade has come with a new sense of standardization. Trade agreements are technical documents that include lengthy appendices of technical definitions, rules and standards. These appendices are substantially larger than the agreement itself. Hence we should not be surprised that the goods and services that have moved most easily from economy to economy and from culture to culture are those that are easily standardized. We can only hope that the growth of standards will ultimately promote better thinking and clearer expressions, that we will ultimately be able to apply the scientific method in one culture to solve a problem in another, that we can understand enough of colleagues from a different culture that we can honestly share their lives.

Auditions

THREE MILES STOOD BETWEEN MY BURROUGHS OFFICE and the palace divisé, the local theatre that presented itself as a center of the cinematic art. If you took the shortcut through the neighborhood, you could leave the office at 9:00 pm and not only get to the theatre in time for the late show but also be able to grab a bite to eat before the movie began. The place offered a nice collection of the fashionable haute cuisine.

So it was on one relatively mild February night while downing a curry chicken salad with a triple chocolate brownie as a chaser that I heard some one utter the phrase "vectorizing the Livermore Loops." The Livermore Loops were a small set of programs that were used to test high-speed scientific computers. I spent large parts of my days worrying about these programs and knew that they were a pretty esoteric part of the computer science literature. I looked around the room and determined that the words had come from a clutch of people sitting in the corner. Four men were nursing beers and talking. A young woman was sitting on a stool, with one leg gracefully folded over another. She was paging through a magazine and paying little attention to the conversation. A new member of the group, perhaps.

I eavesdropped for a moment and concluded that they were the hardware engineers who were working on my project. I recollected that I had seen two or three of them at company functions but had never been introduced. They worked in the manufacturing building, which was separated from my office by a couple of parking lots and a chain link fence. As I listened, I recognized that they were discussing a hardware test that was scheduled for the end of the month. The test would compare our machine to the competition. The company was offering bonuses if our machine met certain standards. It had also hinted that failure would have consequences.

After a moment, in which I finished my salad, I decided to introduce myself. I circled the group, caught someone's eye and said, "The trouble is that your computer is such a bad match for the 9th loop."

It was as if I had said "I can lick you" or dared the group to cross a line that I had drawn in the sand. The men instantly stopped talking and turned to me. The woman looked up from her magazine. I considered the idea that she might be an expert in scientific programming but concluded otherwise. She was paying attention

Too Soon to Tell: Essays for the End of the Computer Revolution, by David Alan Grier
Copyright © 2009 IEEE Computer Society

to the guy standing next to her. Her face suggested that she was interested in how he was going to handle my challenge.

We stared at each other for a moment or two and then the one standing by the woman spoke. "OK," he said. "You must work for the software division or for Cray," our major competitor, "or perhaps the Soviet intelligence agency."

I let the statement hang in the air. The doors of the theatre opened and the usher called the show. "Software Division," I said. With those words, someone laughed. Apparently they were pleased that I was not a spy. The four relaxed and began to talk. We would have talked longer had not the young woman encouraged us to the theatre door.

"You with anyone?" they asked. When I said no, they suggested that I come with them.

With that introduction, I joined the social circle of the four hardware engineers. It was a male society that included a few other technical sorts. The young woman was a temporary addition to the group. She had been auditioning for the group's leader, whose name was Ziff, as a potential girlfriend. My addition to the company that night apparently changed the nature of the audition. The woman had decided that Ziff should be the one auditioning and that his eagerness to talk with me had suggested that he was not prepared for the role.

The five of us, the four engineers plus me, formed a comfortable group. We were at the same stage of life and had similar patterns in our days. By contrast, most of the programmers were married and were interested in children, mortgages, private schools and homes at the Jersey Shore. The five of us were more intrigued by movies, music, and women, though our collective expertise on this last subject was decidedly lacking. The topic of most interest to us was the benchmarking of high-speed computers.

BENCHMARKING WAS THE TERM USED FOR MEASURING the speed of computers. It was drawn from the vocabulary of mid-19th century surveyors, where it originally referred to the marks on stone slabs (benches) where altitude measurements had been taken. Technically, the benchmark was an arrow that pointed up at a horizontal line.

The process of measuring the speed of computers began in the earliest days of the industry. The IBM 701 was compared to the MANIAC computer at Los Alamos. The MANIAC was compared to the ENIAC at the University of Pennsylvania. The ENIAC was compared, by John von Neumann no less, to an office of 25 human computers. Even with this history, the process of benchmarking was still vague and contentious. Computers "have become much more complex and benchmarks much less meaningful," wrote one contemporary expert on the subject, "even as more people have become seriously concerned with computer economics."

A researcher at Livermore Laboratories, which was a center of computer testing, suggested that economics might be the appropriate way of measuring the speed of a machine. "Strange as it may seem," he wrote, we can "get a measure that agrees fairly well with the others by using the cost of the system as an indicator of largeness."

For about seven months, I worked on benchmarking problems with my hardware friends. They were the "the hardhats." I was "the softie." I regularly made my way across the parking lot, passed through the gate of the fence and took my place in a meeting that was filled with the surplus tools of circuit engineering. Our task was to make our machine faster. Senior engineers had created the basic design. We could only make minor changes to the implementation of that design.

We made our biggest contributions by rewriting the test programs. By making small modifications, we were able get substantial improvements in the system. We recommended only one change to the hardware. We suggested that one of the basic computer instructions be modified so that it would operate faster. Our work often spilled into the evening. The complex was quieter after 5:00 and gave us an atmosphere that was conducive to solving problems. Regularly, we would end the day at 9:00 and make the dash to the Palace Divisé for a quick dinner and a late movie.

By end of the summer, our work was nearly finished. We had gotten the machine running almost as fast as intended. As a reward for our accomplishments, the company sent the technical staff to the National Computer Conference in New York City. It was supposed to be a chance for us to look at the competition and compare our device with the machines that had already made it to market.

About a week before the trip, the senior boss took me aside and told me that I would not be going on the trip. "It's a matter of seniority," he condoled. "We have a finite number of spaces and we have to make a choice. You can go next time."

There would be no next time. I would quit the firm and move to Seattle before the year was out. However, I would eventually get a good description of the conference. This description came not from my colleagues, who were not that good at telling stories, but from the writer Tracy Kidder, who visited the National Computer Conference that year while writing his book *The Soul of a New Machine*.

The Soul of a New Machine entered my life when I needed a nostalgic look at my time in industry. I was struggling with exams and problem sets and yearned for the kind of camaraderie that I had had with my friends in industry. The book told a story that paralleled my own, the tale of a computer engineering group that had worked at exactly the same time as my team. Kidder's group had designed a new machine, just as we had. They had programmed late into the night, struggled with performance problems and had attended the same National Computer Conference in New York. I wanted to think that Kidder's "Hardy Boys," the name he used for the hardware engineers, were my "hard hats"; that Kidder's long nights of programming were the nights that I stayed up until dawn; that Tom West, Kidder's dynamic central character, was my mentor Ro.

I recommended the book to friends and family, in much the same way that parents circulate photographs of new children. None of them received it with the same enthusiasm with which it was offered. Most of them enjoyed it. A few of them thought it gave them an insight into my life. None embraced it as I had. One friend, when she returned it, said that she thought that the book was sad.

"Sad?" I said. Kidder is "a young explorer standing on the threshold of a new age, looking for the outlines of uncharted regions of human experience," I replied. This judgment came from the *New York Times Book Review* and I liked to quote it.

"Sad," she said. "They thought that they were building that machine for love but Kidder thinks that they are doing it for money."

I returned to the book and saw her point. The book opens with a discussion of market value and repeatedly touches on the issues of money and reputation and desire. It does suggest that the Hardy Boys and their software counterparts, the Microkids, were partially motivated by something beyond money but it also acknowledged that computers were firmly grounded in commerce and hence could never be separated from money. Even my favorite review of the book acknowledged that the story was touched with sadness, even though the group designed a successful computer. After "the triumph and glory," wrote the reviewer, "comes the tragic recognition that for each individual the quest must start afresh, and that life may never again be as exciting."

I had spent 18 months on the computer design project. I would not describe the time as exciting but it was certainly fun. We were creating something out of nothing, a calculating machine that was intended to be special. Because I didn't have to worry about budgets or schedules or personnel, I could enjoy the present accomplishments without concern for the future. In fact, our machine was failing the three goals that the management had set for it. The project was behind schedule, substantially above its budget and far from its performance requirements.

Within a few months of my departure, one last bit of news ended the project. Our one customer cancelled its contract and bought a Cray. Apparently, we had only been a trial boyfriend and we had failed the audition.

Annie and the Boys

ANNIE KEPT A KITCHEN FOR TEENAGERS. The air smelled of freshly baked cookies; the cupboards were filled with snacks that claimed to be both good and good for you; and the refrigerator was covered with calendars and notes and instructions for getting each child to some activity at the appropriate time.

Annie was the mother of three teenagers, all sons. One was about to depart for college. The next was in the second year of high school. The last, who had just crossed the frontier into the teenage years, was still young enough to accept still his childhood nickname, "Little Bear." He stormed into the house one afternoon as Annie and I were sharing a cup of tea at the kitchen table.

"Is that you Bear?" Annie asked when she heard the front door slam.

"Yeah," came a voice from a distance hall.

"Are you home to stay?" yelled Annie.

The conversation was punctuated by a certain amount of banging and crashing. I would have compared the experience to the noise produced by Fibber McGee's closet on the old radio show, but no one there was old enough to understand the joke. We caught the words "I'm off to practice" and then heard a loud screech.

"Roger, let go of the Bear," said Annie in calm but forceful voice that implied that she could see all. The door slammed a second time and then a third. We then found ourselves listening again to a quiet house.

We talked for a time about teenagers and families, about the unbounded energy of adolescence and our tendencies to look backward at the child rather than forward to the adult. "There are days that you pray for your kids to make a sudden miraculous leap into adulthood," Annie said. "But most of the time you are simply in awe of them."

The conversation continued for a short period before Dan, Annie's husband, returned home. Dan was my new boss, a friend of my father's who had moved to Seattle to start his own firm. He was the champion of new technology, the one who could see the kernel of a good idea in some piece of hardware or software and convince others of its worth. At this point in our friendship, he was promoting the personal computer to senior executives.

"Most of the stuff out there is garbage," he said as he led me to his office at the back of the house. "They are programmable calculators with a big ego. But then I

Too Soon to Tell: Essays for the End of the Computer Revolution, by David Alan Grier
Copyright © 2009 IEEE Computer Society

found this machine." He pointed to a pile of equipment on his desk that looked vaguely like a window air conditioner with a portable television strapped to its back. It was made by a short-lived company named Divergent. "This kid has everything that you can find on a real mainframe: multiprocessing, report generators, COBOL."

"If it were only a small mainframe," he continued, "there would be no reason to get it, because it is slow as bad plumbing but it has one piece of software ..." At this point, he started to boot the machine, pushing buttons and flipping switches. Eventually the green and white screen came to life and displayed a grid of cells.

"This, my friend, is a spreadsheet," Dan said, "and it is going to change the world." He then took me through a demonstration of the program's capabilities, describing each function with concepts that were familiar to computer scientists of the time: database, general ledger, matrix, calendar, compiler. He finished his informal presentation with a line that he must have been preparing for the senior officers of the company. "Without spreadsheets, these machines are nothing. With spreadsheets, they are unstoppable."

AS WE HAVE COME TO TELL THE STORY, the fortunes of the early personal computer were indeed tied to the fortunes of the spreadsheet. More than any other piece of software, the spreadsheet demonstrated that the personal computer could be a useful business tool. The first prominent spreadsheet, Visicalc, was released in the fall of 1979 and sold 200,000 copies in less than 18 months.

The spreadsheet went through a compressed childhood, as a string of vendors tested the various ways of developing and marketing the software. The original spreadsheet creators, Dan Bricklin, Dan Fylstra and Bob Frankston, decided to organize their business around a publication model, a plan that divided the tasks of designing and programming the system from the work of selling and promoting the final product. The three of them owned the company that produced the spreadsheet, Software Arts, while a second company Personal Software (later Visi Corporation) was responsible for sales and distribution.

The distance between the development and the marketing teams made it difficult for the programmers to respond to customers and bring new features to the market. The market was volatile, with new machines entering and departing in rapid succession. The combination of Software Arts and Visi Corporation was not able to respond to these changes. In less than four years, their partnership collapsed in acrimony and legal actions. The Visi Corporation claimed that the programmers were not adding enough new features to the product and the programmers claimed that Software Arts had failed to sell the system properly. "They were young, immature and not disciplined," remarked one observer. The business did not end well.

Between 1983 and 1993, the spreadsheet industry went through a period of rapid growth and consolidation that paralleled similar processes in the hardware industry. Visicalc was no longer the only spreadsheet on the market. The young Microsoft, far from the dominant player in the field, offered Multiplan. A program called Context MBA garnered good reviews from users. A new company, Lotus, was preparing a sheet called 1-2-3.

All three of these firms abandoned the idea that software would be produced by one firm and published by another. They all combined development and marketing activities in a single organization. "I reluctantly concluded," recalled Lotus executive Mitch Kapor, "that I needed to start a firm to publish the software myself." The "publisher makes a set of decisions and really controls the product."

Of the competing products, Lotus 1-2-3 proved to be the big success. It not only outsold the other spreadsheets, it helped fuel the rapid sales of the IBM PC. "I was shocked at how successful it was," Kapor recalled. "I was probably as surprised as anyone on the planet or more. I knew the product was good. I liked the product, but I had no sense that the market was going to explode." The company went from no revenue in 1982 to $53 million in 1983, and three times that the following year. In 1984 it was the largest software company in the world. "Lotus grew from 20 people to 250 employees," Kapor added, "to 750 employees at 12 month intervals."

As the hardware and software markets of the personal computer began to mature, they both began to acquire more sophisticated identities. In the hardware market, the alternatives to the IBM PC started to falter. A dozen different brands— Osborne, Vector, Victor and similar firms now forgotten—failed between 1983 and 1987. These companies had offered machines that were similar to the IBM design but not similar enough to use the same software. They were replaced by companies that copied the IBM computers, that manufactured machines that could run software that had been written for the IBM PC. These machines soon acquired the nickname of "clones."

IBM had plenty of experience in dealing with clone machines. The architecture of the IBM 360 mainframe had been copied first by Amdahl Computers, a firm created by a former IBM designer, and then by a pair of Japanese companies. IBM reluctantly tolerated these firms, knowing that an aggressive move against clone-makers could be interpreted as an illegal attempt to monopolize the market. Nonetheless, IBM took steps to blunt the impact of the competing machines by modifying the operation of its own computers machines and by introducing new features.

In 1987, IBM tried to reclaim leadership of the PC hardware market by introducing a modified architecture, the PS/2. At a public demonstration of the new hardware, IBM technicians showed how the new technology could emulate the IBM mainframes and run the same kind of COBOL code that operating on large systems. As a whole, the market was not impressed. A few models of the PS/2 sold well but most languished. The clone manufacturers gained strength at the expense of IBM. The market was more interested in low-cost hardware than in the kind of innovations that IBM had to offer.

The spreadsheet market faced a similar problem in 1987 with the introduction of software clones, programs that copied the behavior of other packages. As Lotus 1-2-3 dominated the spreadsheet market, it was the obvious target for cloning. It was first copied by a product called VP Planner, which behaved exactly like 1-2-3 but sold for one fifth the cost. A dozen other packages were clones or near clones of the Lotus product. The most threatening was one called Quattro, which was marketed by Borland, and it could be programmed to emulate any form of spreadsheet.

The software market was younger than the hardware market, simpler and more vulnerable. Hardware manufacturers could employ many different techniques to lower the cost of a product and increase profits. They could reduce manufacturing expenses, find more efficient ways of distributing goods or expand their production runs. Their efforts led to strategies that seemed paradoxical to outsiders. Many of the early vendors used a single production line to build several kinds of computer models, each with a different level of performance and a different price. To do so, they would actually build computers from a single design and then install additional electronics to slow the processor speed.

One summer, in that distant time when I was working as a customer service representative, I helped a senior colleague upgrade a slow, low-priced mainframe computer to a faster version of the same design. We took the skins off the machine, identified the board that slowed the system and removed it. We then readjusted a few internal cables and then put the skins back on the computer. I asked if we needed to install a faster processor or something but my supervisor shook his head. "It is cheaper," he explained "to build a single model that you can run at three different speeds than to build three different computers." One large production run is less expensive than three smaller ones.

The software companies have fewer ways of reducing their costs, as they generally have very simple ways of reproducing and distributing their product. Usually, their largest fixed expense is the cost of developing the software: preparing specifications, designing the program, writing code, and testing the final system. They usually have two strategies for reducing the development expense. First, they attempt to make their staff as efficient as possible. Second, they will attempt to acquire the underlying intellectual property as cheaply as they can.

By the middle of the 1980s, several small software firms had produced low-cost spreadsheets that resembled 1-2-3. Most of them had duplicated the Lotus design by purchasing a copy of the 1-2-3 spreadsheet and then writing a program to replicate its behavior. These programs were soon identified as "clones," like their hardware progenitors, and quickly drew the wrath of the Lotus Corporation. Lotus acknowledged that these programs were new products that had been created independently of 1-2-3 but argued that they represented a form of unfair competition, a way of using others' intellectual property without compensating the owner. According to Lotus, the clones had stolen the "look and feel" of their product.

In 1987, Lotus claimed that the "look and feel" of software was legally protected property and sued one of the makers of a clone spread sheet, a company called Paperback Software. Paperback Software claimed its innocence and took the case to court. Three years passed as the two parties debated the similarities between their products, the screen layouts and menus, the file structures and outputs. In June of 1990, the courts ruled that Paperback Software had indeed violated the rights of Lotus and ordered them to cease marketing their product. Flush with victory, Lotus turned its sights on a second competitor, the Quattro spreadsheet of Borland Software.

Borland was a more formidable foe than Paperback Software. It was a large and sophisticated company that had grown wealthy by marketing a series of successful language compilers under the trademark "Turbo." It also argued that it had not created a clone of Lotus 1-2-3. Instead, it offered an entirely new spreadsheet, which it claimed was superior to the Lotus product. One of the features of this product was a macro language that could modify the operation of the spreadsheet. Borland demonstrated the power of this language by including code that could emulate 1-2-3.

Lotus v. Borland was a conflict of high drama, though of course such drama is really the conceit of outsiders. It is difficult to characterize any activity as dramatic as where the primary exchanges are filings of legal briefs rather than a fight between rival gangs of teenagers that are armed with chains and switchblades. Nonetheless, the two rival firms were just as brutal in their efforts to get the other firm to concede. As the case moved through the courts, Lotus used the ruling from its case against Paperback Software to remove other 1-2-3 clones from the marketplace. None of the cloning firms had the resources to mount a vigorous defense against Lotus and quickly retired from the field.

For its part, Borland worked to narrow the claims of the "look and feel" suit. It demanded that Lotus identify the exact ideas that it claimed were copied and to demonstrate how such ideas were protected by law. Eventually, the suit finally focused on a narrow question. Borland admitted copying aspects of the Lotus design. In particular, it agreed that its programmers had copied the fundamental structure of the Lotus command menus. However, it argued that those menus were not copyrightable. Lotus, of course, claimed the opposite and continued to press its suit. On July 31, 1992, the court ruled in favor of Lotus and required Borland to remove the Lotus interface from its spreadsheet. Borland complied with the order and then immediately appealed the ruling.

The United States Constitution guarantees the right of a speedy trial to individuals charged with crime. It does not offer that same guarantee to law suits or to appeals of law suits. Eighteen more months passed before a court reviewed the Lotus v. Borland decision. During that period, the software market began to shift, in much the same way that the hardware market had shifted under IBM in 1987 and 1988. In this new market, Microsoft had become a major institution, having surpassed Lotus as the largest software company. It sold both applications, including a spreadsheet that competed directly with 1-2-3, and operating systems. The new version of its Windows operating system was gaining widespread acceptance and was changing the environment for software development.

In contrast, Lotus remained largely a one product company. It experimented with other systems but never developed any of them into a major product. "Lotus 1-2-3 was always 90% of the revenue," remarked one observer, "people would say: 'How can we make a case for continuing to invest in something else?'"

The appellate court made its judgment in December of 1993. "Whether a computer menu command hierarchy constitutes copyrightable subject matter is a matter of first impression in this court," wrote the judge. "While some other courts appear to have touched on it briefly," he added, "we know of no cases that deal with the copyrightability of a menu command hierarchy standing on its own … Thus we are navigating in uncharted waters."

The judge chartered a course that favored Borland's tack across the competing winds. He ruled that menus were not copyrightable because they were part of the spreadsheet's control apparatus and such apparatus could not be copyrighted. Using a metaphor that became widely quoted, he compared the menus of 1-2-3 to the control buttons of a video cassette recorder and noted that, since the size, placement and operation of the control buttons could not be copyrighted, neither could the menus of a spreadsheet. He overturned the lower court ruling and returned Borland to safe harbor.

The ruling produced an immediate reaction from the software community, though that reaction was divided equally between those who supported Lotus and those who wanted Borland to gain the advantage. Lotus appealed the case to the U.S. Supreme Court. The court accepted the case, heard the arguments and then ended the debate with a decision most unsatisfying. Four justices supported Lotus. Four supported Borland. One did not participate in the case. With a tie vote, the appellate judgment stood.

LOTUS V. BORLAND WAS A FIGHT in an adolescent industry. It was brutal, angry, loud and almost irrelevant the moment it was resolved. For a brief time, the two sides tried to gain some advantage from the decision. A group friendly to Lotus argued for changes in the legal system. Existing "intellectual property laws are fundamentally ill-suited to software," they argued. "We believe a durable solution requires a new approach to the problem. We suggest one such approach that is founded on the notion of market preservation, that is, constructing just enough machinery to head off the ways in which marketplaces fail."

A second group, generally more favorable to Borland, suggested that the basic copyright laws would be adequate if they described things the way that computer scientists conceived of them. "As long as the courts considering computer software copyrightability persist in crafting new terms of art and ignoring the more precise and relevant computer science terms," wrote one attorney, "we will have unpredictability in computer software copyright law, which in turn will impede full throttle progress in the development of computer software. That result is bad for the economy, bad for consumers, and contrary to the directive of the Constitution's Copyright Clause."

Neither set of ideas long held the attention of the software industry. They looked back to the child and not ahead to the adult. Lotus v. Borland quickly vanished from the computer literature and lingered only a little longer in the legal journals. The case ended one way of protecting software and had little other influence.

The protagonists in the case also vanished, absorbed into more mature companies. Borland had already sold the Quattro package to a firm that wanted to include the spreadsheet in a suite of office productivity tools. Lotus, its revenue in decline, was purchased by IBM. The 1-2-3 spreadsheet lost its place at the top of the software market to other products.

WHILE WE WOULD LIKE TO THINK THAT TEENAGERS move gently into adulthood, we know that maturity grows more quickly in adversity than in ease. We don't always know what our kids need and are all too tempted to cling to the vision of a child that is vanishing before our eyes. Though we try to be a place of comfort at difficult times, we are often surprised by the lessons that teenagers need to learn and the events that teach those lessons. "They don't remain teenagers very long," Annie would say of her boys. "One day something happens. They wreck the car, they get an A in French, they are dumped by their girlfriend, they score a goal against the top goalie in the league. In a moment, they are adults and you never saw it coming."

Mergers and Divestitures

HAD WE BEEN BORN IN A COMMON CULTURE, Watanabe and I would never have become friends. We simply didn't have enough shared interests to sustain a relationship. We both enjoyed music, but he didn't like pop music or jazz or opera, the forms that I preferred. We found some common ground in the majestic rituals of Sumo, a spectacle I still find oddly compelling, but had no other shared appreciation of sport or culture. Watanabe was never able to convince me that ceremonies of any other martial art were intrinsically interesting and I could not get him to appreciate the culture of American politics. When I tried to explain American ideas to Watanabe, he would often shake his head and give a little nervous laugh that indicated that he didn't quite understand what I was saying and had no idea why he should care.

Watanabe was an attorney for a Tokyo technology firm. He had spent eight years dealing with the routine legal problems of a corporation: liability suits, product regulation, export licensing. He had worked the long hours of a Japanese salariman, usually leaving his Yokohama dormitory before the sun had risen, staying at his desk well into the night, and looking the other way when one of the female clerks had tried to catch his eye. His discipline was rewarded by the opportunity to travel to Seattle, study at an American law school and to get an American degree.

Watanabe and I had been introduced by my fiancé, a term that we never used in public and rarely acknowledged in thought. She had come to Seattle to study Japanese law and had soon befriended most of the Japanese lawyers on campus, about a dozen in number. Six months after we met, she had won a scholarship to study in Japan and had departed, leaving me responsible for her American affairs and her Asian friends.

Of the group, Watanabe was the most interested in trying to establish a friendship with me. Though he had many reasons for this interest, he was partially motivated by a desire to learn more about computing technology. He had learned a little about computers at his company, which made printers, scanners and modems. The firm offered some training classes for employees. However, he had gained only a superficial knowledge from the experience. He wanted to know more, especially about software, which he viewed as a mythical entity that held some kind of strange power over the physical reality of hardware.

Too Soon to Tell: Essays for the End of the Computer Revolution, by David Alan Grier
Copyright © 2009 IEEE Computer Society

In his apartment, Watanabe kept a little shrine to his computer in the breakfast nook next to the kitchen. The table was a little island of order in otherwise cluttered space. Housekeeping was neither his strength nor his interest. Yet, he kept the area around the machine clean and neat. The computer, an early Macintosh, occupied one end of the table. Manuals were stacked to one side in alphabetical order. A new notebook occupied the other side of the table. In front of the keyboard was a new teacup that had been thoroughly scrubbed. It was marked with the Chinese character for "Everlasting Peace" and filled with freshly sharpened pencils.

I decided that I would teach Watanabe about programming by showing him how to write a Japanese word processor for the machine. Though the project impressed some of my colleagues, it was not particularly novel. Japanese language processing had been an early project of IBM. In 1961, IBM had demonstrated Katakana characters (one of the two syllabic Japanese alphabets) on its 1401 machine. By 1969, it had created a word processing program for its 360 series that used Kanji, the Japanese equivalent of Chinese characters. Within a few years, this system would be used by a major Tokyo paper, the Asahi Shimbun, to typeset its daily editions.

We never got very far with our Macintosh program. I was devoting most of my energies to finishing my graduate study and Watanabe had to write a paper about intellectual property rights. Our system could handle only a single page of text. Once that page was filled, the program would stop. However, it did lay down the Japanese characters in columns rather than rows. As you typed, the cursor would steadily move down the screen. When you pressed the return key, it would jump to the top and move one space to the right.

The cursor proved to be the most intriguing aspect of our work. It captivated a group of Watanabe's lawyer acquaintances, who believed that a computer screen naturally operates from left to right, just like a typewriter or a printer. They congratulated Watanabe on his tremendous engineering achievement and suggested that he patent the idea so that he could collect royalties from the hapless individuals who might want to use this alleged innovation without his permission.

For several weeks, Watanabe's word processor was a useful topic of conversation for me. It convinced my colleagues at school that I was a bit nuts and should be left alone. It reassured my fiancé that I was interested in the things that interested her, even though Japanese word processing was not the same thing as Japanese law. Finally, it intrigued my father, who was dealing with uncertainty at work. His employer, Burroughs Corporation, was considering a merger with Sperry Rand, the company that owned Univac.

Like many, Dad was mystified by the potential merger. The two companies had similar lines of business but very different kinds of computers. Burroughs offered three different computer models, including one that it had acquired from the ElectroData company in the 1950s. Univac had three. One was extended from the original Univac of Eckert and Mauchly. The next had begun its life at Engineering Research Associates, where the young Seymour Cray had worked. The last had been acquired from the RCA Corporation. All used different operating systems and were programmed with different dialects of computer languages. "It's kind of hard to see the synergy here," said one baffled industry analyst.

The prospect of the merger fluctuated over the course of a year, like an uncertain romance or a poorly founded friendship. As the talks progressed, they slowly revealed the business strategy behind the potential deal. The leaders who initiated the merger hoped that they could generate the revenue of the combined companies with the employees of only one firm. One commentator speculated that 10,000 jobs might be lost in the merger.

As the talks moved into their final act, the protagonists took steps to protect their positions and their people. No manager wanted to contribute their own staff to the list of the newly unemployed. In these maneuvers, the Sperry officers found strength in weakness, a surprising ability to force new demands upon Burroughs. They could not repel the advances of their suitor, one Sperry officer noted, but they were able to "make clear to Burroughs that it did not have the ability to get the company on it's own terms."

When the deal was done and the papers signed, the new corporation sponsored a contest to find a new name. A surprising number of employees suggested "Sparroughs," a label that suggested two organizations rather than a single company. The officers wanted to look forward rather than backward. Burroughs took its name from the founder of an 1890s adding machine company. Elmer Sperry, of course, was the engineer who adopted the gyroscope for navigation at the start of the 20th century. They finally selected a name that had no historical reference but suggested a modern, unified entity.

The new company had one too many directors of customer relations. Dad was ready go and so departed with several thousand other surplus employees. He collected the trappings that come with early retirement: a new personal computer, a book of memorials, and a consulting contract. He was one of the few who had worked for both firms and was one of the few who could remember when the two technology companies tried to present themselves as an extended family of happy employees and grateful dependents.

Univac had urged its workers to live in common neighborhoods and had encouraged the spouses of current employees to welcome the wives of new additions to the company. Burroughs had a country club for families and sponsored a singles club for the younger workers. Both firms made liberal use of casual clothing imprinted with their respective company logos.

Dad's departure from Univac, some 25 years before, had been marked with a twinge of disappointment. He felt that the company had failed to take advantage of its historic link to the invention of the computer and its early entry into the high-technology market. Hence, he tended to identify quite strongly with Burroughs. He took great delight in identifying every company that had purchased Burroughs computers. Wayne County? A Burroughs User. Vernor's Ginger Ale? Also a Burroughs User. So was Ford Motor Company and the Detroit Zoo. As a child, I was pleased that my father had some connection to the zoo, though I somehow thought that such a link would have a useful benefit for me, such as the opportunity to bring a crocodile home for the weekend.

On one particular Saturday, our family toured the zoo grounds, which gave my siblings the opportunity to ask if each animal was indeed a "Burroughs User." In later years, when I had my own job at Burroughs, I was tempted to embellish the story of that Saturday at the zoo. I would claim that we believed that the ostrich was a systems operator, that the tapir kept the tape library and that the cockatoo knew COBOL. It's a clever addition to the tale but it is also was not true. As children, we never felt that we were part of a Burroughs family. Burroughs was downtown. It took Dad away from us. It made him do things that we didn't understand. Our sense of family was expressed in other ways. By going to the zoo. By reading stories at night. By going to the ballpark. By doing Saturday chores while listening to the opera.

Old Bottles

"I CAN'T QUITE HEAR YOU," DAVID SAID.

"Sorry," I replied. "The phone slipped off my shoulder."

"You're clear now," he assured me.

"What do you see?" I asked.

"Lots of things."

"What file is open?" I pressed.

"How do I know?" David responded.

"It's in the upper right corner," I said.

"Cardbox," he replied. "The file is named cardbox."

"You've found the right one," I assured him.

"It doesn't look like a cardbox," he said. "It looks like a little kid has been pounding on the keyboard."

"Old bottles for new wine," I replied. "An old name for a new process."

"I'm not sure I like that," he noted after a moment. "For the bottles shall be split and both shall be lost."

"Let us hope that that parable doesn't apply here," I responded.

David and I had become friends because of the personal computer. He was an early adopter of the technology and I was his programmer. On the surface, David was not a likely advocate of these machines. He was a man of the cloth, a religious minister. Though he had not completely forsworn the comforts of material life, he relied little on worldly goods. He spent his most of days with no technology beyond the reassuring sounds of his resonant voice. That voice was central to his profession. It comforted and taught, exhorted and calmed.

David had discovered the personal computer in the early 1980s, when he spent a brief time at a church on the East Coast. "Almost from the start, I knew that I would have to have one," he said. He had learned how to use a word processor and had discovered that the computer gave him a new ability to refine and organize the words that were crucial to his trade. It would allow old notes to be updated with new inspiration and old talks to be revised for new situations. "It will give me the services of a secretary without having to impose on others," he suggested.

At the time, the personal computer market was still very small. "What today goes by the name of home computer," noted the *New York Times*, "is and always has been a hobby product for computer enthusiasts and not the average homeowner." For most people in the United States, the computer was merely a luxury good. Few individuals could understand how a machine costing two or five or even ten thousand dollars might be of use to them. "The new arrival on the status appliance circuit is the home computer," trumpeted one publication. This publication quoted two "home fashion experts" who claimed that no well-designed home should be without one. "If you want to give a dinner party," claimed the article, "it will tell you what to buy." Furthermore, it "takes up very little room in the kitchen."

Through the early 1980s, few individuals accepted the claim that a personal computer could be useful in the home. "Compiling endless computerized lists of telephone numbers, recipes or record albums is generally a waste of both the user's time and the computer's power," argued an industry observer. "Similarly, using the computer to balance a checkbook quickly takes on make-work characteristics." About the only applications that received an enthusiastic reception from the public were the entertainment programs. "Playing Star Trek and other computer games," wrote one homeowner, "is more addicting than potato chips."

David read few secular publications beyond the front pages of the newspaper and hence was unaware of the limitations of the personal computer of the time. He also had no idea about how to purchase a machine or how to select software or how much work was required to keep a system in good operating condition. He believed that the Lord would provide and I became that provision. A mutual friend introduced me to him as "the guy that knows all about computers."

The purchase of the machine was straightforward except for the utter incomprehension of the sales people. None of them were ready to sell a computer to a minister. They had no insight about how the machine might be of use to one such as David and no idea about how to behave in front of him. They stumbled over their words in a vain attempt to avoid cursing. All made an embarrassed confession that they hadn't been to church in some time. Each made misguided attempts to explain the operation of the computer. "It's like a boxful of Monks," sputtered a salesman who had a very dim sense of the nature of Protestant clergy. "But they are new Monks. With a television screen."

We took the computer to David's apartment. I installed a word processor, and taught David how to use the system. I left him that evening, thinking that our contact had come to an end and that David would be able to handle his own needs from that point but I was apparently mistaken. A few days later, I received a call from him.

After a brief exchange of pleasantries, he got to the point of the call. "I need to have you show me some things on the computer."

"Like what?" I asked.

He then described how he wanted to make notes about the people he visited, add to those notes, sort them in various ways and print reports.

"We'll need to create a database to do that," I said.

"OK," he responded without missing a beat. "How do we do that?"

Initially, I believed that I would have to create the database system from scratch and write programs in a one of the languages that were then available for the personal computer, languages that seemed primitive in comparison to the mainframe languages that I had used as a child. I was relieved to discover that a local computer store sold a simple database program, called Dbase, which was similar to the database packages that were available on mainframe computers.

Dbase was created by Wayne Ratliff, who was a contract programmer for the Jet Propulsion Laboratory in California. While working at the laboratory, Ratliff purchased a microcomputer kit. "It took a year to put the thing together," he complained. "I had to solder more than 2,200 joints." Once he had assembled the machine and debugged the circuits, he had nothing more than an empty box. "Nothing was included except 1K of memory," he stated. After thinking about a couple different projects, he decided that he would fill the box with a database system.

Using a specification from the Jet Propulsion Laboratory, Ratliff wrote a primitive system that he called "Vulcan." "I got it working and a little over a year after I started, I did my taxes on it," he remembered. Deciding that the program might have commercial value, "I began to polish it up and get it to a sellable stage. In October 1979, I went to market and put my first ad for Vulcan in BYTE magazine." The ad brought customers and soon he had more responses than he could handle.

Like other developers of this time, Ratliff divided the tasks of programming and marketing. He sold his software through a firm named Software Plus, an entity that was known as a software publisher. Among the publishers could be found the progenitors of the more sophisticated software firms of the 1990s, including Novell (1979), Satellite Software International (Word Perfect) (1978), and MicroPro (1978). As a whole, these companies were gingerly exploring the software market for personal computers and trying to find useful lessons from the existing business community. Many quickly failed but a few found success as software distributors. The "distribution and marketing efforts [of these firms] were improved from the early years [of the personal computer industry]," observed one commentator, "but were still rudimentary."

Having only the most elementary description of the Dbase system, I required several months to create a database for David. In the process, I discovered that my mainframe experience was not the best training for the work. As the system became operational, I realized that my design was backwards and inefficient. It made the small processor struggle to sort and organize records. I had to restructure several of the data structures and routines in order to make good use of the machine.

When I taught David how to use the system, I briefly explained why I had to rewrite the programs but I decided that I didn't need to tell him about the technical aspects of the system. Our version of Dbase had several unusual features, including the ability to process code that was not syntactically correct. Usually, the code would produce an acceptable result but under certain circumstances, it would stop the computer dead and turn the screen to blue. After encountering this problem, I had worked hard to avoid certain commands and I honestly believed that David would never experience the fatal blue screen.

THOSE BRIEF MONTHS WITH DAVID CONSTITUTED my time on the frontier of the personal computer, the era when the technology was new and the institutions surrounding that technology were primitive. "From the conditions of frontier life came intellectual traits of profound importance," wrote the historian Frederick Jackson Turner. It produces the "buoyancy and exuberance which comes with freedom" and the "practical, inventive turn of mind, quick to find expedients." I had written many programs by myself, including the word processor in college, but I had never developed a product for someone else without the full structure of a company and a programming team. Everything on this system had been designed by me, including the expedients, which I believed to be quite clever, that avoided the problems in Dbase.

In addition to reinforcing the practical nature of expedients, the frontier also exposes the weaknesses of shortcuts. When you have left one region, you cannot easily travel back to your former home to correct incomplete work. When I left David's neighborhood, I knew that my program was not perfect but I also believed that the system would be stable for several years. I did not anticipate that David would begin a cycle of improving and expanding his office computer.

Nothing in this world is permanent, even a job that has 2,000 years of Western Civilization behind it. David did his work in an age that measured the sands of eternity in the 18 month cycles of Moore's Law. First, David needed a new hard drive. Then a new monitor. Next a faster processor. So the cycles progressed. I made three or four trips back to his house to help with the system. Twice, I transferred his programs to a new computer and hoped that any problems in my code would survive the move. Each time they did. At one point, I even thought that I could dispose of my notes on the project but then I received a call in the night.

"It's not working," David said in an anxious voice.

"What's not working," I replied.

"The system. Your program. It's not working."

"What's wrong," I asked.

"There are messages," David said, "and the screen is blue." He then began to read the phrases that had filled his screen. There were messages about buffers and exceptions and illegal instructions and fatal errors. From what I heard, I concluded that the problem was similar to the one that I had identified earlier but was found in a different piece of code.

After he finished, he asked "Do you know what is the problem?"

"New wine in old bottles," I said. "A new operating system and the program are interacting in an odd way."

He paused and then laughed. "Tell me," he said. "Exactly what is the wine in this case and what are the bottles?"

The process of fixing the bug took several days. Over the phone, I had to guide David through the key parts of the program, identify the bad code and write the corrections. In the end, we got the program working properly and David could return to his ministerial tasks. It was a dramatic incident but it would not be the last time that I would be called to fix my program over the phone lines. Though the system pleased David, it had not really given him complete freedom. It has loosed him from secretaries and church volunteers but tied him to the cycles of innovation and, hence, linked him more closely to me.

The Days of Cyberspace (1986–2007)

The network has engendered considerable enthusiasm on the part of the participants.

Orenstein, Heart, Crowther, Rising, Russell and Michel, 1972

Alley Life

I WAS LOATH TO LEAVE SEATTLE. For me, as for the essayist E.B. White, Seattle was the place where I learned to see myself as an adult, the place where I explored what I might accomplish. There is "a period near the beginning of every man's life," White wrote, "when he has little to cling to except his unimaginable dream, little to support him except good health and nowhere to go but all over the place." I explored Seattle as I had explored no other area. I walked through the neighborhoods, biked the streets of downtown, and probed the old industrial corridors that were tucked between the hills of the city. I stood on Pine Street, where the future author of *Charlotte's Web* paused after being fired by the local newspaper.

White's city was not mine. He lived in Seattle for nine months in 1923 in the midst of lumber mills and fish canneries, anarchists and steamers to Alaska. Mine was the Seattle of the 1980s, a city where labor was tightly under control and where the local fortunes still rose and fell with the prosperity of the Boeing Corporation. The region's software powerhouse, still a minor presence at best, occupied a mid-sized office building at one end of the Evergreen Point Floating bridge, a structure that I kept calling the "Floating Point Bridge" in homage to my time with supercomputers. Its future coffeehouse empire was a single store in the Pike Place Market that bore the name of the cook from Herman Melville's novel *Moby Dick*.

I found a connection with E.B. in those odd corners of the city that harbored young people possessed of energy and ambition but little interest in high technology. The old Nickelodeon that served as the artist studio for one acquaintance and the machine shop was the apartment of another. I particularly enjoyed the abandoned right of way from the old Interurban, which ran through the back yards of houses and revealed remnants of old industry. When I left Seattle for the District of Columbia, I left these little treasures for the planned elegance of Washington. I left the West Coast for the East, cyclist's clothes for business suits, software research for policy studies. I also thought that I had left the eclectic landscape of the northwest for the bland urban geography of a planned city but then I discovered Washington's hidden alleys and recognized that these passages would be the connection to my old life in Seattle.

In Seattle, alleys had been pretty ordinary affairs, a parallel street that held garbage cans and boat trailers. In the District, they were communities unto them-

Too Soon to Tell: Essays for the End of the Computer Revolution, by David Alan Grier
Copyright © 2009 IEEE Computer Society

selves, communities that gave local residents an alternative way to move through the city. The District alleys were formed in the middle of large square blocks. The outer edge of the block would be ringed with row houses, good, solid homes fifteen feet wide with no space between the northern exposure of one building and the southern wall of the other. In the middle of these blocks was the alley, a courtyard that had been built to be the home for 8 or 10 or 20 families. In these courts, residents had lived in small buildings, usually no more than ten feet across, and had shared the space with a variety of dirty businesses: stables, farriers, rag pickers, small forges, dustmen. "Resourceful people lived for years in attractive residences on the avenues," observed a civic activist, "without knowing or affecting in the slightest degree the life of the alien hovels just behind them."

By the time that I arrived in the District, the character of the alleys had been radically changed by the reformers of the 1960s. The alley businesses had been closed and the families had been moved to housing projects on the far side of town. The old buildings had been torn down, or converted to storage bins or renovated as apartments for Capitol interns. A few were showing signs of radical gentrification. In one alley, not far from our house, a senior politician from Washington State had built his home.

Once I had learned the basic geography of the neighborhood, I didn't give much thought to the alleys until I got in a discussion with a friend named Evelyn about the difficulties of driving in the city. Evelyn had grown up in the city and clung to the illusion that the District was still a southern town. She acknowledged that the Confederacy had been defeated and that Liberal New Dealers had taken every good apartment in her hometown but she would never surrender the idea that we lived in a little southern village on the banks of the Potomac.

"What'd y'all mean that it's hard to drive here?" she asked.

I explained that in our neighborhood, the main streets ran one way from west to east and so made it difficult to leave our home and drive downtown. We commonly took a route that went three-quarters of the way around a local park and was interrupted by four stoplights in the process.

Evelyn was shocked at my explanation. "But don't y'all drive the alleys?" she said. "That's what they're for."

We took Eve's advice but we needed several weeks before we were truly comfortable with the idea. Driving through the alley seemed like driving through someone's back yard. The entrance was a narrow lane between two houses. The central courtyard was ringed with porches and clothes lines. We might see a child's toy snuggled beneath a telephone pole or a dog sunning itself by a garage or an unfinished home project waiting to be completed.

We soon found that the alleys provided shortcuts for both cars and pedestrians. Many of the routes through the courtyards were obscure little walkways that allowed you to cut from one street to another without walking halfway around the block. During our early months in the city, these walkways had a brief role in a sex scandal that involved a prominent politician. This politician was charged with spending the night with a young woman in his home. He defended himself by claiming that the woman had left the house late at night and had traveled through the alleys to the home of a friend. Though this story was plausible, no one accepted it. The press didn't believe the explanation because they were convinced that the politician was an inveterate womanizer. Those of us who lived in the neighborhood didn't believe the story because we thought that no man of manners would have allowed a woman to travel through the alleys at night.

THE ONE-WAY TRAFFIC OF DISTRICT STREETS was not the only navigation problem that fall. My move from Washington State to Washington, D.C., had ended my email connection. In Seattle, I had been working at a major research institution and had been able to claim all those perquisites of those organizations that study science in the name of national security. We had a full battalion of computers, many not fully used. A few of these machines were gifts that had been proffered by companies that somehow believed our organization to be influential. We also had a high-speed network connection that allowed us to communicate with friends at like-minded institutions. Bell Laboratories. U. Cal Berkeley. Chicago. IBM Yorktown. Programs. Data. Manuscripts. News. Gossip.

For me, the District provided no such technology. My new colleagues believed, not without some justification, that they lived at the center of the known universe and needed no connection to any other part of the globe. The National Science Foundation was a few blocks away, the National Academy of Science a short distant in the other direction, and a daily parade of black limousines drove past their front door.

Still I persisted in my search for an email connection and eventually found an office, located in the basement of a parking garage, that operated my university's data processing systems. "We don't do that here," replied the office's director when I explained that I was seeking email service. I had already learned something of the ways of Washington and persisted. I found some member of the organization who had a friend that was owed a favor by one of the computer operators. Leveraging this debt, I was able to claim a precious email account and the rather lengthy list of regulations that guarded its use. Rule 1: The account may be used for University work only. Rule 2: Only important messages can be sent over email. The restrictions continued to Rules 3, 4 and on and on.

I asked how to address email to computers outside the university and got a shrug of the shoulders. "Never done it," was the reply. With those words, he turned and left me to find my own way back to my friends in Seattle.

The path across the country was not easy to find. The landscape was flooded with dozens of networks, network technologies and network standards. The kind of email address you had depended upon the kind of network you used and hence upon the kind community to which you belonged. Research institutions had one kind of network. Commercial firms had another. Computer hobbyists had a third. The different kinds of networks seemed to increase daily. "Computer networks have spread to larger and smaller machines," wrote network observers John Quaterman and Josiah Hoskins. They have embraced "different protocols and many nations."

To send email from one network to another, one had to begin by learning the addressing rules on the recipient's network. There "is as yet no universally accepted network addressing convention," concluded Quaterman and Hoskins. Though many networks were starting to adopt the now common three-part address scheme, many more had other conventions for addressing mail. On one system, you might address a message to mom@home.com. On another, you would use home!mom. On a third, you could type mom%home%ibm.com.

Once you had determined how to address the email, you had to route your message to the recipient's network. Often you had to explicitly identify a computer that was connected to both networks and then direct your email to that machine. "Practically everyone agrees that users should not have to supply source routes manually," acknowledged Quaterman and Hoskins, but most users of the networks had at least one correspondent that required a manual routing of email.

I needed nearly three months to find a stable route from the District to Seattle. An early success through computers at the University of California at Berkeley proved to be illusory. The route was well-documented in the computer literature but it did not work well for me. It delivered my messages slowly, if at all. After an extended period of trying to find a problem with the route, I abandoned the California machine and started looking for an alternative passageway, an alleyway that would give me a clear path to the West Coast.

My explorations of the network were tentative. I looked at system routing tables on my host machine, which were both public and surprisingly easy to find, notes from other computer users and postings on the electronic bulletin boards, which then served as a primitive kind of blog. Someone suggested a link through a machine at Montana State University. I tried the connection and found that it worked easily. Having left my community in Seattle, I was finally back in touch with the friends that I had left behind.

After a time, I became curious about my Montana connection. Why was this machine a good connection? What was it supposed to be doing? Like my university's computer, this machine offered a surprising amount of information to the public. I learned that it had no more than three or four regular users and that it ran a couple of programs that never seemed to demand much of the processor. It was used as a word processor by one individual and as a gaming machine by another. It was busy only in the early afternoon, when it would host a couple of rounds of the Adventure game. As far as I could tell, I had found my alley, my quick path through the network to Seattle.

Finding a path to Dad proved to be harder. He had ended his career at Burroughs and had taken his retirement gift, a fairly substantial personal computer, to a small home by a river in rural Michigan. After mastering the basic operation of his machine ("This is nothing like a B-5000," he complained) he decided to subscribe to one of the early network services. "Email looks interesting," he said, "as does the news service."

Dad soon came to enjoy email. He found that he could stay in touch with his friends from Burroughs, his cousin in Cheyenne and a couple of Army buddies. Try as he might, he could not get a message to me. I worked from my end, also without success. As the weeks stretched to months, I began to wonder how it might be possible that our two networks were not connecting. Both were part of large organizations. Both had substantial investments in network technology. However, neither was based on the TCP/IP protocol, the protocol supported by the U.S. Government, and neither used the software most commonly found on networked computers.

We finally solved the problem during a winter visit. He and I sat at the computer, burned a couple of hours of connection time, and probed the different options on the network. I was surprised how cautious he was about trying new solutions. "I know that this shouldn't hurt the machine," he would say, "but is it the right thing to do?" I pointed out that he had once had no qualms about reprogramming a Univac 1103 to play Christmas music but he objected to that comparison. "That was different," he said. "I knew what I was doing." He thought for a bit and then said "And there was no operating system. It was simpler."

We eventually found a system note that gave us a clue about how to connect our two networks. It suggested that we might be able to route our mail through a computer at Ohio State University. We gave it a try and waited. Nothing happened. "Maybe they're still mad about the Michigan–Ohio State game." His alma mater had recently triumphed in the traditional interstate rivalry of November. We tried again with the same results and decided to quit for dinner.

When we returned, the mailbox had its little iconic flag raised and the little copyrighted phrase "You've got mail!" below it. The connection had worked. It had a delay but it would serve as the alley between our computers. When I had a chance to explore the connecting machine, I discovered that it was a fairly busy alley. Carloads of messages sat at each end of the passageway and would wait their opportunity to pass from one end to the other. Usually, a simple email would take about an hour to make the trip. During busy times, the transit might take as long as a day.

"The moral of all this is that there is no magic formula to get mail between any two points," wrote Quaterman and Hoskins. "It is a jungle with trails that may cross and conflict, lead to the wrong place or become overgrown." Of course this jungle was only a temporary phenomenon. Step by step, the networks adopted standard protocols, standard software and standard operating procedures. Slowly, the need for the different alley passageways vanished. When my school got a connection to the Internet, I was able to abandon the Montana State machine. When Dad was able to connect to a standard network, he was able to leave the Ohio State bottleneck with its unpleasant association to the wrong Big 10 football team.

E.B. WHITE ENDED HIS SOJOURN IN THE NORTHWEST with a note of regret. "My spice route to nowhere was behind me," he wrote. "I would soon be host again to the specter that I commonly entertained – the shape of a desk in an office, the dreaded tick of the nine-to-five day, the joyless afternoons of a Sunday suburb. ..." The end of alley communication did not bring the same emotion to me or even to Dad. Yet, once we had a systematic way of corresponding, we no longer paid attention to the operation of the network. For all we cared, the Internet was a fiber optic cable that ran between our houses. We knew nothing about bottlenecks or alleyways or games of Adventure. Alleyways tell better stories than Avenues. Back yards are more interesting than front yards. For a time, I missed the clever route that carried my emails but that emotion soon faded, like a cherished memory of youth. Eventually, we must all leave Seattle.

On the Camino Real

I HAVE NEVER FELT SO FAR FROM CIVILIZATION. The plane ride had been long enough, a restless all-night flight from Miami to Lima, Peru, but it had only taken us part of the way. The next segment of the trip was a bruising 14-hour drive over the 14,000-foot Ticlio Pass. Once we arrived at our destination, we faced one final journey: the hike into the dark tunnels of the lead-zinc mine.

The trip was part of a consulting job, an assignment that had seemed intriguing when it was offered. The mine's owner, a friend of a student, wanted me to come to Peru and teach a computer science course to his engineering staff. In particular, he wanted to develop software to prepare the daily production plans for the mine.

When I accepted the job, I joked that all I knew about Peru was a story that it had been considered the site of El Dorado, the fabled city of gold that had to surrender its wealth to Spanish invaders. As I walked into the mine, I received the first hints that cities of gold were not places of leisure but civilizations built with hard labor. The mine itself was Miltonic, the "dungeon horrible" of *Paradise Lost*, "As far removed from God and light of Heaven as from the centre thrice to th' utmost pole."

My headlamp peered weakly into the fog of dust and diesel fumes that filled the air. I heard the crash of ore in the distance as front loaders dropped ore down deep shafts to rail cars that waited on levels below us. I had been told to keep my eye on the tunnel roof, as rocks could free themselves from the earth's grip and fall on the heads of unsuspecting miners. I was so anxious about this charge that I failed to watch my steps and regularly stumbled over rubble on the mine floor.

After a half hour of walking through the darkness, we came across a culvert, a pipe 30 or 36 inches in diameter. My guide, a tall, slender engineer named Tito after the Yugoslav dictator, indicated that I should get on my knees and begin to crawl. "This is an unstable area," he said, "so we put in the pipe."

As I crawled through the tube, I found that the culvert turned upward and that I had to press my back against the top of the pipe to keep from slipping. After proceeding in this manner for 75 or 80 feet, I emerged into a little chamber with a door. Behind the door—in the heart of the mine—was the engineering shop. It was a cavern sheathed in corrugated iron, lit with fluorescent lights, and filled with machine tools.

Too Soon to Tell: Essays for the End of the Computer Revolution, by David Alan Grier
Copyright © 2009 IEEE Computer Society

"This is where we run the mine," said Tito as he advised me to turn off my head-lamp. "We want to put a computer station here and connect it to the mine office."

As I looked around the room, I saw shelves of drawings and chests of tools. I heard the dripping of water on the iron ceiling and the whir of an electric fan. "So this is technology transfer," I thought to myself. "So this is what it means to be at the frontier."

THE COUNTRIES OF SOUTH AMERICA were late recipients of computing tech-nology. The most industrialized South American countries—Argentina, Brazil, and Chile—purchased their first computers in 1962 and 1963. The number grew steadily but slowly. When a researcher from MIT conducted a survey in 1972, he identified fewer than 2,800 computers on the entire continent. Of these, 75 percent were located in Brazil and Argentina. Peru had only 100 machines, less than 4 percent of the total. "Most of the installations in Latin America are running conventional data processing applications," the researcher noted, "deviating very little from the North American pattern."

At the time, Peru had a simple economy. The country's largest businesses were engaged in mining and agriculture. In contrast, both Argentina and Brazil had growing industries. In Buenos Aires, Siam Di Tella was manufacturing automobiles. The Brazilian government had just moved part of its aircraft industry to a private firm, Empresa Brasileira de Aeronáutica S.A. (now known as Embraer). Yet, neither of these companies was ready to start a computer firm. "No computers, aside from tabulating equipment, are manufactured in [the region]," noted a regional expert. "All must be imported."

Through the 1970s and early 1980s, observers of the region noted many factors that were limiting the growth of a high-technology industry. A report by the National Research Council pointed to "persistent internal economic and social problems," which included such things as "obsolete land ownership systems, a markedly unequal income distribution, inequities of ethnic integration, segmentation of production and marketing systems, inequities for various socioeconomic groups in education and training, and restricted social mobility." Yet, by the mid-1980s, most of these observers noticed a change in the region.

"A visit to Latin America has always seemed like a journey into another era," wrote a visiting scholar in 1985. "Whereas it used to be that there were 30, 40, even 50 years of difference, no more than a decade separates the U.S. and Latin America when it comes to computers." To clarify his point, he added, "Computer use is clearly on the rise in Latin America and at an accelerated pace."

The new computer for the mine's machine shop was a system that used the Intel 386 chip. It had accompanied us on the truck ride over the mountain pass, carefully snuggled beneath the truck seats. Noting that it was one of the more powerful machines then available, I asked Tito where he had purchased it. I knew that the Peruvian government had severely limited all imports. Tito smiled. "Puerto del Este," he said. "Paraguay."

If you believed the economic statistics, Puerto del Este was the high-tech capital of the region, the largest importer of high-tech goods in South America. However, the city was only a transshipment point. Goods arrived on one flight only to leave on the next. The merchants of Puerto del Este were smugglers. They had learned how to circumvent the tariffs of Brazil, Argentina, Chile and Peru.

We carried the new computer to the machine shop and installed it in a plastic box to give it some kind of protection from the water. We snaked the network cable out through a ventilation shaft. It was a longer path than the route through the culvert, but it was less likely to be broken by shifting rocks. The total distance between the computer in the mine and its host in the engineers' office was slightly longer than the maximum length specified by the machine manufacturer, but it didn't seem to matter. The two machines were able to communicate with only occasional difficulty.

With this network, Tito and his colleagues wanted to plan the day's production. Each morning, they determined which sections of the mountain should be blasted, which tunnels should be reinforced, which piles of rock should be moved to the rail cars, which routes the miners should take. Such plans were not that difficult to make, though the process was time consuming. Once the engineers had gathered the basic production data, they could create a production plan in an hour or two of work.

However, like the mountain itself, the production plans were never stable. A tunnel could collapse. A pile of ore might prove to contain too little or too much zinc. A front loader might fail. Under such circumstances, the engineers would have to redraw the plan and redeploy the miners. Their goal was to keep the refining plant operating 24 hours a day. When forced to redraft their daily plans by hand, they would regularly fall short of that goal.

Writing the planning program was not very difficult. It used a simple search algorithm. You entered the relevant constraints: the quantity and quality of ore needed, the tunnels that were open, the piles of ore available, the areas ready to be blasted, and the equipment that was operational. The program would then search through the various possible plans. It was not a very efficient program, but it didn't need to be efficient as the mine was not very complex. The system generally could create a new plan in six to eight minutes.

AFTER WE GOT THE SYSTEM RUNNING, I had to explain how the programs worked and how the engineers could modify them. We held a programming course in the engineers' office, a large plywood building with windows that opened into low winter sun and the vistas of the high jungle. We created a classroom space by pushing tables to one side, moving a small computer to a desk, and taping paper to the wall. I stood at the front of the room with a list of information that I wanted to convey: the database's structure, the search algorithm's nature, and the programming language's syntax.

We had planned two hours for the class, but two hours stretched to three, three to four, and four to five. Part of the added time came from the need to translate the ideas for those who could not follow my English. The remainder came from the desire to test all the ideas as I soon as I presented them.

As I began to describe the first idea, one of the engineers walked to the computer, took a seat, and began to program. Even if I had tried, I doubt that I could have stopped him. The others gathered around the screen and added their comments, criticized the results, and joked about any mistakes.

We ended the class at the sixth hour, when the declining sun made it difficult to see the notes that I had written on the wall. We finished the day tired but happy with what we had accomplished.

We had dinner in town that night, a celebration of sorts. I had a chance to walk the town square as I waited for the mine's truck to shuttle the engineering staff from the mine. The sight did indeed look like a vision from 50 years back in time. Women in bowler hats squatted in front of the church and sold roasted meats: chicken, pork, and guinea pig. Men watched a cockfight in an alley. People stood in a queue at the telephone office waiting to use the public radio phone, the only way to communicate with Lima and the outside world.

We took our meal at the town's most prominent restaurant, a building that was little better than the engineers' office. The floor was concrete, the sides were open to the weather, and the table was nothing more than a strip of plywood sitting on galvanized pipe. In our honor, the owner entertained us with his favorite American music, a worn tape of Jimmy Rogers tunes. "My pocketbook is empty and my heart is filled with pain," sang the scratchy voice. "I'm a thousand miles away from home just waiting for a train."

We talked about many things that night, but the conversation often turned to the isolation these men and women felt. They complained about how far they were from Lima and from the centers of computer science. They said that it was very hard to get technical information and that they had to spend hours trying to glean new ideas from the few manuals and books that they had been able to procure. They were pleased that I had been able to visit them, that I had brought them a stack of computer books, and that I had spent the time to give them a few insights into the current state of computer development.

Only rarely can we recognize that we are standing at a point of inflection, a time when the twig is bent and a tree begins to follow a new curve. I left the mine honestly believing that I could return in two or four or eight years and find that nothing had changed. If anything, I believed that the pull backwards was stronger than the push forward, that the combined economic and social forces were more likely to keep the country in a primitive state than to build a modern economy.

DIGITAL NETWORKS STARTED TO REACH SOUTH AMERICA that summer. Bitnet, the network based on IBM protocols, had reached Argentina just before I had arrived in Peru. "The advances of knowledge, science, and the arts know no boundaries, because they belong to all of humanity," raved Argentine President Raul Alfonsine. "When any nation, whatever its motivation, inhibits free access to information from within or outside itself, it is doubtless condemning itself to isolation and underdevelopment."

A network connection reached Peru six or eight months after my visit. For a time, the network was our Camino Real, our royal road that carried information from an engineering shack in the bowels of the Andes to the offices of the industrialized world. Tito posed technical questions from his machine in the high mountain valleys and I responded from my computer in Washington, D.C. The mine's general manager sent production reports down to the Lima office and the Lima office responded with directives. The employees of the mine, when they got access to the computer, mailed electronic letters to their families in Lima and the families responded with news of their lives.

After a year or two with the network connection, the mining engineers began to realize that they could use the network to operate the mine. They could prepare the daily production plans in the relative comforts of Lima and evaluate the day's accomplishments without being anywhere near the cramped and dirty shop in the mine. One by one, the engineers relocated to Lima. They visited the mine only when they needed to inspect the operations. Tito was the first to resettle but he was soon followed by the others.

Unlike the original Camino Real, the computer network was not a simple path in the mountains, a single road from the Peruvian capital to a distant source of wealth. It put Tito and the other mining engineers in touch with the world's industries, industries that offered special opportunities to Spanish speaking engineers. Just as they had taken the path way from the mine up in the mountains, Tito and his friends traveled the computer network to new jobs with software firms in El Norte. Tito was again the first to take the path. He found a software support job with Siemens AG. From his home in Lima, he worked with clients across South America. The other mining engineers soon followed the same path. One went to IBM, another to Novell, a third found a career with Computer Associates, a fourth became a software retailer. In only a short space of time, all the engineers I had met in that mining office, once so distant in the Andean highlands, had left their homes and had traveled the digital Camino Real out of old Peru.

Dirty Electricity

THE HOUSE ON BAGLEY AVENUE was a mystery to the residents of its quiet, suburban neighborhood. They knew little about the owner, a former executive from a local telephone company, and less about the two men who arrived each morning in separate cars and left in the early evening. Some speculated that the residence might be an illegal methamphetamine laboratory or a safe house for the CIA. One individual called the city government to see if the building was using an inordinate amount of electricity. Another homeowner, a retired office worker, decided to conduct her own investigation.

This neighbor began her study of the Bagley Avenue address by walking her dog past the home twice a day. She would peer at the big front window and wave if she saw any shapes moving behind the glass. Occasionally, she would intercept the postman and volunteer to deliver any mail to the front door but she gained no information about the activities within the house from her efforts. Her raps on the door would bring a polite reply from Andy, the owner of the home, but they brought no invitations to step inside and no further information.

Eventually, she abandoned this tactic and would linger at the front lawn long enough to allow her little poodle, who was clearly not built for extended exercise, to empty his bowels on the front lawn. Judging from the expression on her face, she might have been hoping her puppy's actions would draw the wrath of Andy or one of the other occupants of the home, and from the ensuing confrontation, she might learn the secret of the house. If this was her plan, it was never fulfilled. No matter how often she visited the house, she was unable to discern what was happening inside.

Andy, the owner of the home, was wary about talking with his neighbor. He was using the house as the office of a new technology firm and was aware that, in doing so, he might be violating local zoning covenants. He was the president of the company and was doing the financial work in the guest bedroom. The company's server was installed in a spare bathroom. Roger, the vice president for marketing, was preparing the sales plan in the den. Les, the technician, was developing the first product in a laboratory that began at a 220 volt outlet in the kitchen, snaked past two workbenches in the hallway (with acid burns on the carpet) and ended at a large computer installation in the living room.

Too Soon to Tell: Essays for the End of the Computer Revolution, by David Alan Grier
Copyright © 2009 IEEE Computer Society

The condition of the house belied the fact that the three partners had once been highly successful employees of a large technology firm. Andy had produced record profits from the division that he had overseen. Roger had managed a dozen of the company's products and found large markets for each of them. Les was a designer without a peer at their old firm and was known for his creative, efficient designs.

Andy, Roger and Les had been operating their firm, "Bagley Systems," for over a year. They had produced a business plan, found initial funding, recruited a distinguished board and had even gained the interest of a few potential customers. However, they had yet to produce a working prototype of their first product, a device that would transmit data at high speeds over ordinary power cables. No matter how hard Les worked, he could not make the prototype function properly. "The oscilloscope looked like the original scene of the first Star Wars movie," recalled Andy. "Flashing points of light would appear at the bottom of the screen and slowly float to the top. If you stared at it long enough, you would believe that you could see a giant spacecraft traveling through the universe."

Andy was worried about the state of the prototype. Every day of delay made another demand on the firm's precious capital and increased the likelihood that the company would be exposed by an inquisitive neighbor. After watching Les struggle for four months with the prototype, he decided to ask advice of an individual who had a reputation for fixing other peoples' computer systems, a programmer named Kai.

Les was not pleased to learn that Andy had hired a consultant, especially one that was clearly not trained in engineering. He was cool when Kai arrived at the house. After the initial pleasantries, he wasted no time in challenging the newcomer. "How much do you actually know about circuit design," he asked.

"Nothing," Kai said after a brief pause, "or maybe a little bit less than that."

Given a sigh of obvious contempt, Les took Kai over to the oscilloscope and showed him the picture of little green stars rolling through the lumineferous ether.

"What do you think that you can do with it?" he asked the consultant.

"Depends," Kai replied, "on what it is supposed to look like."

"A straight line," Les responded.

The two stared at the screen in silence. Les took comfort in the idea that Kai's tenure would be short.

"What do you think is wrong?" Kai finally asked.

"Everything is perfect," Les stated confidently. "I've checked every element of the circuit and looked at every line of code. I believe that the problem is dirty electricity," a term that normally described a power source that occasionally had random fluctuations.

"Hmmmp," replied Kai, "So you think that the electricity passed through a porn video on its way to the house?"

This remark irritated Les but before he could respond Kai asked a second question. "Are you sure that the input to the device is correct?"

Feeling that he was being mocked, Les decided to put Kai in his place. He uttered a well-known expletive, disconnected a cable, flipped a switch and turned back to the oscilloscope. A green sign wave appeared on the screen.

"Is that the right signal?" Kai asked.

"No," said Les.

"Good," said Kai. "Let us begin here. It is time for us to remove the bugs."

IN THE FIELD OF COMPUTER SCIENCE, the concept of the "bug," the small error in design or implementation can be traced back to earliest days of the field. In February 1944, one of the staff at the Harvard laboratory of Howard Aiken wrote that they were running test problems on the electro-mechanical Mark I in order to "find 'bugs'." In a story that was recounted by Grace Hopper, Aiken's staff actually found a moth in their second machine, the Mark II, and taped it in their log book with the notation, "first actual case of a bug being found." In fact, the term is much older than the computer era. Thomas Edison used the term as early as 1878 to describe problems with electrical systems. "Bugs," he wrote to a friend, "show themselves and months of anxious watching, study and labor are requisite before commercial success—or failure—is certainly reached."

Debugging, the process of removing conceptual errors from programs, has been one of the crucial skills of computer science. Only in those brief days of naiveté that followed the introduction of high-level programming languages did anyone profess that a computer system could be built without hours of debugging, and yet, debugging has held an anomalous role in the field. "Program testing and debugging occupies more than 50% of professional programmer's time," complained an early author in the field. He noted that the process of debugging a program was "time consuming, difficult, poorly planned, and often slighted." At the same time, he noted that most computer scientists could offer little guidance on the subject. "Students and teachers are encouraged to minimize errors by having good work habits, being methodical and neat, and checking for clerical details. This is certainly good advice, but it doesn't really help when it comes to fixing a problem."

The topic of debugging has never been able to command enough attention to create its own comprehensive theory, or its own journal or even a regular conference of devoted to the subject. Indeed, debugging has largely been ignored by the theoretical literature. The journals devoted to computer theory have published only a couple of dozen articles on the subject in the years since the ENIAC began operation in 1946.

Debugging receives better treatment in the applied computing literature but, even in these journals, the coverage is incomplete. "Debugging is said to be the least established area in software development," observed one set of authors. "Industrial developers have no clear ideas about general debugging tools, yet they debug programs anyway."

One of the aspects of debugging that separates it from other aspects of computer science is the fact that it is an empirical task rather than a synthetic activity. Good debuggers must reason from effects back to causes, a process that is fraught with problems. They must build a mental model of how the machine should behave under the control of the program and hypothesize the state of the machine at points during the execution of the code. From observing the actual state of the machine and comparing it to their hypothesis, they must assess their model and determine how they should first adjust their ideas and then modify the code itself.

Much of the literature on debugging has presented ideas for software tools that would help with one part of the debugging process, the part that connects the code to the state of the machine. Articles on such tools began to appear in the 1960s when high-level computer languages began to separate programmers from the logic circuits. "It appears that many programmers of large scale computers today do not understand and often do not even wish to understand symbolic machine language," wrote one author in 1963. "This puts severe restrictions on the types of debugging procedures that may be used, and, in fact, restricts them to debugging at the complier language level." Such judgment was harsh and shortsighted. In 1963, several systems had symbolic debuggers, software that would connect user programs to the operations of the machines. Within a decade, symbolic debuggers would be common on most computers.

During the 1980s, the literature of debugging expanded for a second time with the introduction of more sophisticated ideas such as concurrency, parallelism, distributed programming and optimizing compilers. For programs that made use of these concepts, the old symbolic debuggers no longer gave a clear picture of machine operation. Such ideas complicate "the mapping between the source code and the object code due to code duplication, elimination, and reordering," observed one research team. They also make "reporting values of source variables either inconsistent with what the user expects or simply impossible."

However, the problem of connecting a program to the underlying state of the machine is only a small part of debugging. The bigger task, that of hypothesizing the proper state of the machine and reasoning from the actual state back to the logic of the program, had defied a general engineering solution. "Debugging," wrote one author in 2001, remains "as labor-intensive and painful as it was five decades ago." Some researchers have been able to develop algorithms to handle some of the debugging work or to automate the task of checking all possible paths through the code but the basic work remains unchanged. It is no easier to find the bugs in a program than it is to discern the activities inside a home by standing on the lawn and observing the shadows inside the windows.

AT BAGLEY AVENUE SYSTEMS, the debugging took four days. The hardware was the easiest part to fix. The software was considerably harder. It controlled two processors, one that processed the incoming data and another that prepared the output. At each step of the code, Kai demanded to know how the joint flows of information were to be transformed by the machine and asked Les to demonstrate that the processors were behaving correctly. Les responded to each request but he remained just as impatient with this process as he had in the initial encounter with Kai.

As they came to the end of the system, they were no closer to working as a team then they had been on the first day. Kai continued to make his requests, often punctuating his questions with comments that irritated Les. Les did all that was asked of him but still resented the idea that he was working with someone who couldn't understand the technical details of his design.

By the end of the last day, the rolling stars had vanished from the oscilloscope. In their place could be seen a gentle wave and a few dots that would appear at arbitrary moments and quickly vanish. Les was not pleased with the picture and turned on his partner. "You've added a new error to the code," he claimed in frustration. "It's supposed to be straight."

"Prove it," was Kai's response.

Les pushed a pile of cables to one corner of the table, found a piece of paper and started to write the equations that described the operation of the system. When he reached the end of the page, he started to search for a second sheet but Kai stopped him. Pointing to one line, Kai said "This statement is only an approximation."

"But it's good enough," blurted Les.

"Perhaps," said Kai, "but if you add a second term you will see that there is a wave in output."

Kai paused to let Les fully comprehend the issue. "If you add a third term ..."

"What ..." Les interrupted.

"If you add a third term, you will see that the system is sensitive to small changes..." he hesitated and then corrected himself. "Sensitive to dirty electricity."

Because We Were Different

MY LECTURE HAD BEEN PREPARED THE PRIOR FRIDAY. It was a combination of statistical analysis and computer skills that I taught every term to graduate students in the public policy program. I placed the notes on the podium, slipped out of my suit coat and started to roll up my sleeves. It was a theatrical touch that I used to signal that I had left my office and was joining the students in the act of learning. I picked up the chalk and was about to start my lecture when a student in the third or fourth row raised her hand. "Can you explain what happened last weekend?"

The date was Monday, November 7, 1988. The story of the weekend was the Internet worm, a computer program that had attacked the nation's research computers. The worm was an invasive program, an unwelcome visitor that sucked up the free process cycles of every machine that it infected. It crawled from machine to machine by exploiting security weaknesses in the late 1980s versions of the Unix operating system. It had been first spotted on the prior Wednesday night by the computing staff at Cornell University. It was soon seen at MIT, which had strong research ties to Cornell. Shortly after midnight, it had spread across the country and had reached the machines at the University of California, Berkeley.

The worm used three different methods to propagate. It might drop a little piece of code in a remote machine by feeding a string of text to a common operating system command. It could also enter a machine through the debug option of the mail program, an option that was commonly left open in those less sophisticated days. If those two methods failed, it could gather a list of user ids from the machine and attempt to guess the correct password. Most passwords of the age were short or simple or obvious. A surprising number of young graduate students selected their passwords from popular culture. One computer manager speculated that every research computer in the nation had at least one user who protected his account with the password "darthvader."

By early Thursday morning, the worm had attacked all the major centers on the Internet and had drawn the attention of the network operators. Some of the operators thought, at first, that they just had a malfunctioning program that was consuming all of the machine time. When they were unable to purge the program from their computers, they concluded that something was wrong. "A virus has been detected on

Too Soon to Tell: Essays for the End of the Computer Revolution, by David Alan Grier
Copyright © 2009 IEEE Computer Society

media-lab," wrote a worried researcher at MIT, who added that "The virus is spread via mail of all things." Desperate to bring their machines back under control, they took the radical step of terminating their email system. Unable to communicate with their computers, they were reduced to calling each other over the telephone. "This situation will continue," apologized the MIT researcher, "until someone figures out a way of killing the virus and telling everyone how to do it without using email."

At MIT, Cornell and a half dozen other sites, the computer staff worked through the day and into Thursday night, as they tried to isolate the program and determine how it worked. Some researchers grabbed images of the machine code, as it worked to spread itself through the network. Others traced the actions of the code. While they labored, the story of the worm started to spread through the research community. By the end of the day, the news had reached the public press, who sent reporters to MIT and Cornell to learn what was happening to the nation's scientific computers. Most of the reporters knew little about computer operations and even less about networks. The network managers found that they had to explain the most basic activities of the network, including email, file transfer and remote access. "The media was uniformly disappointed that the virus did nothing even remotely visual," explained an MIT researcher. "But the vast majority of the press seemed to be asking honest questions in an attempt to grapple with the unfamiliar concepts of computers and networks."

By Friday morning, the researchers were starting to understand how the worm operated and how they could keep it from spreading. They reconfigured their mail programs, changed the name of their language compilers, patched weak code and hid their password files. By Saturday morning, the worm started to disappear from the computers, which allowed the researchers to return to their routine tasks. By Monday morning, only two problems remained. They needed to determine who had created the worm and find a strategy to block such programs.

On that Monday, standing in my classroom, I could do nothing to help solve these two outstanding problems but I knew enough to be able to explain the worm, in broad terms, to my students. Even though it was entirely improvised and had nothing to do with the goals of the course, that class was one of the most satisfying that I have ever taught. The students drove the discussion, asking how the worm worked and how it might have spread. As the hour progressed, we moved a fairly detailed discussion of computer processors, operating systems and network protocols.

Midway through the time, the student who had started this discussion, raised her hand again. "Why were our computers not touched by the program?" she asked.

Her voice was almost plaintive, disappointed. An event of great import had just happened but it had not touched her. The tone made me pause before answering. "Because we are different," I said.

I explained that the worm only worked on a certain kind of operating system and hence only touched a few brands of computers. The computers that had been infected ran Unix and were made by Digital Equipment Corporation or Sun Microsystems. Our school had IBM equipment and they were connected to a network using IBM software. The plague passed over our house because we were different.

AS I WAS ADDRESSING MY CLASS, the federal bureau of investigation was starting to draw up lists of individuals who might have created the worm. Though some in the public press suggested that the worm might be an act of espionage from the tottering Soviet Union or the creation of organized crime, most investigators assumed that the perpetrator was "bored graduate student." Only a graduate student, they reasoned, would have the necessary knowledge, access to networked computers and the time required by such a project.

On the whole, the graduate students who were developing computer networks formed a fairly privileged class. To be sure, a number of them slept in their research labs and ate nothing but macaroni and cheese, but they worked at the elite research universities, had good educations and came from comfortable homes. No one should have been surprised when the FBI asked for warrants to search university computer laboratories but they were. We "all gasped," recalled one researcher "and hoped it had not really been one of our students." By Thursday, the FBI was focusing its attention on Cornell University and one graduate student, Robert Tappan Morris, who was the son of a nationally known computer security expert.

The community of computer scientists did not know how to react to the news of Mr. Morris' arrest. He was one of their own, a young man who had been born into the world of digital technology. Yet, he had badly transgressed this community's standards of behavior. These standards reflected the ideals of the scientists and engineers who had created the network. They had never been formally codified but they permeated the community that worked on the network. The network was disciplined, explained one researcher, "almost exclusively by peer pressure." If someone misuses the network there is "a good chance that you may get 500 or 1,000 pieces of electronic mail telling that's not an appropriate thing to be doing."

Even though Morris had violated the standards of the network community, he found a fair amount of sympathy among his peers. "I don't know of too many who want to see this kid rot away for the next few decades in a jail," confessed one computer scientist. He claimed that Morris had made a bad judgment and seemed to be aware of his error. Most computer scientists were relieved when the young graduate student received only a mild punishment for his actions: three years probation, $10,000 in fines and 400 hours of community service. "He was playing with fire," admitted one witness who had testified against Morris, "but he didn't really mean to burn anybody."

The strongest objections to the sentence came from those interested in commercializing information technology. "Industry was counting on a tough sentence for Morris," wrote two members of the U.S. Congress. Viewing Morris as representative of a renegade segment of society, they argued that "Destructive computer hacking would largely stop if a few computer vandals were put behind bars."

THE INTERNET WORM OCCURRED at a key point in the development of the Internet. The news stories that explained network operations and network services introduced digital communication to millions and laid the foundation for the effort to build a commercialized Internet four years later. Yet, it also marked the end of the Internet as a close, little community. Prior to 1988, most of the major network managers knew each other. They shared information and handled their responsibilities with a personal touch. Users might feel that they were part of an inner sanctum. Yet, this world was slipping away as the network expanded.

The expansion of the Internet brought a greater uniformity to computer hardware and software. When the original progenitor of the Internet began operation in 1970, the idea of a common operating system running across dozens of different platforms was unknown. "The types of machines and operating systems involved in the network vary widely," explained an early article on networking. "The only commonality among the network membership is the use of highly interactive time-sharing systems; but, of course, these are all different in external appearance and implementation."

After the 1988 worm attack, software designers moved to secure the network but they focused on a few, common pieces of software, such as the Unix operating system. When the next generation of worm writers began to test their skills, they aimed at a target that may have been better protected than the 1988 Internet, but was also more standardized. The new Internet software may have been able to defend itself better from most attacks but it was also vulnerable to a virus that attacked an email interface that was found on most office computers.

In May of 2000, the Internet was struck with another debilitating worm attack. This one was carried in emails that were marked with the phrase "I LOVE YOU" in the subject line. These emails contained an attachment that would use the email interface to replicate itself and send copies to every address stored in the email database. Within hours, the new worm had circled the globe and had paralyzed the computers of many institutions, including Ford Motor Company and several investment firms.

Unlike the attack of 1988, the "I LOVE YOU" virus was studied by a group of institutions that had been given the job of defending the network from intrusions. These institutions had developed a great deal of expertise about worms, Trojan horses, viruses and other programmatic attacks on the network. "It frightens me to think about what is out there," confessed one security expert. Such attacks came daily and were no longer caused by a "bored graduate student." Many different sorts of people possessed the expertise, the access to equipment and the time to prepare such a program.

Early in the attack, someone claimed that the "I LOVE YOU" virus had originated with a German graduate student but this idea was quickly dismissed. The virus code contained several clues that it came from the Philippines. It included, for example, the word "barok," a Tagalog term meaning "fool" or "crazy person." It also had the phrase "I hate to go to school." A security consultant suggested that "They're either trying to look like a teenager or they are a teenager."

The investigation soon focused on a small group of friends from a lower-middle class neighborhood of Manila. The most likely suspect appeared to be a student at a local computer school, named Onel de Guzman, who lived in a weary and worn apartment with his sister and her boyfriend. In their world, there was enough money to purchase an inexpensive desktop computer but there were no family connections to the computer world like those possessed by Robert Morris' father. de Guzman had shown talent in computer programming at a local computer school, but he had accomplished nothing that would have given him entry to the laboratories of Harvard or Cornell.

de Guzman found no sympathy from computer scientists, or business students, or the computer industry, even though he made a few statements claiming that he was defending the freedom of the Internet. Most users of the network were disappointed when de Guzman did not have to face prosecution on charges of disrupting the Internet. "A Panel of prosecutors dismissed the charges," reported the *New York Times*, "saying the laws cited did not apply to computer activity and there was insufficient evidence showing an intent to gain from the e-mail program."

OVER THE YEARS, THE STUDENTS OF 1988 taught me how far the Internet had extended into our lives. Their letters followed a common pattern. They began with the hope that I remembered them, gave a brief sketch of their life and perfunctorily asked for news of me. At the end, appearing to be an afterthought, they would add "and could you write a recommendation for me?"

As a group, these students were delighted to discover the growing scope of the Internet. They wrote messages from a luxury hotel in Atlanta that delivered coffee and chocolate to their keyboards; a public library in Alaska, where the crews of fishing boats waited in line for a computer; a technology center in rural Germany; a café in Yerevan, Armenia, that had electricity for only eight hours a day; a massive room off New York's Times Square, where the air hung heavy with the smell of sweat and the computers clicked with the anxiety of 80 people rushing to finish their work before their precious time came to an end.

Yet, these students were wary of network technology in a way that subsequent students were not. They had been eager to leave our school with its non-standard machines and restricted protocols. Yet, they were not surprised when public machines were crippled by viruses or when their messages were blocked by security software or when they received enticing offers of quick wealth from the distant relatives of central African dictators. Their first introduction to the network had been the Internet Worm. They knew the price you had to pay when you wanted to be like everyone else.

A Winter of Hope and
A Spring of Despair

THE OLD X AND O COFFEE SHOP was a great place to get gossip. If I arrived early, I could usually get the table by the window, the one that had both an electric outlet for my computer and the view of the United States Capitol building. As my machine went through its boot cycle, I would clear the table—taking the china mugs back to the counter and recycling any abandoned reading material. You'd usually find an old issue of the *Economist*, the op-ed page from the day's *Wall Street Journal* and a ratty copy of the trade journal *Campaigns and Elections*.

The shop was frequented by young congressional aides who were apparently not particularly essential to the nation's business. They would lounge on the tattered couches and threadbare chairs, sipping esoteric brews of coffee and swapping lies about their lives. Most commonly, they spoke about their social activities: the committee aide that they were dating, the lawyer they would like to date and the intern that they would prefer never to date again. Between these conversations, you would hear snippets of legislative strategies and expansive monologues on the roles that they were playing in the Republican or Democratic Party.

The monologues were often little soliloquies on power and ambition. They spoke of the leadership they intended to express, the political office they hoped to gain, the good they hoped to accomplish. Each of them had a plan for their career. All of them were willing to share that plan to a room full of strangers and every one of them was confident that their organizational strategies would succeed.

JUST TWO OR THREE DOORS AWAY FROM THE OLD X AND O is an office that advertises "Power Tools for Politicians," computer software packages for political campaigns. It is housed in a building that suggests the old stereotypes of political deals and smoke-filled rooms rather than the clean lines of the modern high-tech firm. The structure was built in the decade that Herman Hollerith completed his first punched card equipment and delivered it to the U.S. Census. Its brick façade is worn

---

Too Soon to Tell: Essays for the End of the Computer Revolution, by David Alan Grier
Copyright © 2009 IEEE Computer Society

and cracked, its stairs slant and creak, its window frames are caked with years of paint.

If you explore the world of political software, you quickly find that most of the applications are surprisingly mundane, much like the campaigns themselves. One company provides lists of registered voters. Another provides financial accounting software for Congressional campaigns, including programs that produce the reports that are required by the Federal Election Commission. A couple of firms market software that tracks the needs of constituents. The firms' brochures remind the ambitious political leader that the problems of modern leadership are almost impossible without the assistance of computers. "In the aftermath of the 'Storm of the Century'," it reads, "the governor and key legislators must respond to tens of thousands of requests for emergency assistance and information."

The stories of computers in politics often restrict their scope to the newest and most sophisticated of technologies, as if the parties only recently discovered digital technology. Yet, computing technology had been associated with politics and government since the days of Hollerith. Punched card equipment tracked the needs of farmers in 1900, helped organize the mobilization for the First World War and shaped the economic climate of the 1920s.

During the Great Depression of the 1930s, political leaders started using computing technology as a means of communicating with constituents. "Like a great business corporation," wrote on observer, "a political party endeavors to maintain agents in every 'sales' territory in the country to attend to its election interests." By 1932, the United States had grown so large and so diverse, that both political parties and governing administrations needed mechanical tools to assist with their work. "The complexity of the job that government has to do is great," remarked the American Vice President Henry Wallace. Wallace was a strong advocate for computing technology among Franklin Roosevelt's advisors. If an "administration is not to break down of its own size and complexity," Wallace argued, "continuous lines of communication, in addition to periodic elections, must be kept with the various publics affected by administrative policy."

Wallace oversaw a series of modest efforts to use computing machinery for politics and governance. In his time, the parties acquired punched card equipment, compiled databases of voters and transmitted polling data over telegraph lines. Slowly but steadily, the political parties gained sophistication with the new technologies. As computing firms developed new products, the parties found novel ways to use them in their efforts to promote their interests. This technology remained firmly in the hands of the parties until its cost began to fall in the 1990s. As small organizations were able to acquire a desktop machine, a printer, a network connection, they learned that they could challenge the power of the major parties.

IN MARCH 1989, AN EMAIL MESSAGE BEGAN CIRCULATING among the Chinese students at American universities. "Dear Friend," it began, "I am sorry to have bothered you by E-mail." The writer announced that he was planning on running a "news and information service for you people." He described the kind of news that he hoped to circulate and asked "Would you please tell other Chinese students in your school about this service, or can you be so nice to forward to me the E-mail addresses of your friends?" He added that to "protect readers' privacy, I use "bcc" (blind carbon copy) mode to forward news so that recipients' names do not appear in the mail header."

This email marked the start of Democracy Spring, a period of political protest in China. The pressures that created the protests had been building for a decade and were reaching a crisis point. Students were gathering in Beijing's Tiananmen Square and calling for political reforms, greater democracy and government transparency. Separated by an ocean, Chinese students in the United States, some 25,000 in number, yearned for news of their homeland and friends. They shared gossip at social events and shared news by letter. Students in the technical fields found that they could correspond with email but they found that email connections were still a novelty at many universities. Only the large research institutions, the schools engaged in defense work, had connections to Arpanet. A second group of schools were linked to NSFnet or csnet or another of the small networks. Even at these schools, only the science and engineering students tended to have access to network services. The only network that was easily accessible to general students was Bitnet, a store and forward network that was based on IBM protocols.

Bitnet was slow. It was awkward. It had choke points that could delay email for days. "When I send Bitnet email to Israel," complained one friend of mine, "the letters stall in Paris." At one point, he claimed that his intellectual work had spent so much time on the computer of the Ecole Politechnique that he "should be considered a French author." Yet for all its problems, Bitnet had three unassailable advantages. It was accessible to general students, it had global reach and it had Listserv, a program that allowed an individual to manage a large and complex email list.

In late March, a group of four Chinese students, two in Canada and two in the United States, began circulating a short electronic periodical that they called *News Digest*. The two in Canada edited the digest while the two in the United States handled the distribution. They claimed that this division of labor was designed "to evade the pressures from the Chinese Consulates in Canada," which they claimed "had a higher degree of control on Chinese students than their U.S. counterparts."

From the start, the *News Digest*, was a political journal. It made some effort to carry cultural and economic stories but these efforts were half-hearted. One of the first issues carried a 50-word notice of the annual Academy of Awards Show with the comment that it would be "Aired by Five Stations in Toronto Area at 9:00 p.m., Wednesday" but gave no indication of what would be seen on the show or why anyone should watch it.

As March turned to April and April to May, the *New Digest* followed events in Beijing: the construction of a statue called the Goddess of Liberty, the large demonstrations on May 4, the visit of Mikhail Gorbachev from the Soviet Union, and the gradual waning of the crowds during the last days of the month and finally, the first reactions to the events of June 4, when the Chinese Army cleared the square. "EMERGENCY!!! BLOODSHEDDING IN BEIJING NOW !!!" read the subject line. With little more than a quick summary of events, the editor ended the posting

"I cannot type more, my fingers are twisting, my heart is breaking, tears are dripping for our homeland, our fellow students and our people."

Behind the dramatic stories of world politics, the *Digest* carried the backstage discussion of local activities. It told of the students who had established a communications office in Boston, a group that had raised $36,207.54 for the Tiananmen protestors, of the committee that was working to change American law so that Chinese students could remain in the United States. By the end of the summer, the organization had acquired a new name, *China News Digest*, and was closely following the activities of a new political organization that was called the Independent Federation of Chinese Students and Scholars.

During the fall of 1989, the *Digest* staff devoted much of its coverage to the political activities of the Independent Federation, particularly the Federation's efforts to change U.S. immigration laws. *China News Digest* was "not affiliated with any political organization and [Independent Federation] is no exception," explained one editor. "However, we do keep a good working relation with [the group] and other organizations in the Chinese communities." The "good working relationship" included the publication of reports from the Independent Federation. These reports circulated stories about lobbying activities, instructions on how to contact members of Congress, calls to rally on Capitol Hill and analyses from the Federation's lawyers. "Many students seem to be very panic now," read one hastily written report from the Federation. "Under the current situation, it is very IMPORTANT to talk POSITIVELY."

The *Digest* reports show how the Chinese students were struggling to use network communication to manage a national political effort. They clearly appreciated the benefits of the technology, particularly the ability to reach a national audience with a unified message. At the same time, they learned that network communication was an unruly animal. Dissident groups established their own communications channels on the network. Angry individuals would undermine the students' efforts with postings that questioned the integrity of the Federation. "Some times, there are things we can not post," said one leader, "and some times it is not the best way to have massive response."

It was an age of wisdom and an age of foolishness; a season of light and season of darkness; a winter of hope and a spring of despair. Step by step, the Chinese students brought their network correspondence under control. They learned, as other leaders had learned before them, that political communication needs to disciplined, focused and organized. They limited opportunities for dissent and stopped debating strategy over the network. For their efforts, they were awarded the legal changes that they sought. In early December, the administration of George H.W. Bush gave the students the opportunity to remain in the United States.

The success of this effort was noted by the members of Congress. Senator Alan Simpson (R-WY) ruefully noted that the student leaders "are good and they know exactly what they are doing." He was aware that they had "used the computer systems of every major university" to contact every member of Congress. From those students, "I received 1,000 Christmas cards," he said, adding "that is more than I get from [my home state of] Wyoming."

THE OLD X AND O IS LONG GONE FROM CAPITOL HILL. It has been replaced by one of those franchised sandwich shops that move hungry people along a high-speed assembly line, thereby ensuring that the business of politics is not long neglected. A few of the old regulars still linger at the tables, though they are more likely to be poking at their laptops than to be gossiping about the social life of congressional asides. They will be writing a report for some committee or redistricting the state of Delaware or planning a massive lobbying effort for a bill of deep importance to a small minority of American voters. All of them will get the chance to learn, as the Chinese students did in 1989, that the quality of the "power tools" is less important than the quality of the organization behind it.

Coming into the Country

I HAVE RECEIVED AS WELL AS GIVEN unsolicited career advice. Such advice, we know, is worth only the price offered for it on the open market, but occasionally some ideas can make you reassess your decisions. Twice, over an interval of 15 years, I was told to avoid the field of computer science. I first received this advice when I was a young programming intern and found that I had a free day when no one wanted me to program. Thinking that it might be good to learn something about hardware, I volunteered to help one of the field engineers re-cable a large mainframe. We spent the morning chatting about our days and complaining about the company. We proved to have little expertise in any of these subjects so we were soon working quietly.

We finished the technical work by the middle of the afternoon and started to replace the outer shell—called the "skins"—back on the machine's frame. As I handed one of the larger skins to my partner, he stopped and looked at me.

"You should get out of computers," he said. "There's no future in it."

As I had thought that computers had nothing but future, I was surprised. "Really?" I sputtered.

"Yup," he said. "Data communications. That's the future."

This conversation was repeated 15 years later when I was purchasing my first home computer. The clerk, who was probably no more than a year or two younger than myself, had taken apart the processor in order to install a graphics board and a hard drive. He tried to engage me in a discussion of sports but I was no more knowledgeable about the subject than I had been a decade and a half before. I tried to switch the conversation to his job but he quickly grew silent. As he was reassembling the processor, he suddenly spoke. "I want to get out of computers. I'm looking for a new job."

"Really?" I said. "Why?"

"There's no future in it," he said. "I'll be doing the same thing for ever. I want to get into networking." And with that, he clicked the box shut and moved to the register.

The year prior to that purchase had not been good for the computer industry. The economy was lingering in a recession that had begun when the Dow Jones

Too Soon to Tell: Essays for the End of the Computer Revolution, by David Alan Grier
Copyright © 2009 IEEE Computer Society

Industrial Average had fallen 22% in a single day. The computer industry had survived the first 18 months of the recession with few changes but had started to reduce its payroll in 1989. In 1990, the industry eliminated 20,000 technical positions. By that time, no one believed that the economy would recover quickly. "Many jobs lost during this global downturn are likely to be gone from corporate organization charts forever," concluded one professional journal.

At the time, only a small part of the industry believed that computer networking would be a major aspect of the industry, an aspect with a future. Only a few commercial networks were open to the general public. The academic networks were restricted to research and teaching. In particular, such networks generally required all communications to either begin or end at a college or university or a government laboratory.

That winter, Congress began to look at computer networks and think about the future. "Advances in computer science and technology are vital to the Nation's prosperity, national and economic security, industrial production, engineering, and scientific advancement," read one bill that was circulating through congressional offices. This bill, the High-Performance Computing Act of 1991, would build a new national computer network and encourage the development of commercial network services. Congress wanted to promote the commercial use of computer networks and directed the government to study "the technological feasibility of allowing commercial information service providers to use the Network and other federally funded research networks."

The computer industry pushed hard to get Congressional approval. They already had a technology, digital packet switching, that could be used to construct the new network. They also had a name for the network: Cyberspace.

"Imagine discovering a continent so vast that it may have no end to its dimensions," wrote John Perry Barlow, an advocate of computer networks. "Imagine a new world with more resources than all our future greed might exhaust, more opportunities than there will ever be entrepreneurs to exploit, and a peculiar kind of real estate that expands with development."

Barlow was not a computer scientist. He had been born in southwest Wyoming and had spent almost 20 years working as a rancher. For a time, he had served as lyricist for the Grateful Dead and, through connections in San Francisco, had learned about the early Bay Area communications system, the Well. By 1991, he was a well-known advocate of computer networks and a friend of many leaders of the computer industry. That winter, he published "Coming into the Country," an essay that compared computer networks to the western frontier. "Cyberspace remains a frontier region," he argued, "across which roam the few aboriginal technologists who can tolerate the austerity of its savage computer interfaces, incompatible communications protocols, proprietary barricades, cultural and legal ambiguities, and general lack of useful maps or metaphors."

Perhaps only a native of Wyoming could recognize the connection between the settlement of the inter-mountain west and the new digital communications technology, and also appreciate the political forces that would shape the new technology. Southern Wyoming was developed only after the Union Pacific Railroad built its part of the transcontinental railroad across the state. Like the proposed national computer network, the transcontinental railroad was sponsored by the federal government (identified as the Union government when it passed the necessary legislation in 1862) and built for reasons of national security. Furthermore, the new railroad brought the influence of New York City to Wyoming.

The state of Wyoming did not have the resources, financial or physical, to build the new railroad. "Everything needed had to be brought into that barren country," wrote the historian Ray Allen Billington, "ties from the forests of Minnesota, stone from the quarries of Wisconsin, rails from the steel mills of Pennsylvania." The town that eventually became the state capital began its life as a worker's encampment, "Hell on Wheels," where supplies could be stored and sin could be leased for market prices.

Even after the railroad had been completed, Cheyenne could not exist without a connection to the east. The land did not provide sufficient resources to support local industry. Chicago was the source of most manufactured goods: clothing, bricks, steam engines parts, and stock for Wyoming's finest furniture store. When prices changed in the east, the residents of Cheyenne knew it within days. When Union Pacific's board of directors made a decision in New York, the merchants of Cheyenne would feel the impact.

In writing about his beloved cyberspace, Barlow was concerned that the new computer networks would be controlled by the government and the major telecommunications firms. "Sovereignty over this new world is not well defined," he argued. "Large institutes own much of the hardware which supports it and therefore claim, which some justification, to hegemony over the whole thing." Yet, Barlow knew that the state of Wyoming had built a local government that had occasionally challenged the Union Pacific and he felt that the residents of the new cyberspace should do the same.

Barlow argued that those involved in computer programming and engineers were "well suited to the task of civilizing Cyberspace." You "are almost certainly more knowledgeable about the legal and cultural ambiguities surrounding digital communication and property than your computer phobic fellow citizens," he wrote. "Only by bringing awareness to this task, will we create the sort of place we would want our children to live in."

The founders of Wyoming had created a good environment for children. Children could safely walk the small town streets, explore the land, and test themselves. They could spend the afternoon climbing the rocks at the edge of town or riding horses on the open plains or run through the buildings of Cheyenne and Casper and Evanston. Their parents had found a good livelihood in the stores and businesses of the state but these children would still have to someday ask if Wyoming held a future for them. For all of them, Wyoming would always be their home and would be the land that they knew best. For more than a few, the future was to be found at the other end of the Union Pacific line.

Outposts

THERE WAS A YEAR, MAYBE TWO OR PERHAPS THREE, that our children will never understand. We will tell them the story again and again, but they will never take the point. When we launch into a discussion of the great lessons we learned in the 1990s, they will close their ears, roll their eyes and say to themselves that mother is blathering again or that father is speaking into his soup. No matter how hard we try, they will never grasp that we once found tremendous pleasure in merely connecting to a distant machine, making its disk drive spin and its lights flash. Like many a dilettante adventurer, we cared little what we found on these machines, we only cared that it came from far away. We marched through the forests in search of life and were grateful for every smoldering kitchen fire and every abandoned dump heap.

On such travels, we would uncover ordinary bits of information that we would treat as rare bits of exotica: the computer policies of a university in Florida, the lunch menus of a research laboratory in Geneva, the schedule for a faculty club in Tokyo. The discoveries were not important. We took pleasure from the mere fact that we could command a machine that sat on the far horizon.

As we traveled the world's machines, we occasionally find a lone outpost, a missionary's hut, where a dedicated individual was trying to teach hymns to the natives, trying to use digital communication for some noble purpose. These outposts were not quite blogs nor even personal web pages, through they pointed in the direction of both. They were usually just a collection of writings, crude simple essays, that found shelter in some digital archive. Near this archive one could find a small body of followers who would discuss the texts over email.

On my travels through the network, I passed dozens of these outposts, little communities devoted to obscure computer languages or science fiction or the lyrics of heavy metal songs. At first, I would spend a little time investigating these groups but I soon found that they held little of interest for me. I would leave them quickly and wash my hands on the way out. Traveling through the Internet was proving enough of an adventure.

My interest changed when I found a digital library called "Letters from Sarajevo." It was not, as I had originally hoped, actually located in the former Yugoslavia, but

Too Soon to Tell: Essays for the End of the Computer Revolution, by David Alan Grier
Copyright © 2009 IEEE Computer Society

in the general purpose computer of a small, Midwestern college. It was the kind of school that tried to instill a global vision in its students but had limited success. Most of the student body had trouble thinking beyond the boundary of their own county. They found it extremely difficult to look beyond the border with Missouri or Illinois and impossible to conceive of themselves in a different country.

The organizer of the group was a student named Holden Caulfield. This name, he explained was a nom de plum, which he had taken from his favorite book, *Catcher in the Rye*. He admitted that the book had nothing to do with Sarajevo, Yugoslavia, or computers. He even acknowledged that it was a little paradoxical to take a false identity from a literary character who professes to hate phonies and fakers. He merely liked the name and felt comfortable writing behind it. "It gives me a sense of distance," he explained. "I occasionally have a bit of a thin skin. When someone writes something that attacks Holden Caulfield, I find that I can put a buffer between me and that identity. I can pause, think for a bit and then respond calmly or rationally."

It was a time when there was little calm or rational discussion about the Balkan states. The fragile trusts that had bound them into the single country of Yugoslavia had been snapping and unraveling for a decade and an half. One by one, the largest constituent states, Bosnia, Slovenia, Croatia, Serbia, had stepped away from the union. Slovenia and Croatia moved first to declare their independence. Their actions were accompanied by justifications on their part and accusations by those that remained. Every slight, every historical precedent, every ethnic snub was recalled and flung into public view. "We have been wronged," claimed one side. "Not, it is us who has been slighted," responded another. "You both are lying and we are the victims," argued a third.

By the early years of the 1990s, the global computer networks found that they had been invaded by the conflict in Bosnia. Partisans argued their points over email and in discussion groups. At times, Usenet would carry two or three heated discussions about the Balkan region. Many computer scientists found these discussions disturbing. "Where is truth to be found" they asked, "and why is it our job to find it?"

In the winter of 1992, as Bosnia became the battle ground for the dissolving state, some researchers began to argue that computer networks were not the appropriate forum for such political discussions. "Have the networks been inappropriately used?" asked one observer "Do or should the organizations running the networks have policies on this matter?" The answers to such questions were controversial in themselves. Some favored excluding all political commentary. Some were willing to draw the lines at mass mailings. Some demanded a fully open network. "It would be a major blow to freedom of speech to take such calls [for restrictions] seriously," wrote one computer scientist. "They are remnants of communist thinking where it was possible to forbid any activity under the pretext that it is political."

Caulfield cared little for the debates over the proper use of computer networks. He saw digital communication as an interesting tool and wanted to use it for his own purposes. "I was lucky enough to be in on the ground floor," he admitted. "I had dreamed for years for a chance to communicate globally, to be in on the opening of the 'Soviet bloc' to Western computer interaction." But from his corner of the world, there was precious little global communication that he could do. He could listen. He could gather information. He put his thoughts into words, but he stood at the headwaters of a small tributary to the Internet. He knew no one in the former Yugoslavia, no Balkan partisan who might want to communicate with him. All he could do was to stand on the river bank, stuff his message into a bottle and cast his ideas onto the waters with the hope that they might find a sympathetic soul.

Caulfield was not alone at the water's edge. Through the trees he could see the fires of other small settlements, people who used the same software and the same systems to support some little community. There was a group that discussed Republican politics. Another that read European history. A third that was interested in the general problems of political discourse. Yet another discussed the rock and roll, both important and obscure, that was coming from Eastern Europe. None of these communities was at the center of the Internet, at some major server that would attract attention. Each was lead by a single individual who posted essays and called for responses from interested readers.

In time, the different groups began to establish paths between their organizations. The leader of one group would read the essays posted on another group and add comments to the public discussion. "I spent about 8.5 hours a day online monitoring 41 discussions," admitted Caulfield. "I've developed a methodology for deciding what I want to read, and what is gibberish or garbage." He paused and then added "I probably miss some things, but not much." He claimed that he read about 70 percent of all the material in the discussions and contributed about 10 to 30 messages a day to the server. "I feel like I'm trying to keep the standards of debate and discussion on a high plane," he said, "tempered by a good dose of reasonability."

At the start, Caulfield, like many a network pioneer, had faith that any discussion on the network would be naturally well behaved and intelligent. He believed that the contributors would respect the technology and use it wisely. This idea proved to be a naïve faith, a false trust in the kindness of strangers or inherent goodness of primitive men and women. This faith was justified during the early days of the Bosnia conflict, when Caulfield's discussion group was new and the participants were eager to demonstrate their mastery of the technology. When one got out of line, the infraction was minor. Within a day or an hour or even a few minutes, other discussants would correct the improper behavior of single individuals. The group seemed to be committed to his high standards of debate and was willing to enforce a common etiquette.

After a few quick months this idyll was threatened a by a new voice in the group, a young man who was very sure of his own opinions and was not prepared to be contradicted by others. At first, the young man was a minor irritant, a commentator who wrote a note about every posting. However, he quickly grew bold and insulting. He mocked the contributions of others and began comparing Caulfield's essays "to the writings of Hitler." Soon, he was dominating the group and threatening the discussion leader. "He refused to stop despite both public and private entreaties," Caulfield recalled. "After a week of agonizing, I finally deleted him from the group. I really did not like doing it, but felt he had backed me into a corner."

The incident was a moment of growth, an event that taught Caulfield much about networked discussions. He found that his participants would not behave out of respect for technology and that bad behavior could easily destroy the group. His outpost would not prosper if a single individual was able to hold the conversation hostage. He was soon confronted with a second incident. This one came from a pair of individuals who were calling for the assassination of American President Clinton because of his policy in the Balkans. Caulfield intervened quickly in this case. He collected all the postings from the two commentators and sent the material to the manager of their home computer. He was pleased to report that the manager "froze" the accounts of the two perpetrators "until they had a sharp lecture from senior computer staff about acceptable net behavior, and appropriate ways of saying things."

Caulfield lived and worked in an age that passed quickly and left him behind. By the middle of the 1990s, users were starting to bypass the discussion groups on file servers and were expressing themselves in the new HTML language on web pages. In 1997, they were starting to use the term "blog" for "web log," to describe such an activity. These blogs developed their own formats, structures and technologies. By 1999, bloggers were able to find a number of software tools that eliminated the hand coding of HTML and allowed opinions to be posted directly to the net.

As I began to follow blogs, I lost track of Caulfield. With the change of technology, I found other discussions easier to follow and more engaging. The troubles in the Balkans were starting to recede and other parts of the world were demanding more attention. I had entirely forgotten about him when I heard the announcement, in 2004, that the American political conventions were going to admit bloggers as accredited members of the press. This announcement also stated that several of the bloggers had been engaged in network discussions for many years and had developed large communities who were interested in their writing. This statement reminded me of Caulfield, who had once claimed to have "worked on 51 political campaigns in my life." I wondered if his little network outpost had flourished and if he had become an eminence gris of the blogging community.

I was pleased when my efforts quickly found someone who used the name Holden Caulfield but was disappointed to discover that this blogger was a different person. He had none of interests and none of the high standards of my Caulfield. Instead, he behaved more like the Holden Caulfield from *Catcher in the Rye* and hurled accusations of phoniness and falsehood at anyone and everyone.

After a little more exploration, I found traces of my Caulfield, the Caulfield who had once tried to organize discussions about the Balkans. Exploring different servers on the Internet, I found a reference to one of Caulfield's essays. I followed the link and discovered a small server with a collection of old postings. For an hour or two, I poked away at that machine and made its disk spin. The more I probed, the more I came to believe that the server was a ghost town, an outpost that had been abandoned by its owner. It was filled with files from 1994, 1995, and 1996. Nothing in the directory had a date after January 1997. Bill Clinton was still president, the Boston Red Sox had not won a World Series for three generations, and programmers had yet to face the problems that might occur when the calendar rotated from 1999 to 2000.

In the decade since 1997, computer networks have become an arena of opinions and reactions. There are now at least 12 million bloggers in the United States, roughly 4 percent of the country's population. Many of these bloggers are isolated writers, individuals who send their ideas into the void and hear nothing in return. They write diaries of their lives, close observations of common tasks, comments on the events of their neighborhood. Such work has its value but it is little more than the abandoned server of Holden Caulfield. Most bloggers want to be part of a community, want to write words that draw the interest and comment of their neighbors. Most are satisfied being part of a group of three or four or five bloggers. The most ambitious look to be part of the grand blogosphere and gain the attention of the prominent blog writers such as Arianna Huffington or Steve Clemmons or Matthew Drudge. Without the attention and comments of others, they know that they are merely playing with an expensive toy, pushing distant buttons that make some lights flash and a small disk or two spin.

The Captured Imagination

FOR A YEAR, I WORKED IN AN OFFICE that looked across a four-foot airshaft into an apartment that was shared by two young men, neither older than 25, who had apparently taken a vow to live their lives in full view of the public. The two never closed the curtains on their windows, if indeed they had curtains to close, which gave me a detailed view of their home. The decorations showed the tasteful touch of the male hand. The walls were covered with posters that proclaimed the pair's interests in medievalist fantasy drama, women's specialty fashion, and sports that were sponsored by brewed malt beverage companies.

A second wall held a large video game console, which commanded much of their attention. They would spend most evenings in front of the screen, sitting on an old couch and playing round after round of games. Their bodies swayed in time to the simulated motion of the games and their voices would occasionally penetrate the windows that separated their rooms from mine.

Many a day, they would start in the late afternoon and continue their play into the night. More than once, I opened my office in the morning and spied one of the two, sitting on the couch with a game controller clenched in his hands. Looking tired to the point of exhaustion, he would be struggling to master some aspect of a game. Observing this scene, I could only wonder how his imagination had been captured by this play.

We have reached a point where many, if not most, people get their first exposure to computers through video games. Interactive computer games are a major sector within both the high-technology and entertainment industries. It has become the "killer app for multimedia" according to Nolan Bushnell, a founder of the game manufacturer, Atari. In 2005, computers games and game software generated over seven billion dollars of revenue. Though computer games now seem to be an obvious form of entertainment, they actually grew out of a series of different efforts to represent the natural world, to abstract complex activity, to analyze organizational problems.

THE GAME OF CHESS QUICKLY CAPTURED THE ATTENTION of early computer researchers. "Although perhaps of no practical importance," wrote Claude Shannon of Bell Telephone Laboratories, "the question is of theoretical interest and it is hoped that a satisfactory solution of this problem will act as a wedge in attaching other problems of a similar nature and of greater significance."

Of practical importance or not, chess-playing computers attracted the attention of both Shannon and the English mathematician Alan Turing. Between 1946 and 1954, these two researchers developed the fundamental theory of chess playing programs. In 1950, Shannon outlined his ideas in a paper and Turing incorporated his thoughts into an elementary piece of code. Both knew that their accomplishments were modest. Much "further experimental and theoretical work remains to be done," acknowledged Shannon.

Unlike many early applications of the computer, chess could be understood by the general public. Many individuals were familiar with the game and knew that it was difficult. They were more impressed with a machine that played chess than with one that solved partial differential equations.

Shortly after the publication of Shannon's paper, a small California computer manufacture, Computer Research Corporation, learned how chess could command the public attention. One of the company's executives, Richard Sprague, grabbed on to the idea of a chess-playing machine in an attempt to explain the computer to a bored reporter. The "power of the stored program idea was so great," he claimed, "that eventually computers of this type would be able to play a decent game of chess."

Sprague's claim was dramatic and quickly produced a series of newspaper stories. Much to his dismay, the stories quickly shifted away from the capability of his machine and proposed a chess tournament among different computers. The calls for a tournament embarrassed Sprague, as his firm had no plans to write a chess program. As the stories began to draw the attention of the New York media, Sprague had to disentangle himself without admitting that he had exaggerated the capabilities of his machine. "To avoid the admission that the machine could never play chess," he stated that the computer "was scheduled for far more important defense work at Cambridge Air Force Research Laboratories. Thereby we graciously ducked the matter."

Chess remained a central part of computer science until 1996, when Deep Blue became the first computer to beat a grandmaster, Gary Kasparov, in tournament play. During the intervening years, the development of chess programs created new forms of searching, new ways of organizing memory and new types of hardware. Even with all these accomplishments, it had little influence on the modern video game. Video game technology came from researchers who were attempting to simulate the social world with a computer.

Unlike computer chess, computer simulation has never captured the imagination of either the public or computer scientists. It "was not then and is not now part of the mainstream of either computer theory or applications," lamented one of its pioneers. Computer simulation developed as an engineering tool, as a means of understanding complex systems. Like so many other facets of computer science, the field of computer simulation found an important advocate in the airline industry.

In the 1950s, airplanes formed only a small part of the transportation infrastructure but their role was growing rapidly. American Airlines, the largest U.S.-based carrier of the time, had only 85 planes but possessed a grand vision. "Any employee who can't see the day when we will have 1,000 planes," argued the company's president, "had better look for a job somewhere else."

The engineers at American Airlines wanted to use simulation to understand a key part of the organization: the reservation process. This process was a large, complicated activity. It involved reservation agents, clerks, phone lines, airports, travel agents, and paper records. At the heart of the system was an electro-mechanical device, the Reservisor, that counted the number of tickets sold for each flight. The engineers had tried to analyze the system but had concluded that the standard mathematical methods did not accurately capture the flow of information from person to machine and back again.

The first simulation of this reservation system was neither glamorous nor an event that might draw public attention. "For an entire week," recalled one young engineer, "the table of random numbers was manually consulted, transactions were generated and a printing calculator was used to perform the mathematical operations." The work was hard because it was repetitive and demanded concentration on details. The engineers tried to translate their work into a computer program for the IBM 650 but were thwarted in their efforts. It was "beyond the state of the art in the late 1950s," the engineers reluctantly acknowledged.

Step by step, engineers began adopting the tools of computer science for such simulations. An early success can be found in 1957, when traffic engineers at the University of Michigan wrote a computer program to simulate the movement of automobiles moving on the streets that connected four intersections. "[E]very quarter of a second of problem time the contents of the computer were scanned," reported the research team. In order to analyze the simulation, they developed a primitive form of computer graphics. On an oscilloscope, they drew points "corresponding to those of cars within the computer model." They then photographed the oscilloscope with a movie camera. "The resulting film provided an animated cartoon-like version of the flow of traffic within the computer."

Like the engineers at American Airlines, the Michigan researchers never completed their project. "Funds were not forthcoming," they claimed. Yet, they established the pattern that other researchers in simulation would follow. They worked unobtrusively. They concentrated on analyzing their simulation. They made use of the newest contributions of computer science. Computer simulations were some of the early applications for innovations such as object-oriented programming, interactive graphics, and parallel processing and distributed systems.

The technology of computer simulation caught public attention only when it became the technology of computer games. This transition occurred in the 1970s, when the cost of computation fell. When computers were expensive, they had to be used for important tasks, like fundamental engineering, basic science or corporate operations. As they became commonplace, they could be used as a source of entertainment.

The early games of this period directly simulated physical reality. A well-circulated Basic program of the 1970s simulated a landing on the moon. The classic game of Pong simulated the physical game of table tennis. Simple though they were, these games could captivate an individual for hours. Many an individual spent long evenings hunched over a teletype terminal while playing with the lunar lander program, rejoicing with each success and cursing with each failure.

The games of the early 1970s were often ill-conceived and badly written but by the middle of the decade, the best of these programs were borrowing the technology of computer simulation. As more and more programmers became skilled with the tools of simulation they realized that they did not have to model their games on physical phenomena but could set them in fantasy worlds. "The computer is a playing field on which one may play out any game one can imagine," wrote one commentator of the time. "One may create worlds in which there is not gravity" or situations "in which time dances forward and backward," or societies that obey alternative laws of economics. "In short," he argued "one can single-handedly write and produce plays in a theatre that admits of no limitations."

The computer game industry began in 1977 and it grew as if it faced few, if any, limitations. As it has grown, it has used the technology of simulation to create a host of artificial and imaginary worlds. It has given us artificial air flight, artificial spelunking, artificial warfare, artificial city planning and an equal number of environments that have little parallel in the natural world.

FROM TIME TO TIME, I have spied my former neighbors on the streets of Washington, usually as I came into my office in the morning. They would be striding down the street, wearing the style of suit favored by the ambitious young men of our city but sporting the kind of shoes that mark them as people who have not yet discovered the importance of formal footwear. Occasionally, they are met by women who appear to be their girlfriends. They are greeted with a peck on the lips, a rub on the shoulder and an attentive gaze that suggests a special relationship. On Thursday nights, I have seen them gathering with other young people who are clearly headed for an evening at the clubs of the Adams Morgan neighborhood. Nothing marks them as serious gamers. Nothing suggests that they are capable of spending long nights exploring the intricacies of a simulated world.

I am unable to determine the artificial world that captures my neighbors' attention. From the body movements of the two young men, I suspect that they are playing something that simulates physical activity in some real or imagined world, such as artificial football or imaginary space motor cross. No matter what game they are playing, they are utilizing the common technologies of computer simulation. Within their gaming program, one can find all the technical elements that have been used to simulate factories, airline reservations systems and global telephone networks. By itself, that technology would not occupy them for a minute. If you place simulation technology in a competitive, interactive story, you can command their attention as long as you might like. You can cause them to forgo sleep, to curse at inanimate objects and to leave their curtains open so that their captured imaginations may be observed by all their neighbors.

Shutdown

"WE ARE ABLE TO BORROW SOME HARDWARE. We can get the software for a dollar. The engineering school will give us a connection to the network. We should test the project now. Otherwise, we will be too late."

The language at the Steering Committee had suddenly become heated and angry. After weeks of meeting in the backroom of a library, the group had suddenly split in two. The more radical faction was tired of the lengthy information sessions and gentle descriptions. They had heard all that they wanted to hear about electronic bulletin boards and the WELL social network of Silicon Valley. They wanted their own network and they wanted it now. They believed, deep in their hearts if not in their heads, that a digital service based in Washington, D.C., would change the fundamental nature of American politics. They saw themselves distributing government reports to every citizen in the country and rallying the electorate to new and better informed points of view. With the network connection big enough and place to stand, they would move the world.

For a time, the committee had been content to discuss the future of computer networks as if that future was some pleasant country beyond the horizon, the land where people wore aluminum suits, drove space cars, and received the vague blessings of a beneficent technology. The mood changed when Thomas Grundner came to speak. Grundner had created a public access computing service in Cleveland and had the fire of a true activist.

Almost a decade before, Grundner had been working at the Case Western Reserve Hospital and had become interested in computer bulletin boards. Seeing them as a way of disseminating medical information, he created one that he called "St. Silicon's Hospital." Unlike the common bulletin boards of the day, he organized St. Silicon's around the metaphor of a hospital, and called one section the emergency room, another the pharmacy, the third surgery. Furthermore, he recruited individuals from the real units of the hospital to run the equivalent electronic divisions of St. Silicon's. They would both post information and answer questions.

The service proved so popular, that Grundner expanded it, to cover the entire city of Cleveland. He extended the hospital metaphor to cover the civic landscape and recruited supporters from the city library, from the mayors' office, from the

Too Soon to Tell: Essays for the End of the Computer Revolution, by David Alan Grier
Copyright © 2009 IEEE Computer Society

police and from the fire station. Users would connect to this service, named Cleveland Freenet, over a phone line and would make their choices from a screen decorated with a drawing of the city skyline that had been neatly sketched with typewriter characters.

Grundner's presentation pushed the more radical members of the committee to action. They embraced Grundner's approach and claimed it as their own. At the next meeting, one pair of the radicals, two long-time users of electronic mail, demanded that the committee start, with no further delay, an information service with Grundner's software. "We are ready to move," they said. "We need wait no longer."

The decision was not as obvious to the committee as it was to the radicals. Some urged caution. Some said that they had not done enough study. Some felt that the time had not yet come. For most of the evening, the radicals were able to characterize their opponents as timid and frightened of technology but as the clock passed 9:00 pm, the suddenly faced an idea that was harder to dismiss.

The new argument came from Milton, who was the vice president of an organization that was thinking of supporting the new service. Milt was not very articulate. He had a way of twisting sentences into odd, cramped shapes—ill-formed balloon animals that were made out of words rather than rubber. Many on the committee dismissed him.

"What is the commitment?" he kept asking that night. "What is the prerequisite organizational commitment required to our plans?"

Most of the committee thought that he was talking about the organization's finance and kept telling him that the group had no monetary risk in a trial but Milt was apparently talking about something else. He held the floor against the radicals, returning time and again to the idea of "prerequisite commitment." Some members of the committee become frustrated. The radicals got angry. In the end, no one could get a consensus out of the group. As the meeting broke up, at least a few of the group realized that the two sides were arguing different points. The radicals thought that the new technology would empower the individual. Milt, as far as anyone would tell, was arguing that the new service would require the support of an organization, a collection of people that would be responsible for each part of the electronic service.

THE RADICALS HAD COME TO BELIEVE THAT TIME WAS NOT ON THEIR SIDE. They knew that other organizations were trying to establish an electronic service in Washington. Several universities and at least a few news organizations believed that they could be the provider of government information to the nation. The biggest player on the horizon was the United States Congress. In 1992, both the House of Representatives and the Senate began deploying personal computers and network connections throughout the Capitol complex. This technology replaced minicomputers—Honeywells, Data Generals, Primes—that had been used to manage Congressional offices for a decade or more.

Most members of Congress had used the minicomputers as a means of organizing their correspondence. Their staff would match the incoming mail and phone messages to "robo" letters, responses that had been prepared in advance. These letters would be updated as events unfolded and members refined their positions.

When each letter left the office, it would be recorded in a database. A "quick look at the constituent history may reveal that this individual wrote a letter on the same issue only weeks before," explained one congressional staffer. "Sending the standard robo again would be a mistake but a slightly modified version might thank the sender for following up, and provide an update on where the issue currently stands and a birthday greeting for a family member."

Initially, Congress considered the new networked computers to be internal tools, devices that would be used by the congressional offices only. The Senate Rules Committee, which had direct control over the Senate network, proclaimed that staff members could only use the networks to get information from the Congressional Quarterly, and from the news services. The new office computers "did not allow for dialing out to any phone number not approved by the Senate Rules Committee and built into the system by the Senate Computer Center."

In the summer of 1993, the House of Representatives began to deploy an email system that was connected to the outside Internet. Seven members volunteered to test the system. None of them knew how to treat the new communication technology. They first adopted a policy of requiring all potential correspondents to register, to send their office a postcard to verify that they were a constituent. The Senate, which deployed email six months later, was equally reluctant to engage the citizens of the state with the new technology. "Thank you for sending an email message to my office," read the standard reply from Senator John Warner (R-VA). "If you have included an address I will respond through the U.S. postal system as soon as possible."

Senator Ted Kennedy (D-MA) broke with the rules committee and began to use digital means to promote his ideas in the fall of 1993. This effort was lead by a young staff member, Chris Casey, who had studied political science in college and had developed an interest in computers. Kennedy had originally hired him to maintain his office computers. Other candidates for the position "had much stronger technical credentials that I did," he wrote. "But during my interview I had demonstrated an understanding of what the office hoped to get out of their computers, and that prevailed over the technical expertise of my competitors."

With his boss' blessing, Casey began posting press releases on a Boston bulletin board system. Initially, he was cautious about engaging the users of these systems. "Our posted guidelines made it clear that we would not be responding to online inquiries," he explained. "I was not conversant with every issue that we covered in our posted material," and "I had not been authorized to (nor would I always have been able to) argue any details."

In spite of his reluctance Casey quickly found that his press releases generated a substantial amount of email. As "soon as it became apparent that my experiment with putting Kennedy online could not be one way," wrote his staffer, "I carefully began to participate in the [discussion] myself." These posts were soon copied by other bulletin boards in Massachusetts and were eventually transferred to Usenet with the help of a researcher at MIT.

In the winter of 1994, Kennedy's office was also able to post its material on an official Senate file server that ran the Gopher protocol, a form of communication that would soon be replaced by the World Wide Web. Still, Kennedy was one of the few legislators to use digital communications. When the Congress ended that fall, only 7 Senators and 36 Representatives had public email addresses.

DIGITAL COMMUNICATION EXPANDED RAPIDLY during the 104th Congress, the Congress inaugurated in January 1995. Capitol Hill offices added to their technological capability and reorganized their staffs to handle email and develop webpages. The change was signified by the announcement, on January 6, of the Thomas system for distributing digital documents. Housed in the Library of Congress, it provided a systematic way of handling the public records and reports of each congress. It was far from technically perfect. "You could take a shower while you wait for some of this to come in over a regular line," one library official admitted. Still, it gave citizens new access to the workings of government.

The 104th Congress brought Republicans to power in both the Senate and the House. It also bore witness to the rivalry that was growing between the Legislative branch and the Executive branch of the Government. Both the new Speaker of the House and the Vice President considered themselves to be champions of digital technology. The Vice President had recently held an open chat on the CompuServe network, and had urged the White House to create its own document server.

Of course the rivalry between Congress and the White House had deep roots that went far beyond the new network technologies. That rivalry concerned fundamental goals, control of the national agenda, and the direction of the country. Over the year, it developed through a series of conflicts between the Republicans and the Democrats. Increasingly, those contests were discussed over digital networks. Email lists circulated reports on partisan debates in Washington. Chat rooms gave people an opportunity to argue their opinions. Major media outlets, such as the *Washington Post*, operated news sites. Document servers contained the writings, both official and unofficial, of congressional offices.

Some members of Congress, dissatisfied with network options on Capitol Hill, turned to local Washington network services, such as the bulletin board that was being organized by my library steering committee. This bulletin board finally become operational in January 1995. As it was not associated with the government, it soon become a substantial repository of the partisan documents that were being produced by the 104th Congress.

THE PARTISAN POLITICS OF THE 104TH CONGRESS CAME to a head in November and December of 1995. Unable to agree on a Federal Budget, the Republicans and Democrats let the funding measures expire and shut down parts of the Federal Government. On Tuesday, November 14, a total of 800,000 employees, 40% of the non-military payroll, found that they could not go to their offices and could not do their work at home. The shutdown lasted for four days as each side tried to out maneuver the other. Opinions on "the standoff in Washington," wrote one reporter, "seemed to turn less on whom voters support than on whom they blame less."

"Lawmakers in both parties agree that the debate has become personal and nasty this fall," reported the *New York Times*, "in part because of the raw animosities that have flourished in a bitter year and in part because of cold blooded political strategy."

Over the weekend of November 17, the Democrats and the Republicans found a deal that allowed them to reopen the government temporarily. Over the next three weeks, the two sides worked to find a permanent solution but found no common ground. On December 15, they shut the government a second time.

The second shutdown was smaller than the first. Less than 290,000 workers were sent home. However, neither side was willing to compromise, so the closures stretched into the Christmas holidays. Citizens looked for a way to express their opinions on the closures and aired their views on any web site that seemed to be connected to the Government. Many individuals posted their opinions on a tourist web site that had been designed for visitors to washington.

"We wanted to help these poor people," wrote the company that operated the site. "But editorial comments are running 10 to 1" over tourist messages. The company had thought that the site would be a clever way to advertise their services but they found themselves in the midst of the political battle. The comments ranged over the entire political map. Some blamed the Democrats. Some blamed the Republicans. Some blamed government workers, claiming that they were strikers. Some thought that the entire exercise was a grand and gaudy farce. The company lacked the staff to do anything with the comments but they concluded, as so many in Washington had before, that even bad publicity was good for their organization.

DAD, WHO HAD RECENTLY TAKEN AN INTEREST in Internet news sites, found little noble in the shutdown, and decided to see what he could do about the problem. He was not convinced that an email would be read by his member of Congress, so he decided to place a phone call. After poking around a couple of Internet sites, he found the number for his Representatives' local office and placed the call.

The phone was answered by a young man. ("Full of himself," were Dad's words.) The young man listened briefly to Dad's complaint and then leapt to the defense of the Republican strategy. Two or three times, Dad tried to interrupt the flow of words but the young man rebuked him. "You don't understand," he would say before resuming his argument.

Finally, Dad raised his voice. "Here's the deal," he said. "I'm a life-long Republican. I'm retired. I have a computer and I'm not scared to use it. If your boss doesn't want to see a flier about him on the bulletin board of every supermarket and every drugstore in his district, he better call me back and listen to my concerns." He then hung up.

Later that day, or perhaps the next, a legislative director called from Washington. He was apologetic and deferential, though he still offered a tempered version of the Republican strategy. By the end of the call, he found an accommodation for Dad but was clearly worried about what my father was planning to do in response to the shutdown.

"That computer," the director said as he ended the phone conversation. "We hope you use it for the good of the Republican organization."

"We'll see," replied Dad.

Force of Nature

WHEN I FIRST MET THEM, Jeff, Jeff and Will were inseparable. Un pour tous, tous pour un. As far as I could tell, they spent every waking moment of their lives in each other's presence. I could commonly find them at the local coffee shop or huddled together in some corner of a college building. The younger Jeff would be telling an elaborate story to whatever audience was ready to listen. The elder Jeff would be typing on a computer keyboard. Will might be doodling in a notebook or flirting with a passerby or playing garbage can basketball with pages torn from the day's newspaper.

Among colleagues, I referred to them as the "Three Musketeers," as they seemed to embody the confidence of the great Dumas heroes. They were masters of technology and believed that their mastery gave them an exemption from the rules of ordinary society. The younger Jeff, for example, believed that he was not governed by the rules of time. When given a task, he would ignore it until the deadline was firmly in sight. Then in an explosion of programming energy, he would pound perfect code into his machine.

The elder Jeff was convinced that specifications were written for other people, individuals with weaker morals or limited visions. He wrote code that was far grander than the project required. It would meet the demands of the moment but it would spiral outward to handle other tasks as well. You might find a game embedded in his programs or a trick algorithm that had nothing to do with the project or a generalization that would handle the problem for all time to come.

Will was comfortable with deadlines and would read specifications but he lived in a non-Euclidian world. He shunned conventional algorithms and obvious solutions. His code appeared inverted, dissecting the final answer in search of the original causes. It was nearly impossible to read but it worked well and generally ran faster than more straightforward solutions.

The unity of the Three Musketeers was nearly destroyed when Alana came into their circle. She was a force of nature, and every bit the equal of the three boys. She took possession of their group as if it were her domain. Within a few weeks, she had the boys following her schedule, meeting at her favorite places, and doing the things that she most liked to do. She may even have gotten the boys to dress

Too Soon to Tell: Essays for the End of the Computer Revolution, by David Alan Grier
Copyright © 2009 IEEE Computer Society

167

more stylishly, or at least put on cleaner clothes, but this could have happened without her direct intervention.

Alana had a quicker intellect than Jeff, Jeff and Will. She could see the solution of a problem faster than her compatriots and knew how to divide the work with others. For a time, I regularly would see the four of them in a corner lounge, laughing and boasting and working on some class project. One of their number, usually a Jeff, would be typing into a computer while the others discussed what task should be done next. Crumpled paper would be scattered around a wastebasket. A clutch of pencils would be neatly balanced into a pyramid.

It was not inevitable that Alana should destabilize the group but that is what eventually happened. Nothing had prepared the boys for a woman who had mastered both the technical details of multiprocessor coding and the advanced techniques of eye makeup. For reasons good or ill, Alana was able to paint her face in a way that made the souls of ordinary men melt into little, simmering puddles of sweat.

After three or four months, the group began to dissolve. The end was marked with little, gentle acts of kindness that were twisted into angry, malicious incidents by the green-eyed monster of jealousy. Soon Jeff was not speaking to Jeff, Will was incensed with the Elder, the Younger had temporarily decamped for places unknown, and Alana was looking for a more congenial group of colleagues. Eventually, the four were able to recover the remnants of their friendship and rebuild a working relationship but they never completely retrieved their old camaraderie. Shortly, they moved to new jobs and new worlds, where they faced not only the pull of the opposite sex but also had to deal with the equally potent and seductive powers of finance and money.

THE YOUNGER JEFF WAS THE FIRST TO LEAVE. He packed his birthright and followed the western winds, determined to conquer the world. With a few friends, he built an Internet radio station, one of the first of the genera. They rented space in a warehouse, bought a large server and connected it to the Internet. They found some software to pull songs off their collection of CDs and wrote a system that would stream music across the network while displaying ads on a computer screen. They christened their creation with a name like "intergalactic-radio-usa.net".

For a year or two, the station occupied a quirky corner of the net. It was one of the few places in those days before mp3 downloading, where you could listen to music over the Internet. Few individuals had a computer that reproduced the sounds faithfully but enough people listened to make the business profitable.

One day, when he arrived at work, Jeff was met at the door by a man with a dark overcoat, a stern demeanor, and a letter from one of the music publishing organizations, BMI or ASCAP. The letter noted that intergalactic-radio-usa had not been paying royalties on the music it broadcast and it demanded satisfaction. A date was set. Seconds were selected. Discussions were held. Before the final confrontation, the station agreed to a payment schedule and returned to the business of broadcasting music.

Under the new regime, the station had to double or triple its income in a short space of time. It pushed Jeff away from the technical work of the organization. His partners had grown anxious over his dramatic programming techniques. They wanted steady progress towards their goals, not weeks of inaction followed by days of intense coding. They told him to get a suit, build a list of clients, and start selling advertising.

Jeff was not a truly successful salesman but he was also not a failure. His work allowed him to talk with new people, an activity that he truly loved, but it did not give him the feeling of mastery that he had enjoyed as programmer. "It's all governed by the budget," he told me when he started to look for a new job. "Everything is controlled by the budget."

THE ELDER JEFF LEFT MY CIRCLE SHORTLY AFTER HIS NAMESAKE. He and some friends moved into an old house in a reviving part of the city, a living arrangement that can only be described as an Internet commune. They shared expenses and housekeeping duties and looked for ways to make money with their computing skills. Slowly, they evolved into a web design and hosting company. They created a webpage for one business and then one for another and finally admitted that they had a nice, steady line of work.

As the outlines of their company became clearer and clearer, Jeff decided that they were really a research and development laboratory that supported itself with small jobs. He took a bedroom on an upper floor and began working on a program that he called "the ultimate web system." Like many of the programs produced by the elder Jeff, the ultimate web system was a clever idea. It is best considered to be an early content management system, a way to allow ordinary users to post information without working with a programmer.

As good as it was, the ultimate web system never became a profitable product. Jeff had to abandon it as he and his partners began to realize that their company needed stronger leadership than the collective anarchy of a commune. They needed to coordinate the work of designers and programmers and salespeople and accountants. As the strongest personality of the group, Jeff slowly moved into role of president. As he did, the company became a more conventional organization. Couples married and moved into their own homes. The large house uptown ceased to be a residence and became only an office.

Long after Jeff had begun purchasing web software from others, he continued to claim that he was a software developer. "I will get back to it someday," he would say. "It will be a great product."

WILL WAS THE LAST TO DEPART. He started a company that installed computers for law firms. Our city holds a substantial number of lawyers so his long-term prospects were good. I once saw him on the street, pushing a cart of monitors and network cables. He looked active and happy. Things were going well, he said. He had plenty of work but still had enough time to do a little programming on the side.

We shook hands, promised to keep in touch, and agreed to meet for dinner on some distant day. That dinner went unclaimed for three and four and five years. It might have never been held had not I learned, through one of the Jeffs, that Will had prospered as a programmer and now owned a large specialty software firm. I scanned his webpage and was pleased with what I saw. "Software in the service of good." It read. "Our motto is people before profit. Do unto others as you would have them do unto you."

I called his office and was connected to "President Will," and got a quick summary of his career. He had started creating programs for disabled users and had found a tremendous market for his work. After a brief discussion we agreed to a nice dinner downtown, with spouses and well-trained waiters and the gentle ambiance of success. We spent most of the evening talking about personal things: families and children and houses. Only at the end of the evening did we turn to work. "How is the business going?" I asked.

"Well," he said, but the corners of his lips pursed.

I looked at him a moment. "Everything OK?" I queried.

He exchanged a glance with his wife and turned to back to me. "Extremely well. We have more business than we can handle."

Again, I paused. "Starting to draw competition?"

He smiled and relaxed for a brief moment. "No," he said.

I sensed that something was happening and so I took a guess. "A suitor sniffing around."

He looked chagrined and shook his head. "Yeah."

"A company with three letters in its name?"

"Yup," he said.

"It would be a lot of money," I noted.

"But then it wouldn't be my firm," he said. After a pause, he added, "and if I don't sell, the purchaser might try to put me out of business."

We moved to another subject, as Will was clearly not ready to talk any more about the potential sale of his company. It was months later that I learned that he had sold the company and had decided to leave the technology industry. The news came in a letter that asked me to write a letter of recommendation for a young man who wanted to become "Reverend Will."

ALMOST EVERY TECHNICAL FIELD feels the constant pull of business demands. "Engineering is a scientific profession," wrote the historian Edwin Layton, "yet the test of the engineer's work lies not in the laboratory but in the marketplace." By training, most engineers want to judge their work by technical standards but few have that opportunity. "Engineering is intimately related to fundamental choices of policy made by organizations employing engineers," notes Layton.

The experiences of Jeff, Jeff and Will have been repeated by three decades of computer science students. They spend four years studying languages and data structures and algorithms, and pondering that grand question "What can be automated?" Then they leave that world and move to one in which profit is king, deadlines are queen and finance is a knave that keeps order. Our educational system does little to prepare them for this transition. An early report reduced the issue to a pair of sentences. "A large portion of the job market involves work in business-oriented computer fields," it noted before making the obvious recommendation. "As a result, in those cases where there is a business school or related department, it would be most appropriate to take courses in which one could learn the technology and techniques appropriate to this field."

Of course, one or two courses cannot really prepare an individual for the pressures and demands of the commercial world. Such pressures require qualities that are learned over a lifetime. One needs poise, character, grace, a sense of right and wrong, an ability to find a way through a confused landscape. Often professional organizations, including many beyond the field of computer science, have reduced such qualities to the concepts of skills, skills that can be taught in training sessions: communications, teamwork, self-confidence. In fact, they are better imparted by the experiences of life, by learning that your roommate is writing and releasing virus code, that you have missed a deadline and will not be paid for your work, that a member of your study group is passing your work as his own.

It is "doubly important," wrote the 19th century pioneer Charles Babbage, "that the man of science should mix with the world." In fact, most computer scientists have little choice but to mix with the world, as the world provides the discipline with problems, with ideas, and with capital. It is therefore doubly important to know how the ideas of computer science interact with the world of money.

One of the Musketeers, safely out of earshot of his wife, once asked me what had become of Alana. I was not in close contact with her but I knew that her life had been shaped by the same forces that had influenced the careers of her three comrades, though, of course, her story had been complicated by the issues that women have to consider. She had moved to Florida and had built a business during the great Internet bubble. She had taken some time to start a family, perhaps when that bubble had burst in 2001, and was now president of her own firm. I didn't believe that she had done technical work for years.

"You've not kept in touch," I said more as a statement than a question.

"No," he said.

I saw a story in his face, but that story may reflect more of my observations than of his experience. It told of a lost love, perhaps; a lessoned learned; a recognition that he and his college friends were all moving into that vast land of the mid-career knowing a little something about how to deal with the forces of nature.

Ever Onward! Thanks for Asking!

THE DAY HAD HELD LITTLE PROMISE FROM THE START. The clouds were low and spit drops of rain on the gray water as we gathered on dock to hear a little inspirational talk before we got on the boat. The speaker, an enthusiastic young man with a ponytail down his back spoke about the sanctity of life and the beauty of marine mammals and the importance of preserving these wonderful animals in their native state. He stretched this theme to nearly 45 wind swept minutes and then invited us to come onto the boat and "begin our adventure to the home of the whales."

We cruised the ocean for hours and saw nothing remotely like a whale. We passed floating mats of seaweed, little pods of jelly fish and the occasional seagull diving for dinner. The kids on the boat, there were a dozen of them, began to get restless. Soon they were playing that familiar game of free-form tag that has no goal beyond creating chaos and irritating adults. They ran from deck to deck, screeching and pushing and yelling. Every now and then, a crew member would appear and give a stern little lecture on marine safety and respect for the whales that we were certainly soon to see, but these talks would quiet the children for no more than eight or ten seconds.

Ever the teacher, I decided to take matters in hand. I gathered the kids on the foredeck and told them that I could teach them a sailing song. Something in my pitch convinced them to try the idea. Perhaps I promised that the song would make them famous or bring them new friends or make them rich beyond their wildest dreams. They stood in a tight group on the deck, listening to the words and repeating them.

In common with many men of my generation, I had once cherished the illusion of becoming the next Bob Dylan or Jerry Garcia or Bruce Springsteen. I believed that these singers were continuing the tradition of the work song, the music that told the story of honest laborers, the trials of ordinary people and the redemption of work. I had acquired a guitar and learned a number of those classic folk songs that had

Too Soon to Tell: Essays for the End of the Computer Revolution, by David Alan Grier
Copyright © 2009 IEEE Computer Society

been collected in the 1930s. From that repertory, I selected a song and taught it to the kids.

Like all adults, the tour director became suspicious after a while. The children had become too quiet. Curious to learn what they were doing, he came up to the front deck and found me leading them all in song. Initially, his face glowed when he heard the high pitched voices singing into the wind. It took him a few moments to catch the lyric:

> Tis advertised in Boston, New York and Buffalo
> A hundred brave Americans, A whaling for to go
> Singing Blow ye winds in the morning
> Blow ye winds high-o
> Haul away the running gear and blow winds blow

At that moment, I learned an important lesson for any profession of life. Liberals can have a very imperfect sense of irony. I had long suspected that conservatives suffered lack of humor but I had never believed that this problem could affect all persons of political stances and all educational backgrounds. The tour director immediately ordered the kids below and began rebuking me into the full teeth of the wind. How could I, a cultured person who claimed to love the environment, undercut the mission of this marine mammal cruise by teaching the children a whaling song. He demanded that I go to the cabin and apologize to all.

Of course, no apology was needed or even possible. The kids had sung the song to their parents, who were pleased beyond measure that their children had done something vaguely constructive. We may have seen no whales that day, but at least we had done something memorable. Long before we reached land, I had dismissed the incident. I had concluded that the ponytailed tour director simply did not understand that we were play acting like Dylan or Garcia or Springsteen. We weren't singing about the current trip. We were pretending that it was 1848 and that we were standing on the deck of a Nantucket whaler as it caught the outbound tide and headed out to sea.

THE LINE BETWEEN FANTASY AND MOCKERY CAN BE THIN, even in the best of circumstances. The art that can expand the vision of one individual and transport him or her to a different world can just as easily restrict the moments of another and expose all the weaknesses of that person's life. It is easy to dismiss that line when you are not being mocked.

The folk songs of the information age date to the 1920s and 1930s, when the industry was new. Today, they are impossible to sing without the sense that someone, somehow, is being mocked.

> Ever Onward! Ever Onward!
> We're bound for the top to never fall,
> Right here and now we thankfully
> Pledge sincerest loyalty
> To the corporation that's the best of all

Our leaders we revere and while we're here,
Let's show the world just what we think of them!

So let us sing men - Sing men
Once or twice, then sing again
for the EVER ONWARD IBM!

This song, "Ever Onward," is the touchstone of the information technology folk song cannon, the rough equivalent of Woody Guthrie's "This Land Is Your Land." It is one of 106 songs that were written for IBM salesmen to sing at their annual retreat to Endicott, New York, and published in a compilation entitled *The IBM Songbook*.

"Ever Onward" is one of the few original songs in the IBM songbook. Most of them are new words that were sung to the popular tunes of the day. "Smiles that Make Us Happy" provides the melody for eight songs in the oeuvre. "Marching through Georgia" is used four times. "Take Me Out to the Ballgame" appears once as the song that praises the diligence of Glen H. Armstrong, who was the Assistant Sales Manager of IBM's Tabulating Machine Division.

Many of the songs praise specific individuals: Tom Watson, President; Otto E. Braitmayer, Vice President; W.F. Baitin, Comptroller; C.D. Lake, Chief Engineer. A few tell of groups of people: the 100 percent sales club, the Board of Directors, the office staff, the plant workers. All are written from the point of view of the sales staff. They praise the company that has given them a job and point to the great accomplishments of the organizations. All of them define success in economic terms:

We tabulate statistics the new electric way.
Accounting tasks we do so fast, our customers all say
That our T. M. [Tabulating Machinery] is saving them, materials, time, money and
    men.
Oh, boy! Oh, joy! I. B. M. Hurray!

Even the few songs that speak of ordinary workers reinforce the idea that all company employees are working for the good of the whole:

We're co-workers in I. B. M.—all one big family.
We save materials, time, and men;
increasing profits to all business when
Accurate figures and weights and time—our machines guarantee.
Oh, joy! Oh, what bliss! We are members of this I. B. M. Company.

In the modern age, almost no one could sing "Oh, joy! Oh, what bliss!" about their employer without thinking questions that would give the songs a sense of mockery. "Did my company do the right thing in settling the anti-trust suit?" "Was it a good idea to sell the laptop division to a Chinese firm?" "Will my pension be fully funded when I retire?" "Why are the managers getting such a generous stock option plan?" We have come to believe that unswerving loyalty to a company is tragic not ironic. Such employees have surrendered their ability to think for themselves and have no protection against the day when the company decides that the interests of the employees no longer coincide with those of the shareholders.

FEW POPULAR SONGS EXPLORE THE THEME of working for the computer industry. One of the few, "Palo Alto" by the band Radiohead starts with a lyric that seems to have things in common with the *IBM Songbook.*

> Meet the boss, meet the wife,
> everybody's happy,
> everyone is made for life.

But, of course, this song presents these words ironically. It doesn't really mean what it is saying. It describes a world in which people cannot easily find a role or even find each other. "I'm too busy to see you," the lyric intones, and "you're too busy to wait." The only redemption in this song comes in the chorus, which notes the blessings of little pleasantries.

> Well I'm ok, how are you?
> Thanks for asking
> Thanks for asking.
> Well I'm ok, how are you?
> We hope that you are ok too.

The computer industry provides much material that would be the source for good songs but much of this material is touched with the contradictions of modern life. The employee who devotes extra energy to a project, knowing that they will be laid off. The boss who agonizes over a crucial decision, aware that any choice will likely benefit a competitor. The customer who buys a new product even though they are suspicious that there are better items available.

If you look closely at the lyrics of the old folk songs, you discover that they are filled with the same contradictions. The whaling song "Blow Ye Winds in the Morning" is about men who are leaving their farms to seek their fortune in whaling. Whaling jobs were advertised widely—as far from the coast as Buffalo, New York, because they were dangerous. Many whalers never returned and many a crew member was lost at sea. When the song calls for "one hundred brave Americans" most contemporary listeners would know that the lyrics meant "reckless Americans" or "foolish Americans" or even "desperate Americans with no prospects."

We can also easily imagine a pair of those whaling recruits sitting rowing a leaky boat in the middle of the ocean. They have lost the whale that took them beyond the sight of their mother ship and now they face an uncertain future midst the waves. It is hard to think that any of them might sing a song of unquestioned loyalty to their captain. They might pray to their God, curse their fate or even denounce the ambition that took them on the journey. As they try to decide what to do, they could only inquire how the other is doing under the circumstances and get the reply, "I'm OK." "How are you?" "Thanks for asking."

Emailing from Armenia

"YOU CAN PUT YOUR BAG HERE because you'll be using the front room," Mark advised. "Your cell phone probably won't work and even if it did, you'd discover that it wouldn't be able to send email."

Mark and his fiancée shared an apartment a block from the central shopping street of Moscow. They live as close to Kremlin as is possible for ordinary mortals. A generation ago, their building was filled with loyal apparatchiks, mid-level managers of state factories and devoted members of the Communist party. A few aged lefties are still to be found among those who live in the complex but most of the new residents are entrepreneurs, managers and accountants. They drive luxury cars from Germany and Japan, dress in the latest fashions and eat at ethnic restaurants that are decorated with artifacts from the central Asian republics.

"We do have high speed Internet," he added, "and wireless and voiceover IP phone service."

Such technology was not readily available when Mark had departed the United States, a decade and a half ago, and had traveled to the crumbling remains of the Soviet Union. At the time, the country had only a few network connections. The Zelinsky Institute of Organic Chemistry had a connection through IBM mainframes. RelCom, a commercial venture that had been born in the demise of communism, had link through Finland to the European EU-Net. As such connections were not easily accessible to a young aid worker. Mark had to communicate with me through more primitive technologies: white paper, blue ballpoint pens and return addresses carefully spelled out in Cyrillic letters.

"Dear David," his letters would begin "I am in Kiev" or Riga or Vladivostok. "I am working with emigrants." "I'm programming the computer." "I'm being a tourist in Uzbekistan." Four or five or six weeks would pass between the day that he posted the letter. The envelopes would often arrive with the marks of transit, signs that made you want to believe that they contained the frozen air of the Siberian steppes or the dust of the Silk Road. Yet, the wear that they sustained was really nothing more than the signs of cooperation, the evidence that two very different countries that promoted two different styles of management could make a complicated system work.

MARK FOUND EMAIL IN 1995, when he was assigned to a field office in Yerevan, Armenia, a former Soviet state located on the northeast corner of Turkey. "I was an on-site specialist," he explained in a letter. "I was there to help a new department of the newly independent government be effective and efficient by making sure equipment and funds went to proper use." At the time, Armenia was a hardship post, far from effective and nowhere close to efficient. It had drained its treasury by fighting a ruinous battle with Azerbaijan on its southern border. Its industrial base, built by the old Soviet government, was collapsing and parts of the infrastructure were starting to fail. The power grid was unable to deliver a constant supply of power. "You always had to keep a duplicate of your work," Mark recalled, "in case the power failed when you were programming."

Mark was to help with the reconstruction of the Armenian economy by creating an aid database, records of the resources that might be available to help develop the country. His supervisor envisioned that a user would bring a development problem to the system and then the system would produce a list of possible organizations and activities that could be used in a solution. The organization thought that it would be an innovative use of technology even though it resembled some of the computer applications that had once been commonplace in the Soviet Union.

The Soviet computer industry began in 1950, when Sergei Lebedev (1902–1974) built the country's first computer in Kiev. It grew in parallel with the American industry, developing some machines that were based on Western ideas and some that were unique to the Communist world. It produced the BESM computers, the Strelas, the Urals, the Minsks. By the mid-1980s, it had produced two families of computers that were widely used for data processing, the Unified Systems (usually abbreviated "ES" for Edinenaya Sistema or called Ryad, the Russian word for "series") and the Small Systems (abbreviated "SM" for "Sistema Malaya").

The ES family was the larger of the two. It included 32 different models, 200 peripheral devices and 12 different versions of an operating system. Most of the ES machines were based on the architecture of the IBM System/360 series and, at its zenith, the ES series was "second only to the IBM 360/370 series in the number of installed mainframes." The SM series was based on the DEC PDP-11 and Vax designs.

Through the 1970s and 1980s, Soviet planners spent billions of rubles to place these two families of computers in the management offices of the country's manufacturing and distribution enterprises. They intended that these machines would perform the basic clerical work that was needed to run the country's economy, though, of course, they intended that these machines would answer to the ministry of central planning rather than to the invisible hand of the market.

As a whole, these centers had proven to be a poor investment. In part, they were hampered by the poor quality of Soviet software, poorly trained staffs and slow communication but they were also undermined by the nature of the communist system itself. The central planning office of the Soviet Union wanted reports that would validate their economic goals rather than provide information that could be used to manage operations. Under these circumstances, manufacturing organizations had no incentive to make good use of their machines. "Even computerizing simple accounting can be perceived as a threat," observed one pair of scholars. "It is easier to hide inconsistencies when the accounting system is manual."

The computer industry should have flourished during the period of Glasnost (1985–1991), the six years in which Mikhail Gorbachev tried to bring economic reform to the country. Computers could have provided the information that was needed to move the country towards a market economy. They could have been used to identify efficient sources of production, unused resources, and excess distribution capacity. Instead, the Soviet computer industry collapsed with much of the rest of the old manufacturing base. The state run computer firms lost their government support and failed, taking with them the ES and SM lines of computers. "The engineers did a heroic deed in designing these computers," remarked a Russian journalist, "but they still ran an inefficient industry."

The old state firms, the IBM and DEC of the Soviet Union, were replaced by a collection of small entrepreneurial companies. These new companies were often attempts to capitalize the research of a university computer science department or a government laboratory. They usually had no more than 100 employees and possessed very little business skill. Most of them were overwhelmed by the economic turmoil of the period. "Essentially nothing from before the early 1990s has survived," observed a researcher from that period.

The economic turmoil of the 1990s fell heavily on the old provincial capitals, such as Yerevan. Many full-time workers could not feed themselves from the money that they could earn as salaries and many a job went begging. In this environment, Mark found that he had time on his hands. He could program by day but had little to do at night. Searching the city, he discovered a new independent radio station (HAI-FM, 105.5 on your FM dial) that was financed by an American philanthropist. In spite of the outside financing, the station had little money to offer its employees. Most spent only a few hours at the station before departing to work at a second or third job.

When he introduced himself as a former college radio announcer and a willing volunteer, Mark received a warm welcome and an offer to host four evening shows a week. Mark was pleased with the opportunity but he noted that the station was not only struggling with a failed economy but was also hampered by the old ideas of the Soviet system. "The announcers wrote out scripts beforehand," Mark observed, "and read them in a monotone voice."

Mark brought a Western approach to his shows. "I did a typical pop deejay show in English," he recalled. The music was drawn from his college collection of compact disks: Madonna, the B-52s, the Bangles, Prince. No one quite knew what make of his performance. He was informal. Witty. Relaxed. "The other deejays would literally come in and just watch me," he wrote. "That was kind of creepy."

His stories were predictable to anyone familiar with college radio stations. One day, he reported that he "stuck [his] head out the window with the microphone in hand and described what Mount Ararat looked like at that particular moment." On a particularly snowy day, he "gave the weather report from some Caribbean paradise." "The reaction is tremendous," Mark wrote, "at least in the very small circles of people I talked to."

The letters describing Mark's shows on HAI-FM, 105.5, reached me in minutes, rather than days, because Mark had found an email service. With the economy in shambles, this service was provided by a Western organization, SITA, the Société Internationale de Télécommunications Aéronautiques. This organization provided communications services to support air travel. Strictly speaking, it was not a business but a cooperative society that had been founded jointly by the European airlines in 1949. However, as the airlines wanted to minimize their costs of operations, SITA had a strong incentive to build an efficient communications network, adopt new technologies and maintain an effective organization.

SITA built its first network, a web of manually operated telegraph lines, in 1950. For about a decade, this network proved to be an inexpensive way of handling the relatively small number of messages that were generated by the fledgling airline industry. It carried weather reports, notices of departure, instructions for the pilot and crew. As the airlines began to transmit more and more reservation data, SITA expanded the capacity of its network in 1966 by replacing the manual operators with Univac computers. Six years later, with the airlines demanding that the network handle more traffic and reduce costs, SITA replaced the Univac machines, which relayed messages from station to station, with a packet switched network like the one that was being developed for the Arpanet in the United States.

Mark had access to the SITA network because his aid agency worked closely with the airlines. The agency used the network to make arrangements to move refugees, displaced persons and victims of political persecution. As an extra benefit, the network also gave agency staff access to the Internet. "We dial a local number from Yerevan," Mark wrote, "wait an age and a half for it to connect via Moscow, and then log on to some kind of bulletin board. From there we can download and upload messages."

International email was still relatively new at this time. To jump from network to network, and country to country, one often needed to know how to route an email message through some gateway. Hence, Mark's first communications with me had some of the marks of novelty. He would write lengthy descriptions of his job, his city, his world. I replied with silly questions that showed me to be amazed that I had an observer on the other side of the world. Was it warm over there? Was it cold? What was his apartment like? How did he survive with sporadic electricity? How much did he see of thugs and robbers that were allegedly found on Armenia's roads?

At first, I didn't focus on Mark's role at the radio station. I didn't grasp that an aid worker was moonlighting as a disk jockey. The narrative unfolded slowly, as I began to understand that the shows were important both to Mark and to his Armenian friends. "I am not a rogue personality with some skill at the mixing board," Mark wrote one day, "but rather a live representative of exactly what they want to become." He then added "They just didn't know it until now."

In addition to hosting his shows, Mark was starting to train the local announcers in the skills of the American college disk jockey. He taught them to be relaxed, to improvise, to respond to the music, to feel comfortable, to express their own personality. The Armenians readily accepted these ideas but they also believed that there was something special in Mark's music. "The deejays recorded all of my CDs," Mark wrote. "My music is about 40% of their airtime."

"They sound just like you!" observed one of his friends. For a time, even after Mark retired from his duties at the station, you could turn to 105.5 FM Yerevan and think that you were in an American college town. You heard the hits and jokes of the 1980s. You might be excused for believing that Ronald Reagan was still president, that the iron curtain still descended across Europe from Stettin on the Baltic to Trieste in the Adriatic, that you were on one side of that curtain and that Armenia was on the other.

THE RADIO STATION WAS MARK'S LEGACY TO ARMENIA. His database, the project that had taken him to Yerevan, had suffered a fate similar to that of the old Soviet computer industry. It was delayed longer than anyone had anticipated, was more complicated than they had planned and was rarely used for practical problems. They knew how to build the tool but they did not know how to use it.

Such databases would be useful to a developing economy only as the region developed a new information technology industry. This new industry followed the introduction of email to the region and brought all the faith in the discipline of the market economy. It brought no large manufacturing facilities to the area and established no large software firms. The new firms did only the work that could not be done elsewhere for less expense. Parts came from Kuala Lumpur and Santa Clara to be assembled in Moscow. Software, created in Redmond, and Mysore, was sold in Kiev by young men with BMW's and Italian suits. Yerevan phone numbers, owned by companies in Virginia, gave you high-speed connections to weather reports from Atlanta, news from London and financial reports from Frankfurt. In the end, it brought more to Armenia than it carried away.

The Boundaries of Time

JORDAN WAS THE KIND OF SPEAKER who could have made good use of a backup band. By training, he was an accountant, a small town professor who sold his advice to the local business community. Yet, if he had wanted a career on stage, he would have found it for the asking. He had a smooth, confident voice that commanded not only your attention but also your acquiescence. He was able to use this voice to elevate business topics into subjects that touched on the great themes of mortal existence: good and evil, technical knowledge and human ignorance, uncertain success and incomplete failure. As you listened to his argument, you could easily hear a band adding its contribution to the presentation. First, a high soprano voice would build a long-sustained note above the words. This would be followed by the crack of a drumstick, the rolling sound of an electric bass, and the full harmony of a gospel choir singing of salvation for all who sought truth righteously.

"You trust these machines with your money," Jordan would intone. "You trust them with your health, with your career, and with your children." He would pause at critical moments to make sure that you grasped the full implications of his ideas. "You even trust them with your good name."

"This is a serious time for serious people," Jordan would continue. "When January 2000 arrives, the Millennial Bug is going to touch every aspect of your life. On that day, I would not fly in an airplane. I would not leave my money in a bank. I would not expect that any force on earth would be able to protect me from the chaos in the streets."

During the late 1990s, Jordan had a ready audience for this presentation, an ever-changing collection of business leaders and computer professionals who were ready to be frightened by the potential evils of the Millennial Bug or as it later came to be known, the Y2K Problem. The technical roots of this problem were easy to understand. Many of the computers programs that were operating recorded dates as a pair of digits and hence were not able to keep track of the century. The year "1998" was represented as "98" which was also the representation for "2098" or "1898."

Jordan could convince audiences that this abbreviated form of the date could cause any number of practical problems. "Social Security payments will stop," he prophesized, "because the recipients will suddenly become too young. Dangerous

Too Soon to Tell: Essays for the End of the Computer Revolution, by David Alan Grier
Copyright © 2009 IEEE Computer Society

criminals will be wrongly identified as having served their sentences. Credit cards will be rejected as improperly issued and foods will be given unacceptable expiration dates."

To be a good prophet, one has to offer either a technical wonder or a moral lesson. It is not enough to cry in the corporate wilderness that the day is spent and the time is at hand. Jordan did not understand enough programming to offer a solution and he did not have a vision sufficient to extract a broader lesson from the experience. All he could offer was the vague exhortation to be more diligent, advice that can be applied at almost any time to any computer project.

Without a wonder or a moral, the only thing that might have kept Jordan in the public eye would have been a good backup band. Lacking such a band, he soon found that his golden voice and his message of fear was not enough to hold an audience. As the days stepped towards 31 December, 1999, he pushed himself further and further from the discussion of the Y2K Problem. As calmer individuals began to look at the full nature of the issue, they rediscovered that each generation of programmers and engineers finishes its work with a balance sheet of assets and debts. Living in a world where deadlines are measured in the 18-month units of Moore's law, we work through this sheet in our own cycle of steps and attempt to turn each debt into a wonder.

LIKE SO MANY ISSUES IN COMPUTER SCIENCE, the Y2K Problem had its roots in the interface between the technical environment and the human world, the points where the circuits and commands of a well-engineered device came in contact with hours and seasons of human life. Virtually all of the early computers were designed around a clock, an electronic metronome that synchronized the operation of the different elements of the machine. These clocks kept data flowing in and out of memory, delayed the start of one activity until the completion of another, ensured that the fast electronic circuits did not outrun the slow mechanical input and output devices. However, all of these clocks operated with little connection to civil time. They were hidden deep in the machine's hardware and none were particularly accessible.

Among the early computers, the clock of the 1946 ENIAC was perhaps the most visible but it had a fundamental quirk that made it challenging to use. The clock was a collection of pulses that could be directed to any unit of the machine. It could be sent to an accumulator in order to record the seconds and hours of the day. However, if you attempted to read that clock, you discovered that it would miss a beat and would require a correction. The correction was not difficult to make but it was one of the little open problems that came with a machine was presented as able to solve problems "which could hardly be attempted by more conventional computing tools."

The best timekeepers among the early machines were the Sage computers, machines that had been designed to be part of the American air defense system and to follow events that occurred in the human world. Each Sage machine had a vacuum tube clock that could keep time for 34 minutes and 8 seconds before it returned to zero and began counting again. By itself, this clock was not sufficient for the basic tasks assigned to Sage: tracking Soviet bombers over Alaskan airspace, coordinating fighter intercepts, identifying civilian planes. However, this clock could not be expanded without increasing the size of other machine elements: the data paths, the disk drives, the memory, the input and output channels. Rather than incurring the expense of a more sophisticated clock, the system designers asked the programmers to take the extra steps that would keep track of time.

A decade passed before time keeping became a common feature of the general commercial systems. Even then, any effort to keep track of dates and times required both ingenuity and discipline. The IBM System/360, which was released in the leap year of 1964, had an internal clock that stored the date in five decimal digits. Three digits were used to record the day, a number between 1 and 366 that year (or 365 in regular years.) The remaining two digits were used to record the year. Nothing kept track of the century.

In 1964, the end of the 20th century was far beyond the horizon of every computer designer. The age of electronic calculation was not yet two decades old. No computer had lived a useful life that had exceeded ten years and no computer design had survived to celebrate its 15th birthday. If some engineers had thought about the turn of the century—and some must have pondered that transition—they would have assumed that the machines of 1999 would be four or five generations removed from the machines of 1964 and would possess capabilities far beyond those of the IBM System/360. Certainly they would have expected any problems of dates and centuries would have been solved long before then.

Any complacency over the long years before the century's end was shaken just five years later when the System/360 experienced a problem with its internal calendar. At midnight on 31 December 1969, that calendar caused the System/360s to malfunction. IBM technicians identified the source of the problem in the machines' operating system and told customers to circumvent the issue with a lie—the temporary return of the computer's date to 1 January 1969. By the end of the month, IBM programmers had corrected the problem and returned the System/360 date to the one indicated by the civil calendar.

IN 1980, AS ELECTRONIC COMPUTATION moved into it 35th year, the computer industry began acknowledging, at least tacitly, that some of its creations or their offspring would be operating on the night of the millennial change. IBM, noting that its System/360 design had celebrated its 14th birthday and could plausibly celebrate 20 more, added a century bit to its representation of calendar dates. If the bit was 0, the date came from the 20th century. If it was 1, the date came from the 21st century.

The new IBM century bit was another short-term expedient, a solution that moved a current problem into the distant future. If any of the IBM engineers were concerned about drawing the wrath of the programmers that might face the calendar problem of 2099, they never wrote of it. Perhaps, like the original designers of the IBM System/360, they doubted that their handiwork would survive until that date.

Perhaps they believed that future programmers would honor the technical advancements of the System/360 designers by following the code of never speaking ill of the dead. Perhaps they didn't care.

In the late 1980s, and even in the early 1990s, few individuals were thinking about the calendar problems of the year 2000 and fewer still were doing anything about it. Occasionally, a software engineer would discuss the problem at a conference but these presentations often communicated an air of despair. If we "recognize and fix the problem in our environment while the rest of the computing world ignores it," wrote one researcher in 1990, "the problem will still affect everyone, including us."

As the decade moved towards its mid-point, little had changed. According to one survey, no more than 5 percent of all computer centers were preparing for the change of dates.

As with so many issues in the modern world, the Millennial Bug became a public issue only when someone thought it proper to make a formal statement to the press. IBM took that step on 16 December 1996, announcing to the civilized world that the Y2K Problem would shortly appear in all forms of information technology and that bad effects of this problem could be addressed through services provided by the IBM company. "Although the price tag for making systems Year 2000 ready could be high," the statement proclaimed, "failure to act will adversely affect a broad array of commercial, industrial, educational and government operations."

The news of the Y2K Problem generated some concern among the general public and provided opportunities for speakers to frighten anyone who dealt with high technology. However, most individuals were more puzzled than frightened. "It seems odd," editorialized the *New York Times*, "that in an industry that is downright apostolic about the future [that] no one saw the millennium coming until it was just this close."

Many observers suggested that the world's computers could be saved by lying about the change in the calendar, the same solution that had restored the IBM System/360 computers three decades before. One clergyman, expressing disenchantment with modern life, argued that such an adjustment to the calendar would correct the ills wrought by the 20th century. By returning the calendar to 1900, we would "avoid the countless genocides, the Holocaust and two atomic bombings," he wrote. "Furthermore, it buys us another century in which to fix the millennium bug."

Sadly, a lie twice told loses some of its credibility in the second telling. The adjustment that allowed IBM engineers to address problems with the System/360 in 1969 would not be as effective in 1999. Over the prior 30 years, computers had become increasingly interconnected. They were part of systems that passed messages from machine to machine. They marked these messages with time and date stamps so that they could be stored, retrieved and processed in an orderly fashion. These flows would be completely disrupted by the simple lie about the date.

The system that drew the greatest concern from the public was the network of computers that controlled airplane traffic. They "should not be used beyond December 1999," stated one report, "because they may not operate reliably when the date rolls over to January 1, 2000 and there is no way to predict the effect on air traffic." The air traffic machines had to conglomerate data from multiple radar installations that were "scattered across thousands of square miles," noted one news story, and yet they had problems with their own internal operations. In a test that advanced the date to 1 January 2000, these machines were unable to control even their own cooling systems properly.

Much of the strategy to fix the Y2K Problem followed the standard cycle of quality engineering: Identify the problem. Create a solution. Test the solution. Deploy the solution. Repeat. The only special nature to this problem was the fact that the deadline of 31 December 1999, was immovable.

Commonly, computer centers began their preparation for the 31 December deadline by intending that they would to modify their old programs and recode their databases. As these organizations learned the scope of the problem, many decided that they would be better served by replacing old systems with new. As the deadline loomed, a few writers suggested that the best protection against problems would be to change companies rather than systems, "to merge with or buy a company that has Y2K-safe systems and retire your own."

The effort to beat the millennial deadline proved costly, an estimated $3 trillion in expenses to American firms. Some complained that the money was ill spent, some argued that it could have been avoided with a careful application of those fundamental engineering principles: Evaluate, design, test, deploy, repeat. At the same time, many companies felt, in that last December, that they faced the new world with a better understanding of their old systems. One consultant argued that his client "now has both a baseline and systematic methodology available to improve its computer systems."

I WILL CONFESS THAT I CARRIED A FLASHLIGHT when I walked to the Washington Mall in order to see the fireworks on midnight, 31 December 1999. I was fairly certain that nothing would happen at midnight but I wasn't completely certain. The sky was dark, as the new moon was four days away. I didn't want to pick my way home through unlit streets without a source of light.

All our fears were put to rest when the Washington Monument lit up at midnight and nothing happened. We cheered and hugged, pleased to witness the change of the calendar and grateful that the plague of Y2K had passed us by.

Three or four days later, I was in the one of the local research libraries, chatting with a staff member about the change of year. "Our copier has the Y2K Problem," she said. "It was behaving oddly this morning," said the attendant, "so I changed the date and the machine completely stopped."

I looked at the machine saw a technician replacing a part and thought of Jordan. "Is that true?" I asked. "Was it Y2K?"

"Sorta," he said. "We've had some trouble with the software during the past week that might be Y2K. But this copier came to a halt only when the staff changed the date. It disrupts the billing program, and the company likes to be paid."

Counting Beans

FRANCIS AND GERALD HAVE NEVER BEEN SEEN TOGETHER. Such a meeting is physically impossible. They are the matter and anti-matter of American politics. If they ever arrived at the same place in both time and space, they would annihilate each other in an instant.

Francis is an aged lefty. He marched against all those terrible things of the 1960s and was arrested several times. For a period, he served as the head of the American Association for the Promotion of Goodness and spoke forcefully against the injustice of the world. For most of his life, he was a strong believer in democracy as the solution for all political ills but that faith was tested in the 2000 American presidential election.

Sometime in November 2000, well before the election was resolved, Francis caught me on the street. "We have to do something," he said with urgency. "They're stealing the election."

"Ok," I said. Long ago I learned to be cautious when talking to Francis. "Who is they? And how are they stealing it?"

With a brief snort, Francis suggested that I was a naïve fool. "The moneyed elite," he said. "The capitalists. They couldn't convince enough people to vote for their candidate so they are going to change the rules."

I have always believed that people are more likely to be stupid than dishonest. It is one of the failings of my character. I tried to explain that vote counting was an engineering process and, as such, had an error rate—a certain percentage of votes that would be incorrectly counted. At the current moment, the error rate was larger than the difference between the two candidates.

Francis was unimpressed. "They have the bean-counters in their pocket," he said with obvious disdain. "It doesn't take much to buy a bean-counter."

Historically, Francis was wrong on this point. Once upon a time, the time being colonial New England, bean-counters were people of demonstrated integrity. They were the individuals who oversaw elections. Their name came from the fact that the elections were conducted with dried beans. Voters would indicate their preference by dropping a bean in a pot that was identified with a particular candidate. When everyone had voted, the bean-counters would empty the jars, count the beans and

Too Soon to Tell: Essays for the End of the Computer Revolution, by David Alan Grier
Copyright © 2009 IEEE Computer Society

declare the winner. If they were not people of integrity, the bean-counter would have easily manipulated the outcome. A winning margin could be pulled from a pocket, a close vote transferred from one pile to another or victorious landslide dumped on the ground for the birds to eat.

Francis was not interested in learning the history, admittedly pedantic, of the bean-counter. Neither was Gerald, who used the same term with me a few weeks later. The two of us were attending a meeting at one of those Washington institutes. Gerald saw me, grabbed my arm and began talking loudly. "The bean-counters are stealing the election," he said. "They're under the control of the liberals and the unions. If we don't do something, there will be chaos, utter chaos."

As with Francis, I tried to explain the technical nature of the election process but Gerald brushed my words aside. "Who cares about technology," he said. "We have to have a trustworthy election or democracy is doomed."

As the weeks progressed, both Francis and Gerald concluded that the 2000 election represented a major failure of information technology, a failure far more devastatingly visible than the prior year's Y2K Problem. Like others, they both wanted an immediate reform of voting technology and procedures. "One of the first challenges facing the new Congress," editorialized one paper, "will be to develop a uniform national electoral process that safeguards the sanctity of Americans' right to vote."

Most of people thought that the problems of the 2000 election had a straight-forward solution. "Stop using punched cards," was the blunt assessment of March 2001 report. The American Congress established a commission to prepare standards for voting technology. Election boards discarded old machines, purchased new Direct Recording Electronic devices to capture the vote, and redesigned their bal-loting systems. While this work generally improved the quality of the 2004 election, it also made subsequent problems all the more visible. The next election, the Presidential vote of 2004, brought new claims of voting irregularities and an official challenge to the result.

More damaging was a major failure in a 2006 Florida Congressional ballot. In this election, new, modern voting machines failed to record some 18,000 votes, one out of every seven ballots cast. "A considerable amount of technical investigation has been done into the circumstances of this election," wrote one investigator, but "the exact causes are not known with complete certainty, indeed, they may never be known".

Strictly speaking, many of these failures may have been more managerial than technical. They may indeed have been caused by the actions of the bean-counters rather than by the failure of voting machinery. However, our current body politic is looking for a more robust voting mechanism that is secured by technology rather than by the competence and integrity of bean-counters. Such work is not easy. One author has noted that a good voting system requires us to balance the "often conflict-ing requirements of our democracy," secrecy with accountability, scale with cost.

THE DEMANDS OF DEMOCRACY have grown over the years. The scale and cost have grown most dramatically. In 1800, the United States had to count the votes of some 68,000 white, landholding men who lived along the Atlantic coast. This election had none the trappings of the modern election. It had no fixed precincts, no voter registration and even no common ballot. Voters wrote their preferences on any scrap of paper that was available. Such a system would not have handled the scale of the 2000 election, when 104,000,000 individuals cast their votes in jurisdictions spread over six or more time zones.

As the scale of the election has grown, so has the demand for accountability and secrecy. Secrecy was not an original requirement of the American election system. Indeed, the founders of the country anticipated that voting would be a public activity. The early presidents, Jefferson, Madison, Jackson, Polk, and even Abraham Lincoln, were elected without the widespread use of secret ballots. Through most of the 19th century, voters often used ballots that had been prepared by the candidates or their political parties. These ballots were usually printed on colored paper or had other marks that made them easily identifiable.

The lack of secrecy meant that votes could be easily bought. A political operative could pass a dime and a party ballot to a willing soul and watch as the voter placed the paper in the election box. By 1870, such fraud was common in the large cities. New York had the greatest problem, with several organizations actively buying votes. The largest was Tammany Hall, under the control of Boss Tweed.

For more than two decades, New Yorkers tried to limit the influence of Tammany Hall with little success. Tammany workers found it easy to buy votes from immigrants with money, or a drink, or the promise of a job, or a firmly uttered threat. In 1888, New York election offices gained some control over fraudulent votes with a new technology known as the Australian ballot.

To the modern eye, the Australian ballot is such a simple device that we wonder how it might qualify as a technology or be considered as an invention. It is nothing more than the common paper ballot. Yet, it had four features that distinguished it from the other balloting systems of the 19th century. First, Australian ballots were printed by the state and not by private political organizations. Second, it was distributed and collected by government representatives. Third, it contained all candidates for each office and grouped those candidates together. Fourth, and finally, it was cast in secret.

Taken together, these four features made voting fraud difficult. Political operatives could no longer give partisan ballots to potential voters. They also found it difficult to enforce their bribes. They could no longer watch how people made their votes and hence they could no longer threaten individuals who took their money, drank their whiskey and voted against them anyway.

"Bribery is very greatly diminished, almost altogether ceasing," wrote a Massachusetts advocate of the Australian ballot. Though "we hear these rumors of bribery, there is no doubt the new voting system has placed great obstacles in its way." A few political organizations bragged that they could still control elections. "Oh, we're on to the new law!" proclaimed a New Jersey political leader but a local paper doubted his statements. "It is scarcely to be believed that they would proclaim new villainies in advance if they had found a means of committing them," the paper observed. The paper concluded that such statements indicated that the groups did not know how to circumvent the new ballot law and "that they are merely trying to frighten the people into inactivity."

The Australian ballot reminds us how quickly new technologies can be spread through an economy. In less than 18 months, the major electoral jurisdictions adopted the new ballot. "The Australian system is spreading over the country like a wave," exulted one reformer. "It is constantly appearing in places where you would least expect to find a disposition for ballot reform." However, the new system brought new expenses to communities. They not only had to print the ballots, they also had to provide enclosed places where voters could mark the ballot.

"The fittings in Boston cost $35 for each precinct," admitted a Boston official, "but as the fixtures were made so as to fold up and be taken away and used from year to year, it is safe to say they do not cost over $5 a year for each precinct besides the cost of moving back and forth."

Many jurisdictions tried to reduce the cost of elections by using machinery. The introduction of the Australian ballot coincided with the start of the calculating machine industry in the United States. In 1888, William S. Burroughs of St. Louis, Missouri, was marketing his new adding machine, called the Arithmometer, to banks and businesses. To his north, Dorr Felt of Chicago, Illinois, was selling a lightweight machine, which he named the Comptometer. In Washington, D.C., Herman Hollerith was testing a more complicated system that used his punched cards. In Rochester, New York, Jacob Myers was completing a geared machine that would record and tabulate votes.

"My present invention," wrote Myers, provides a means by which "an honest vote can be had and counted without liability of voters being intimidated." Furthermore, it also prevented individuals from "voting more than once for the same candidate or for different candidates for the same office." The machines could also process large numbers of voters and hence make elections less expensive. There "is great economy in the use of voting machines," observed an official from Buffalo, New York. The city purchased machines in 1900. With them, they were able to reduce by 30 percent the number of election districts and the size of the election staff. The "saving in these and other ways is estimated to be over $10,000 a year," wrote the official, "a sum which will pay the entire cost of the machines in about five years."

THE TECHNOLOGIES OF 1900 DID NOT COMPLETELY SOLVE the problem of voter fraud nor did they provide a technology that could easily expand to meet the demands of a growing electorate. In spite of claims to the contrary, voting machines proved to be expensive to store, expensive to maintain and expensive to transport. By 1960, as populations moved to the suburbs, jurisdictions looked for cheaper, more reliable ways to count the vote. Many of them turned to punched card ballots for the same reason that companies turned to punched card information systems. Such systems were inexpensive. Manual card punches cost little and were easy to operate. Tabulators could count the ballots from dozens if not hundreds of punches.

Almost from the start, punched card voting machines had problems. In was the age when the warning "Do Not Fold, Spindle or Mutilate" was stamped on most cards. Even skilled business organizations could have trouble with the most well-maintained system and the most carefully punched cards. Election systems cards, which were scored to make it easier for the voter, were difficult to tabulate accurately. "It is generally not possible to exactly duplicate a count obtained on pre-scored punch cards," argued a critic of this technology, Roy Saltman, "given the inherent physical characteristics of these ballots and the variability in the ballot-punching performance of real voters." Saltman's recommendation was straightforward. We should stop using such cards as a voting mechanism.

Saltman saw problems beyond the task of tabulating votes at a single precinct. Increasingly, precinct totals were being transferred mechanically or electronically. Jurisdictions would find it difficult to secure the election and identify places where votes could be added or ignored or transferred from one candidate to another, like so many beans in the hands of a bean counter. Jurisdictions needed to test their machines before the election and keep detailed records for a later audit. He argued that audit trails were one of the key ways by "which the correctness of the reported results may be verified."

In 1988, when Saltman wrote his report, almost half of the country used punched card voting machines and none of them was prepared to abandon the technology. Change often comes only through the force of wholesale embarrassment and no one had been sufficiently embarrassed to drop an inexpensive technology. Not Charleston, West Virginia, which faced a contested election in 1980. Not Elkart County, Indiana, in 1982. Not Palm Beach, Florida, in 1984. Not Dallas, Texas, in 1985.

The 2000 election, of course, badly embarrassed the state of Florida, thoroughly frightened electoral officials of the remaining states and forced the U.S. Congress to look at the technology of voting. From the start, most people realized that problems posed by voting machinery were both political and technical. We not only had to design a good, secure system, we also had to get the technology of that system accepted by the electorate, as if that technology were itself a candidate for office. Such a process is not quick nor is it easy to explain to the people who must do the technical work. Ideas that seem obvious to the engineer or programmer or the system designer need to be debated and discussed and even misunderstood for a time before they can be honestly accepted by the people who will use them. There seems to be no other way to balance the "often conflicting requirements of our democracy."

NEITHER FRANCIS NOR GERALD HAVE BEEN HAPPY with the progress of voting technology since the 2000 election. Francis once invited me to a "Hanging Chad," party, an event that flung little bits of paper around the United States Capitol in an attempt to embarrass somebody into action. I saw the results on the sidewalk but I don't think that anyone, other than the street cleaners, took any notice. Gerald, who falsely believes that my opinions are valued by others, has cornered me several times and said, "You have some influence. Can't you get them to dump those stupid voting machines?" I suspect that Gerald believes that the nation would be better if everyone shared his ideas and opinions. Francis probably believes the same thing, though he makes passing claims to "embracing diversity." If either gets their way, then we will find it easy to build good voting machines. We will be able to use bean counters.

The Eyes of the World

OVER THE YEARS, Ray has made peace with his ignorance. That task has not been easy, as he started his career filled with enthusiastic naiveté. During his college career, he had become interested in computer security. He had read Clifford Stoll's classic *Cuckoo's Egg*, about an early hacker infiltration of the computers at Lawrence Berkeley Laboratories and had followed the story of the Internet worm of 1988. As a student, he had found one of the few books on security and had tested the problems that it described on a Unix workstation in somebody's laboratory. He had been able to download the password file, gain access to system commands, and even to modify parts of the operating system. He finished the work with the confidence of youth and an eagerness to do battle with the dark shadows of the human soul.

Over the next five or six years, Ray had become an investigator of computer invasions, a detective who defended the computers of the financial services industry against cyber crime. The work took him to three continents and exposed him to a large range of machines, both big and small. It gave him a badge, heavy enough to stop a .45 caliber slug before it grazed the press of a dress shirt and a fist full of stories that you might not want to share with your mother.

"It is kind of like being a firefighter," he explained. We were sitting in a coffee shop near my office. The place was filled with young men and women who were drinking designer caffeinated beverages and appeared deeply involved in their own conversations. "When the alarm bell sounds, I jump into my boots, leap onto the screaming engine and boldly engage the fire wherever it may be."

Initially, the work had been fun and exciting but the experience had started to drain him. "Our systems are under attack," he explained, "and they are under attack all the time and the attackers are not good people." His eyes were agitated and his face looked tired. This was not the Ray that I had known. "Sure, the big systems are secured but there are hundreds of ways the hackers can get into a system. They can break into the workstation of some contractor. They can exploit the weaknesses of some local application. We just do not know all the problems that are out there."

At the time, his words had the ring of truth. I had recently seen the security weaknesses in a new financial system that our university had purchased. Despite my protests that I might have enough expertise to make the system work, I was told that

Too Soon to Tell: Essays for the End of the Computer Revolution, by David Alan Grier
Copyright © 2009 IEEE Computer Society

I had to take the standard training course. The class was run by a perky young person, the kind of individual who found honest inspiration in those corporate motivational posters that feature bold lighting, dramatic landscapes and slogans like "Dare to exceed."

The training session had been boring beyond measure, as we had to be introduced to the "system philosophy" long before we were to be taught any useful commands. Being unengaged and sitting at a workstation near the back of the room, I had starting fiddling with the commands. I easily found that I could get to the help menu, and from that menu, you could get to the operating system command line and elevate your status to that of a system administrator. I filled the next two hours by sending email to friends, notifying the system administrator of the security hole in his system and sending messages to the screen of the trainer at the front of the room. Unsure of the source of my messages, the trainer did the only logical thing. She ignored them.

"You never know how you are going to get hit," Ray had said at the time. "It might come from inside the organization. It might come from outside. It might be something that you have never even heard of. My advice is to get the strongest protection software that you can find, run it all the time and expect that you will be invaded anyway."

RAY HAD ENDED THAT CONVERSATION with little peace in his heart. Part of his concern may have come from the fact that he was changing jobs and did not know what the future held. Part may have also come from the doubt that eats away at a career, the doubt that suggests that one has accomplished little or done nothing of good in spite of strong efforts and good intentions.

Computer security shares the methods and goals of computer science as a whole but has a couple of features that set it apart. First, it presents an unknown target to its practitioners like Ray. It is one thing to prepare for an expanded business, or changes in the regulatory environment or new operational methods. It is quite another to brace for a new attack by novel software from an unknown quarter. Second, computer security has a vulnerable position in the public mind. When done well, it is invisible. When done badly, "it calls the entire field of computer security into question," according to a pair of critics, "because the public can't distinguish between valid methods [of security] and those that have yet to be proven."

Over the years, Ray came to the conclusion that the practice of computer security was hampered by a third problem: raw embarrassment. Time and again, he would arrive at a site, flash his badge to the system administrator and be told that there was nothing to see. The staff couldn't find the infected machine. Or they had erased the computer's log, cleaned its disk and restored the machine to operating condition. As a group, they were often unwilling to admit that they had been attacked by anything: a virus, a worm or a hacker.

Occasionally, the administrators had been overcome by the reasoned fear that the news of the attack would undermine the confidence of their investors. It was an idea that they justified to themselves and their superiors but it was the kind of lie that has driven the tragic tales of the last 50 years. Public figures are far more likely to be destroyed by hiding an ill deed than by admitting the fact that they actually committed that deed. If Richard Nixon taught us nothing more, he showed the perils of the cover-up.

In the course of his work, Ray discovered that computer administrators, as often as not, were motivated by unreasoned fears, by ideas unsustained by any reasonable logic. System mangers told him that they resisted reporting intrusions because the culprit might be someone beyond the reach of the law, such as a juvenile or a foreign national or, in the worst of all possible scenarios, someone who would gain a better position or more business from the notoriety of the incident.

Such concerns do have a little foundation in reality. "The business side of investigating cyber crime is that it really needs to either put someone in jail or provide network intelligence that can be used to better protect systems on a large scale," Ray told me recently. We had gathered again at my favorite coffee shop to talk about hacking, Denial of Service attacks and other challenges to the modern computer system. A recent incident in Europe had confirmed Ray's historic pessimism about the vulnerability of computers. A network of zombie computers had overwhelmed the machines of an entire country. In spite of this news, Ray seemed remarkably relaxed. Rather than being frightened by an event that many had called the first example of cyber-warfare, he seemed at peace with the world.

"It's not that things are any better," he said, "it's probably that I just more used to it. The operating systems are better, which is nice, but the hackers have more tools at their disposal. Once you needed to understand the actual source code of a system in order to exploit it. Now there are software tools that will help you write a worm, create a virus or even probe the weaknesses of a operating system. There are even libraries of exploit code for the most popular systems."

"Even with all the changes in technology," he added, "each call is more likely to be a porn scare than a real threat against a system."

"Porn scare?" I asked. I must admit that I looked around the room to see if anyone was listening to our conversation.

"You have to know your porn," he said. "Regularly, we get phone calls that claim that someone is running a child pornography web site on their office computer. Ninety-nine times out of 100, these reports lead us to an ordinary commercial porn site that is siphoning money from some poor fool's credit card and there is nothing illegal about that. But even to possess kiddie porn is a felony, so I run through a pornography decision tree to see if we need to investigate."

"A porn decision tree?" I asked, perhaps indiscreetly.

"Yup," Ray replied. "I don't want to inspect every piece of alleged porn to determine if it is legal, so I created a little series of yes/no questions to reach a conclusion. 'Did you see pictures on the site? Are the people clothed? Do the girls have ...'"

"I get the point," I interjected. To my eye, the couple next to us had started to take an interest in our conversation but you can never really be certain about such things.

We paused for a moment, we moved to other subjects: mutual acquaintances, old projects, the state of the world. As we talked, I realized that I would have to abandon one of my plans for portraying Ray and his work. At one point, I had hoped to describe him as a Dashiell Hammett character, a tough-guy detective who used short sentences, active verbs and phrases that conveyed a deep cynicism with the world. But Ray laughed, and tough guy detectives don't laugh. He talked about caring for his parents, and tough guy detectives don't acknowledge their parents. He discussed the new flooring that he was getting for his house, something that would never have entered the world of Dashiell Hammett.

Yet, Ray's job actually has a few things in common with that of the hard-bitten detective who relied on help from the informer, the unscrupulous cop, or the fallen women in distress. "It helps to make lots of friends in this business," he said, "especially friends from other shores." He has friends who will help preserve evidence, give him access to network logs without a warrant, point him towards a likely suspect.

"We just finished a case on a major worm attack," he said. "Once we got the IP addresses, we found that it had been released by three people, two in the Czech Republic and one in the U.S. We have a treaty with the European states and so we were able to put the Czech's in jail for maliciously disrupting computer services." At this point he paused and grinned.

"What?" I asked.

"We were going to do the same thing with the American but we found pictures on his machine, pictures of little naked kids in compromising positions. It's easier to prove possession of illegal materials than to connect a machine with a worm attack. Besides," he added, "the prison term is longer. He went down for child porn."

With that, we turned to the subject of Estonia, the country that had recently been overwhelmed by malicious Internet traffic. The dates of the attack were suspicious and suggested that the Russian government or a friend of the Russian government had initiated the attack. The attacks had begun shortly after the Estonian leaders had removed a Russian statue from downtown Tallin and ended on the day Russians celebrate their victory in the Second World War. However, the Russian government had taken no responsibility for the incident and the meager evidence in the case could point to any one of many possible instigators. Some experts had noted that the attack might have been arranged for as little as US $100,000. It could have been arranged by the Russian Mafia, a wealthy Russian nationalist or some thug who was trying to show how tough he was. No one really knew.

The Lay of the Land

AS WE CAME TO THE EXIT, THE CAB DRIVER was caught out of position. A fast moving truck passed the taxi on the right and blocked our attempt to take the exit. I had been traveling all day and was anxious to reach my parents' home in central Michigan. My driver, a sweet kid who appeared to be no older than 16, was flustered and was unsure of what to do. Thinking for a moment, as we were carried west in the great rush hour flood of cars and trucks, I suggested that we press forward to Ann Arbor and then swing north. The driver was unfamiliar with this route but acquiesced to the idea.

For a moment, the two of us attempted to start a conversation on some meaningless subject but after the exchange of a few sentences, we were interrupted by a loud voice coming from the cab's radio. The voice, which belonged to the taxi dispatcher, demanded to know what we were doing. The dispatcher had been tracking our progress on the company's computer system. He had concluded that we had taken the wrong direction and were lost. My driver, again caught off guard, admitted that he did not know the way and seemed ready to agree to the dispatcher's directions. I intervened at this point and, after a lengthy discussion, convinced the dispatcher to allow me to take responsibility for the route.

The rest of the trip was uneventful, though I noted that the driver was anxious as we approached the Ann Arbor exits. He started talking about the taxi company's computer system. He gave examples of how the system could find obscure addresses, plot the best fastest route and identify problems with traffic. As he talked, I looked around the taxi. Nothing inside the car indicated the presence of high technology. If anything, the interior gave an air of well-established poverty. The carpet was scuffed, the right seat belt was broken, yesterday's paper lay scattered on the floor. A crack, starting from the upper edge of the windshield, was making its way towards the bottom. Yet, this ordinary cab was connected to a sophisticated computer system and that system, though invisible, had altered the landscape for both cab and its driver.

As he reached the end of his explanation, his voice gained a bitter edge. "It tracks you everywhere," spat out. "You can't get a drink. You can't take a leak. You can't run an errand but it will know what you have done."

Too Soon to Tell: Essays for the End of the Computer Revolution, by David Alan Grier
Copyright © 2009 IEEE Computer Society

THE TAXI SYSTEM IS AN EXAMPLE of what we have come to call pervasive or ubiquitous computing, a field that became a major area of research during the 1990s. The basic goal of pervasive computing is to place the power of electronic computation at the common events of daily life. It is, wrote one researcher, "the creation of environments saturated with computing and communication yet gracefully integrated with human users."

A pervasive computing system is usually built upon the technologies that have matured in the last two decades: microprocessors, high-speed data communication, sensors, pattern recognition, sophisticated human interfaces. Yet, the ideas of pervasive computing can be traced back to the origins of mechanical computing. In the 1950s, the U.S. Air Force used several elements of pervasive computing in its Sage system, the system processed radar data from northern Canada in order to watch for invading bombers.

An older, and less well-known example of primitive pervasive computing, is the freight tracking system of Herman Hollerith. Hollerith designed this system in the 1890s, shortly after he finished building punched card tabulators for the U.S. Census Office. The purpose of this system was to track freight shipments on a railroad system in much the same way that the modern package tracking systems of UPS or FedEx follow the progress of a package from shipping point to destination. Unlike the modern systems, Hollerith's creation did not have handheld computers or wireless data links or distributed databases. In his system, the movement of a rail shipment would be punched onto cards. These cards would be returned, by railroad, to a central processing facility, where a card tabulator would recreate the route and compute the cost of the shipment.

Modern pervasive computing differs from these primitive examples because it attempts to hide or at least partially conceal the computer itself. To Hollerith or to the designers of Sage, the computer was an important technology, something to be displayed as a substantial accomplishment. To those building pervasive environments, the computer should vanish into the landscape. "The most profound technologies are those that disappear," wrote Marc Weiser, one of the founders of the pervasive field. "They weave themselves into the fabric of everyday life until they are indistinguishable from it."

Weiser defined the ideas of pervasive computing in 1991, a time when he was serving as the director of the Computer Science Laboratory at Xerox PARC. For over two decades, this laboratory had developed many fundamental ideas of computer science, including the graphical user interface that had been incorporated into the Apple Macintosh and Microsoft Windows operating systems. Though Weiser acknowledged the importance of such ideas, he felt that they were unrelated to pervasive environments. Existing computer technology, he argued "is approachable only through complex jargon that has nothing to do with the tasks for which people use computers" No matter how sophisticated, windowed operating systems only made "the computer screen into a demanding focus of attention rather than allowing it to fade into the background." Once computers faded into the background he believed that, "we are freed to use them without thinking," and therefore can "focus beyond them on new goals."

PERVASIVE COMPUTING SHOULD NOT BE CONFUSED with miniaturization. If a small computing device is ill-designed for its task, it is not woven "into the fabric of everyday life" and hence not pervasive. More important than a computer's size is the way in which it interacts with people and common activities. Weiser argued that a vital aspect of many pervasive systems is the ability to keep track of physical locations. "Little is more basic to human perception than physical juxtaposition," he wrote, "and so ubiquitous computers must know where they are."

Location information helps pervasive systems sort the data and processes that are needed by a user. Taxi drivers need one set of information if they are waiting for a pickup at the airport, another if they are responding to a call, a third if they are waiting at the dispatcher's office. Yet, this same information can change how people react to the physical landscape, as is illustrated by the system in my Michigan taxi or by another canonical example of pervasive computing, the systems that are being proposed for the care of the elderly.

Anyone who has had to care for their father or mother, knows that older persons will often cling to every symbolic act of independence. They will fight to set the day's agenda or pay the bill in a restaurant because it shows that they are still a responsible adult. They accept the loss of independence, no matter what form that loss may take, only with a struggle. By working within a pervasive computing system, an older person might be able maintain their independence or at least the illusion of independence. "By building pervasive computing into the [eldercare] environment," claims one researcher, care facilities can give "residents as much autonomy and even responsibility for themselves and their environment as possible."

The key element of a pervasive eldercare system is a database that contains information on the elderly subject's needs, abilities and medical treatments. Linked to this database is a system that tracks the physical well-being and daily activity of this individual. This system would help the individual operate devices in the home and would inform a family member or a caregiver of any problems with the individual's health. It would track the subject's location through a combination of radio frequency identification tags and motion detectors. It might have sensors in the subject's bed that could measure weight and body temperature. Another set of sensors in the refrigerator or the toilet might monitor the diet of the subject.

Though such a system might sound like a sentence of house arrest for Mom, it could easily prove, for many families, to be more palatable than a nursing home. Yet, for pervasive computing to completely vanish into the landscape of a person's home or even an assisted care facility, it will have to be able to discern the difference between normal and abnormal behavior. The ability to make this kind of distinction is a difficult problem in pattern recognition. When does the data from a motion detector suggest that a person has fallen and when does it record that they take a nap on the floor with the cat? When do the signals from a bed indicate a restless night of sleep and when do they merely follow a long phone call to a sister?

Of course, such distinctions are difficult to make in more conventional circumstances. When my father was taken to bed, I called him three or four times a day and got an energetic, reassuring voice on the other end of the line. I thought that all was well until one day the nurse answered the line. "I don't think you understand what is happening," he said. "Your Dad rallies only when you call. Get here as fast as you can." My bags were packed in a moment. I had a flight within the hour. When I arrived at the airport, I went in search of a taxi that could navigate the distant reaches of the county and, at the end of the line, found a van with a driver who claimed that he could find the address with the help of his computer.

Though much work remains to be done before computer systems will merge into the landscape, we have made at least a little progress in the past decade in building systems that can detect useful information within complex patterns of behavior. Good example of computer systems that have woven themselves into the fabric of daily life while developing a sophisticated means of recognizing complicated behavioral patterns are those that manage credit card transactions.

Credit card transaction systems have simplified business within the industrialized world. They free us from traveling with extra cash or travelers' checks or letters of credit. With the swipe of a card and a few moments of processing, these systems support a wide variety of purchases. At the same time, they scan every proposed transaction to see if it might be fraudulent. This scan looks not only looks at the card holder's credit rating, it also compares it to the transaction to the holder's traditional pattern of consumer purchases. If the purchase is within that pattern and within the credit limits, it will be approved. If it falls outside of that pattern, the transaction will be flagged and you will be notified quickly—as I recently discovered when I attempted to purchase a piece of art while on a recent business trip. The purchase was well within the limit on my card but it was somehow atypical of my ordinary purchases. Within minutes of signing the receipt, I received a call on my cell phone from a nice young woman with the credit card company, who asked me to confirm the transaction. In particular, she wanted me to verify that I was where the credit card claimed I was.

WHEN WE LOOK AT THE LAY OF THE LAND, we rarely see the computer systems that have left their marks upon the vista. These landmarks are often useful, occasionally clever but rarely visible. We somehow believe that we can move from city to city or from one stage of life to the next without following one trail of data and leaving another. We see the signs of pervasive computing only in special circumstances: an unusual transaction, an odd piece of data, a hurried trip to hold the hand of a father.

Circle of Light

I DID NOT RECOGNIZE THE "OLD AUTOMATON," the restaurant that was up the street from my old office. Only later did I consider the possibility that the original building had been removed and replaced with a new facility. I was grateful to find a little respite, as the day was hot and humid. I took a table in the center of the place so that Ro would see me when she arrived.

A woman was standing at the counter, waiting for a credit card receipt to print. Behind her, on the wall, was the photograph of a couple standing at a cash register. Judging from the design of the machine, and the clothes on the couple, I concluded that I was looking at an early 1950s record of the restaurant. Beneath the picture was a framed dollar bill, perhaps the first one to have been placed in that register. As best as I could see, the woman in the picture was the same person who was now standing at the corner. Her hair had turned white. Her jaw had softened a little. But she commanded the place as if she had a lifetime of experience in running a family business.

I had recently attended a ceremony that honored an engineer who had invented a point-of-sale terminal, a device that had been the ancestor, distant or direct, of the machine that was handling the credit card transaction at the counter. The engineer was not particularly well known to the public but his son was a famous executive in the entertainment business.

The son had arrived at the ceremony with more photographic equipment than one normally associates with the most pretentious of local television stations. Two large cameras stood against the back wall. One staffer controlled two banks of light. Another held a boom microphone above the podium. A third, headphones on her head, was recording the proceedings.

The ceremony was dignified and direct. The engineer shared the light with a half dozen others and expressed his profound gratitude for the honor. At the dinner table, the son commanded the spotlight, as members of the audience came to do their obeisance. The engineer sat next to the son, pleased with the award, and presumably happy with the attention given to his son. Like so many technical accomplishments, the point of sale terminal had many parents. It was good to include at least one in the pantheon of distinguished inventors. Though the human ego resists

Too Soon to Tell: Essays for the End of the Computer Revolution, by David Alan Grier
Copyright © 2009 IEEE Computer Society

generosity, no one is an island. When the bell tolls for one, in celebration or in mourning, it also tolls for thee.

Ro entered the place with a dramatic flourish. "I have arrived," her actions intone. "You may begin now." After a warm greeting, our conversation turned to our common subjects: the computer business, Philadelphia in the 1980s, a book I had just completed, our mutual corporation, and, of course, Dad. The news was transmitted almost silently. A word with an upward inflection. A nod of the head. That was all. We shifted to the topics of warm longing that one associates with a wake. There was enough Irish heritage between us to excuse an outbreak of sad songs. The jukebox, however, prevented such a maudlin exercise. "Lift me like an olive branch and be my homeward dove," was the lyric of the summer. "Dance me to the end of love."

We talked until the sky grew dark and I needed to start for home. Dad had spent a lifetime in the computer industry and we were his successors. Through him, we could see almost to the start of the computer era. Through our students and employees, we could see ahead another generation, though perhaps not as clearly. Our best vision was in that little circle of light that had temporarily illuminated our lives.

Beyond the Horizon

THE RUSSIAN MUSEUM OF SCIENCE AND TECHNOLOGY is an impenetrable place. The merciless white marble lobby, a remnant of the Khrushchev era, gives no hint of the building's origin in the age of the czar. The exhibit floors are a little better, as they reveal some of the 19th century architectural features amidst the exhibits. Here, the building is a bit friendlier but it retains the problems that are all too common among science museums. It presents a massive collection of artifacts with little information to guide the casual visitor. The descriptions assert the importance of each object but give no explanation that will ground the technology in the events of the world.

Here is a coil of wire designed A.M. Inductikov. There is a valve assembly that was the creation of a team led by T.R. Ydriansin. By the door is a model of a coal mine that was managed by E.E. Betriovsky. Nowhere can we find a story that explains these objects. They may be examples of Russian technical superiority, or important contributions to the ultimate victory in the Great Patriotic War, or the invention of someone whose uncle was a top party member. They are little drops of oil spilled into a bucket of water. No one has even tried to stir the combination to see if they might mix with the people who come to pay their respects.

The day of my visit, a Saturday when I could convince Mark and his fiancée, Janelle, to accompany me, coincided with field trip by some group of children, the Young Capitalist Pioneers, I suppose. The kids paid far more attention to each other then they did to the exhibits. The adult supervisors struggled to hold the group in order and clearly could not convince any of their charges that the material on display was important. They may have even had trouble convincing themselves of that fact.

The computers are found on the fourth floor, near the space exhibit. The space room was empty of young capitalist pioneers and was surprisingly peaceful. The exhibits, displayed in a jumble around the room, came from the ancient history of the Soviet space program and were no closer to the current crop of 10-year olds than the giant guns of the First World War were to my contemporaries. They recited the exploits of Gagarin the cosmonaut, Laika the space dog, and the technological triumph of Sputnik. The Sputnik exhibit showed a drawing of the satellite and a pair of large springs that were designed to eject the rocket's nosecone and the satellite

Too Soon to Tell: Essays for the End of the Computer Revolution, by David Alan Grier
Copyright © 2009 IEEE Computer Society

itself. I had not realized that Sputnik had been ejected by springs but I hadn't given the subject much thought. For a moment, I wondered why those springs had been selected for display. Were they the only large parts remaining from the project or did they teach a valuable lesson? I left the room unsure of the proper conclusion.

The computer room contained an eclectic variety of old equipment: control panels, memory units, card punches, and Brunsviga calculators. The latter is surprisingly common in computer museums. I moved from display to display, attempting to understand what I was seeing. I do not read Russian, I decode it. I stand before a sign and translate each letter into English. The first is a "D," the second is an "R" and so on. Sometimes I arrive at a word I recognize. Sometimes, I find myself staring at something with no known English cognate and am forced to move on in ignorance.

My decoding had brought me a few interesting facts. One device was a punched card tabulator that was based on a German design. Another object proved to be the control panel for a BESM-6, an early successful Russian machine. My explorations also revealed a pair of certificates that had been awarded to pioneering Russian computer designers by a professional society in the United States. The two pieces of paper had been signed by someone I knew. I was trying to learn the story of these certificates when I heard Janelle's voice. "This computer is interesting. It's called the El'Brus."

To Janelle, the name was intriguing because it came from a peak in the Caucasus Mountains. Like the cars that had been named for beach resorts on the French Riviera or mining towns in the American West, the computer seemed to strive for a connection with something exotic and vaguely powerful. To me, the name was the past returned to life, the confirmation of a story that I had long ago dismissed as a myth.

When I had worked for Burroughs, I had briefly shared an office with a senior engineer named Ralph. His mornings began with a cup of coffee, a pipe of tobacco and a story about his early days with the company. Each story was preceded with a warning, "Never trust an engineer who smokes a pipe," and the warning seemed appropriate. Most of the tales were those of a frustrated technical employee who felt that his contributions had been thwarted by a devious sales manager, an ill-informed marketer, or an ignorant accountant.

One morning, he told me how he had once evaluated a Soviet computer for a U.S. Government Agency. The agency had flown him in to Europe in a small unmarked jet. He was never told which country. Agency personnel took him to a small office building at the edge of town, took him inside, and showed him a machine. According to Ralph's story, that machine was copy of a Burroughs B-5000 computer. "It didn't look like a B-5000," he said, "but it could run B-5000 programs."

Ralph had thought that the device was a clever piece of engineering but he couldn't understand why the Soviets had built it. "The problems in the B-5000 were so well known," he said. "I just don't know why they duplicated the computer instead of trying to fix the problems." Burroughs had quickly replaced the B-5000 with the improved B-5500. The experience had convinced him that all Russian computer engineers were exceptionally stupid. "Not only do they have to copy our designs, they don't even copy a good design." The name of that computer, which he stated with drama at the end of the story, was the "El'Brus."

Long after I had said goodbye to Ralph and had left Burroughs, I learned that the El'Brus, though occasionally called "El Burroughs" by Russian scientists was not actually a copy of the B-5000. It was an attempt by the computer engineer V.S. Burtsev to build a new generation of high performance computers and to narrow the gap between Soviet and Western technology. It borrowed heavily from Western designs, including a number of the basic principles from the B-5000.

The El'Brus was created in a communist economy and never had to feel the invisible hand of the market but was shaped by the same kind of forces that shaped computer designs in the West. Burtsev had to justify each aspect of his design, especially in the points where it deviated from the BESM-6, which was then the most common Soviet machine. He had to compete for manufacturing capacity in the Soviet Union and make use of components that were not as good as he would have liked.

It was not hard for Burtsev to get detailed information on the B-5000. Burroughs freely distributed information about the machine, like so many seeds set adrift on the wind. The Burroughs engineers described several key features in professional journals. They described system operation in sales brochures. They described both the circuits and the system operations in technical manuals. The Soviet Union could easily collect this information through its many agents, both public and illicit, that were located in the United States. These operatives had been collecting information on computing technology from the earliest days after the revolution, when they acquired material on punched card tabulators. In all likelihood, Soviet agents were able to purchase all the information that they needed from a Burroughs branch office or from the trunk of a system representative's automobile.

The B-5000 and its successors were influential machines that pioneered many innovative features but they had shortcomings that limited their commercial success. In particular, these machines tended to be slower than the machines from Burroughs' competitors. By the late 1970s, Burroughs was starting to move away from some of the more restrictive elements of the design and to build more conventional computers. The El'Brus suffered a similar fate. Many "expressed concern that the machine was too complex for the available technology," observed two scholars of the Soviet computer industry. "These fears were realized." It performed only a handful of tasks well. It proved to be poorly suited for much of the work that it needed to do. Ultimately, it had a very short production run. Only 200 processors were ever built.

"So what's so special about the El'Brus?" Janelle asked. "The sign doesn't tell you much." I was in position to do little better. I could attempt to explain the technical accomplishments of the designer or concede that it was a machine of limited importance to the Soviet Union and that it was replaced as soon as the Russians could buy computers from abroad, or I could say that it was a story told to me by a pipe-smoking engineer with whom I had shared an office for three months some 20 years before.

I tried the best idea I had. "It was a machine built for political reasons," I said. "The designer was able to convince the Politburo that they should abandon their existing design, which was borrowed from IBM, and built this one. It was like decreeing that everyone should abandon PCs for Macintoshes."

"For me," I added, "it is a machine that has connections to a computer of my youth. The basic design was taken from the American computer that I first mastered. It is something like a technological niece or nephew."

"Interesting," she said as we moved to the next exhibit. "I wonder why it is here."

Epilogue

Indicator Lamps

I HAD BOARDED THE PLANE, placed my briefcase into the storage bin, and was settling into my chair. I had just finished a couple hectic weeks and was looking forward to a few hours of sitting quietly and listening to some music. I took my mp3 player from its case and touched the power switch. Nothing happened. I pushed again, harder this time. Nothing happened. I stared at the display with the hope that the machine would become embarrassed and start of its own accord. As I did, I began to consider a crucial question. Had I recharged the battery the night before? I wasn't sure. I believed that I had looked at the device, noted that it had little battery charge and had plugged it into a wall socket. That is what I believed at the time. However, the mp3 player was clearly telling me that my memories were not correct.

My plans were not entirely thwarted, as the plane had a new digital entertainment system. This system was fairly sophisticated, with a processor dedicated to each passenger and a screen in front of every seat. I was about to plug my headphones into the system when a voice came over the cabin speaker.

"Ladies and Gentlemen, this is First Officer Yetter," it said. "We're having a little trouble with our entertainment system. We have a technician on board and he would like to see if he can determine the problem it by turning the equipment off for a couple of minutes and then restarting it."

All of the screens went dark for a minute or two and then returned to life. Step by step, each screen started displaying messages that showed how each processor was starting to lead its operating program. In my row, the activity moved from left to right. First, the screen for the window seat starting showing messages. Then the middle screen. Then the one on the aisle. For a little time, I followed the progress of the operation and read the messages as they scrolled down the screen. As best I could tell, the operation system, which was a variant of a popular system in the public domain, was performing properly.

After a few minutes, I found that the messages were less and less comprehensible to me. Some process had not started. Certain files had not been loaded. However, I was reassured when I looked to the front of the cabin and saw the technician standing in front of a screen. She stood in a pose that has marked computer experts since the time of the ENIAC. She was relaxed but entirely focused on her

Too Soon to Tell: Essays for the End of the Computer Revolution, by David Alan Grier
Copyright © 2009 IEEE Computer Society

machine. The cabin could have erupted in a riot but she would not have heard it. Her eyes followed the lines on the screen. Her head nodded approval. Her hands lightly touched the computer keyboard in an act that reaffirmed all to be well.

In an earlier age, this technician would have been looking not at a screen but at a set of indicator lamps, the flashing display that covered the front panel of the large mainframe computers. These lights were wired directly into the memory of the computer. A lit bulb indicated that a certain bit was a 1. A dark one represented a zero. A skilled computer technician knew how to translate these bulbs into numbers and commands. He or she could follow the progress of the machine by watching the patterns of the lights. They would stand by the machine, eyes fixed on the panel, head gently nodding, hands touching the control switches.

At the time, the 1950s and 1960s, all computer users lived in a close relationship to the machine. They not only needed to know how to read a string of bits, they also had to know what those bits represented. Were they numbers? Characters? Program commands? Pictures? Music? How did you prepare a machine to solve a problem for you and how did you interpret the results? Step by step, we began to put layers of software between the actual hardware and the people who used the computers. Program languages. Operating systems. Graphical output. Graphical input. Environmental sensors. Computer controls. Finally, we've reached the point where we forget that we are actually using a computer.

The entertainment system finished loading its programs. The technician gave a thumbs up sign and left the plane. Apparently all was working properly. The entertainment menu appeared on the screen and the passengers applauded. Most looked forward to the music or the movies or the games. Few stopped to realize that the airplane, among all of its sophisticated equipment, dedicated one computer processor to each passenger solely for the purpose of entertainment. In all, the plane had several dozen computers per passenger, as microprocessors controlled every aspect of the flight: engines, navigation, instruments, communication, sensors, heating and ventilation, traffic control, control surfaces, and stabilization. The number of these computers far exceeded the number of laptop computers on board. By my count, the plane had more laptops than the global average of one for every seven people, probably one for every four passengers.

Microprocessors far outnumber laptops. Each year, the semiconductor industry produces at least one microprocessor for each person on earth. Some are big and powerful. Some are small and simple. Only a few are used in devices that are considered computers. Most are used in other kinds of devices: telephones, automobiles, entertainment centers, heating systems, household appliances. In all of these devices, the computer is secondary. An automobile is not really a computer on wheels, it is a transportation system that makes use of computer controls, computer-driven sensors, and computer interfaces. An mp3 player is not a computer that produces music; it is merely a convenient and flexible way of reproducing sound.

Though one billion laptop computers is an impressive accomplishment, it is a symbol that looks backwards rather than forwards. It is an old panel of flashing indicator lamps on a mainframe rather than the display screen that shows how the system is working. The computer has not turned us into a society of engineers and scientists who think in rational, programmatic ways. It has turned us into a world that relies on these machines even though we do not understand fully how they work. We use this technology to shrink time and space, to make efficient use of resources, to extend our capabilities, to coordinate activities, to discipline ourselves.

Looking at the indicator lamps of our age, the flashing signs that tell us where the world had been and where it might be going, we see the past more clearly than the future. For slightly more than six decades, men and women have labored over these computers, feeling that they were changing the world, or improving society or advancing knowledge, or at least becoming rich. They didn't always have a chance to reflect on the way that computing technology changed themselves or their families or their community. They looked at the flashing lamps or printouts or rolling screens and tried to understand what the machine was doing at their moment of time. The past didn't matter. The future was too far away. In 18 months or 24 or 30, the world would spin through another cycle of innovation. The familiar landmarks of machines and software, jobs and companies, would no longer be the same.

Disclaimers, References and Notes

DISCLAIMERS

THOUGH E.B. WHITE did not feel that he had to include a disclaimer with *Points of My Compass*, I feel that the modern age requires such a statement. It probably would not have helped the work of Mr. White, which stands on the clarity of its prose and the simplicity of its imagery, but it may alleviate confusion about a work that falls short of White's standard and appears to comment on the reality of the computer age.

The disclaimer would begin as follows. This is neither a history nor a memoir but a collection of essays based on personal experience. All the characters are real, though some have been given pseudonyms or modified descriptions to protect somebody, perhaps me, from embarrassment. In some cases, they asked that a veil be placed over their identity. In others, I could not contact them to ask their permission. In a few cases, I could not remember their original names.

It would continue by noting that I have often renamed details in order to express something about the way that computer people interact with the world. If you search for the "Old Automoton" restaurant in suburban Philadelphia, you will be able to find the place where Burroughs programmers congregated for dinner and drinks. However, it has a more commonplace name. It is the artist's prerogative and I intend to take no criticism for it.

Perhaps it would also have to address the words and actions of my father and his friends, who are not in a position of defending themselves from the stories that I have told. Most of them are based on tales repeated to me again and again. Dad also left me a manuscript and a file of clippings that I have used to validate the stories. I assume all responsibility for his quotes and the quotes of his friends. While I feel that I am on safe ground, I would gladly accept comments about them from those with more reliable sources.

Because gratitude is good, I need to thank a number of people who shared their experiences with me or read early versions of the manuscript or listened to my stories, including Ro, Mark Brown, Liz Harter, Michael Young, David Stern, Bob Goldfarb, Robin Baldwin, Emily Danyluk, and Robert Vander Boegh. I truly need thank Judi Prow and Scott Hamilton for their support of this work and their efforts to bring this material to the public, and Caitlin House for her help with the final manuscript.

But ultimately, disclaimers have a tedious quality that suggests that the author is not sure of the work and is concerned that the readers will find something in it offensive. This is a work that tries to appreciate those people that have lived in the world of the computer. My modest hope is that it blesses all, injures none, and hence avoids the need for any kind of disclaimer.

REFERENCES

Select Histories of Computer Technology

Abbate, Janet, *Building the Internet*, Cambridge, MA, MIT Press, 2003.
Aspray, William and Campbell-Kelly, Martin, *Computer*, New York, Basic Books, 1996.
Ceruzi, Paul, *History of Modern Computing*, Cambridge, MA, MIT Press, 1998.
Cortada, Jim, *The Computer in the United States from Laboratory to Market*, Armonk, NY, M.E. Sharpe, 1993.
Grier, David Alan, *When Computers Were Human*, Princeton, Princeton University Press, 2005.
Norberg, Arthur, *Computers and Commerce*, Cambridge, MA, MIT Press, 2005.
Waldrop, Mitchell, *The Dream Machine*, New York, Viking, 2001.
The astute reader will note that all of these authors have been affiliated with the *Annals of the History of Computing*, which is another source for material on the history of the age. It may be found under the technical magazines section of www.computer.org.

NOTES

Preface

p. ix "During the recent war there was tremendous development,"
    Archibald, R.C., "Conference on Advanced Computation Techniques," *Mathematical Tables and Other Aids to Computation*, 1946, vol 2, no 14, p 65–68.
p. x "projected to top 1 billion in 2007,"
    Press Release, Computer Industry Almanac, June 20, 2005.
p. xi "American social development has been continually beginning,"
    Turner, Frederick Jackson, "Significance of the Frontier in American History," *Report of the American Historical Association for 1893*, p 199–227.
p. xii "There is nothing new under the sun,"
    Ecclesiastes 1:9,10.
p. xii "The wind whirleth about."
    Ecclesiastes 1:6.

The Computer Era

p. 1 "The desire to economize ...",
    Aiken, Howard and Hopper, Grace, "The Automatic Sequence Controlled Calculator," *Electrical Engineering*, 1948, vol 65, p 384–391+.

Out of Position

p. 3 ENIAC: Electronic Numerical Integrator and Computer

p. 3 "One of the war's top secrets,"
   Kennedy, T.R., "Electronic Computer Flashes Answers, May Speed Engineering," *New York Times*, February 15, 1946, p 1. The *New York Times* was given an early notice of the conference.

p. 3 "The old era is going," J. Presper Eckert quoted in Kennedy, *op. cit.*

p. 5 "the most contented G.I.s in Europe,"
   Dos Passos, John, "Contented GIs," *Time Magazine*, November 19, 1945; see also Haufler, Hervie, "The Most Contented GIs in Europe," *American History*, October 1999, vol 34, no 4, p 58–64.

p. 5 "the janitors [were] German prisoners of war,"
   Winger, R.M., "Biarritz American University," *American Mathematical Monthly*, March 1946, vol 53, no 3, p 134–135.

p. 5 "The American scientific societies kept careful watch,"
   Cain, Stanley, "The Science Section of Biarritz American University," *Science*, New Series, February 1, 1946, vol 103, No 2666, p 129–132.

p. 5 "a disconcerting tendency … to prefer refresher courses"
   Winger, R.M., *op cit.*

Seymour Cray's Cat

p. 7 Seymour Cray (1925–1996);
   _____, "Seymour Cray," *Computing & Control Engineering Journal*, Dec. 1996, vol 7, issue 6, p 294; Murray, Charles, *The supermen: the story of Seymour Cray and the technical wizards behind the supercomputer*, New York: John Wiley, 1997.

p. 7 linear programming
   Dantzig, George B. "Origins of the simplex method," *A history of scientific computing*, Princeton, NJ, 1987, p 141–151; Dorfman, Robert, "The Discovery of Linear Programming," *IEEE Annals of the History of Computing*, July–September 1984, vol 6, no 3, p 283–295.

p. 7 "the diet problem"
   Stigler, George, "The Cost of Subsistence," *Journal of Farm Economics*, vol 27, no 1, p 303–314.

p. 8 George Dantzig (1914–2005)
   Cottle, Richard W., "George B. Dantzig: operations research icon," *Operations Research*, vol 53, no 6, 2005, p 892–898. Albers, Donald J., Reid, Constance, "An interview with George B. Dantzig: the father of linear programming," *College Mathematics Journal*, vol 17, no 4, 1986, p 293–314.

p. 8 "solved by hand"
   See Grier, David Alan, *When Computers were Human*, Princeton, Princeton University Press, 2005, chapter 17.

p. 8 "The problem as set up for solution at this time"
   "Discussion of Linear Programming with Dr. John von Neumann," September 18, 1953, Princeton, N.J., von Neumann papers, Library of Congress.

p. 8 Control Data Corporation
   See Murray, *op cit.*

Songs of Comfort and Joy

p. 12 "Each computer console had a small amplifier,"
Lundstrom, *op. cit.*, p 34.
p. 12 Beer Barrel Polka
Lundstrom, *op. cit.*, p 34.
p. 12 "a beautiful rhythmic tone,"
Rosenfield, Paul, "Plays—Tr La La La La," *Dallas Times Herald*," December 24, 1958,
p A1.

Life on the Frontier

p. 18 "to coordinate activities in the initial programming of machine methods"
Mapstone, Bobbi and Bernstein, Morton, "The Founding of SHARE," *IEEE Annals of the
History of Computing*, October 1980, vol 2, no 4, p 363–372.
p. 19 "A million cards each month"
ibid.
p. 19 "A Broadway singer, a standup comic, a mariachi band"
At one meeting, sometime in the mid-1960s, CUBE hired a satirist called Dr. Nikki Nyetski,
who billed himself as a "stand up Commie." Most of his jokes were aimed at the roots
of capitalism and offended the sensibilities of the group. "The members were angry,"
recalled Dad, "and many walked out." The finale of the evening came when "the wife
of one member jumped to her feet and shouted, "let's all sing Good Bless America." It
was not, Dad recalled, "a very good evening."

Museum Pieces

p. 21 "we do not think"
Leonard Carmichael, quoted in Rabb, Charles, "Univac I becomes Antique at 12,"
Washington Post, October 4, 1963, p A13.
p. 21 "neither fish nor fowl"
Marcus, Mitchell and Akera, Atsushi, "Exploring the architecture of an early machine: the
historical relevance of the ENIAC machine architecture," *IEEE Annals of the History of
Computing*, Spring 1996, vol 18, no 1, p 17–24.
p. 21 "The ENIAC had had a long and storied history"
Neukom, Hans, "The second life of ENIAC," *IEEE Annals of the History of Computing*,
Vol 28, No 2, April-June 2006, p 4–16; Stern, Nancy, *From ENIAC to Univac*, Maynard,
MA, Digital Press, 1981, p 152.
p. 22 "quite small by the standards of the day"
Williams, Michael, *op. cit.*, p 357.
p. 22 "It had been abandoned by the Institute for Advanced Studies"
Regis, Ed, *Who Got Einstein's Office*, Reading, MA, Addison Wesley, 1988, p 113–114.

The Curve of Innovation

p. 24 "increased at a rate"
Moore, Gordon, "Cramming more components onto integrated circuits," *Electronics*, vol
38, no 8, 1965, p 114–117.

p. 24 "there is no reason to believe"
Moore, *op. cit.*

p. 24 "In this revision, he hypothesized that the number of elements"
Moore, Gordon, "Progress in Digital Integrated Electronics," *IEEE Text Speech*, 1975.

p. 24 "This revision has proven to describe the pace of innovation"
Mollick, Ethan, "On the Construction of Moore's Law," *IEEE Annals of the History of Computing*, 2006, vol 28, no 3, p 62–75.

p. 25 "what technologies might be needed to continue"
Spencer, Bill, Wilson, Linda and Doering, Robert, "The Semiconductor Technology Roadmap," *Future Fab International*, January 12, 2005, vol 18.

p. 25 "Of the top ten merchant semiconductor companies"
Committee on Japan, National Research Council, *U.S.-Japan Strategic Alliances in the Semiconductor Industry: Technology Transfer, Competition, and Public Policy*, Washington, D.C., National Academies Press, 1992, p 1.

p. 25 "computer hardware manufacturers could find themselves serving only specialty markets"
Computer Science and Technology Board, *National Research Council, Keeping the U.S. Computer Industry Competitive: Defining the Agenda*, National Academies Press, 1990, p 2.

p. 25 "If this vital industry is allowed to wither away"
Transmittal Letter, Report of the National Advisory Committee on Semiconductors, March 21, 1989.

p. 25 "precompetitive environment"
Transmittal Letter, *op. cit.*

p. 25 "billion bits of memory"
A gigabit static random access memory. The conference considered the problem of producing a gigabit dynamic random access memory chip by 2004.

p. 26 "In cases where more than one technology solution was being pursued,"
Spencer, et al., *op. cit.*

p. 26 "Everyone in the industry recognizes that if [they] don't stay on essentially that curve"
Gordon Moore quoted in Schaller, Robert, "Moore's Law, Past, Present and Future," *IEEE Spectrum*, June 1997, p 52–59.

p. 26 "chip structure, testing, assembly and packaging."
International Technology Roadmap for Semiconductors, 2001, p ii, 2.

p. 26 "It has become more and more expensive to develop the next technology"
Interview with Jon Stoner, December 2005.

p. 26 "We just will not be able to go as fast as we would like because we cannot afford it, in spite of your best technical contributions"
Moore, Gordon, "Lithography and the Future of Moore's Law," *Optical/Laser Microlithography VII:Proceedings of SPIE*, May 1995, vol 2437, p 2–17.

Public Image

p. 29 "Even my 12-year old son has learned this"
Grier, Thomas, "Remarks by Thomas Grier," June 29, 1965, Speeches of Thomas Grier, CUBE Records, Unisys Records, Charles Babbage Institute.

p. 30 "intelligent, constructive and beneficial application"
Grier, Thomas, "Communication between Man and Computer," April 16, 1969, Speeches of Thomas Grier, CUBE Records, Unisys Records, Charles Babbage Institute.

p. 30 "He argued that the computer would improve the business environment,"
   Grier, Thomas, "Technology for 1999," May 14, 1970, Speeches of Thomas Grier, CUBE
      Records, Unisys Records, Charles Babbage Institute.

The Enduring Myth of Hardware

p. 32 "The industry was born almost literally like a rib out of IBM"
   Rick Crandall quoted in *ADAPSO 2002 Reunion Transcript*, Luanne Johnson, Editor,
      iBusiness Press (Software History Center), 2003, p 253.
p. 32 "independent meant non-IBM"
   John Maguire quoted in *ADAPSO 2002 Reunion Transcript*, p 242.
p. 33 "Eventually, we had a $150,000 loan from the bank"
   Doug Jerger quoted in *ADAPSO 2002 Reunion Transcript*, p 102.
p. 33 "It was such an entrepreneurial industry"
   Luanne Johnson quoted in *ADAPSO 2002 Reunion Transcript*, p 65.
p. 33 "Some of the software guys started showing up at ADAPSO meetings"
   Luanne Johnson quoted in *ADAPSO 2002 Reunion Transcript*, p 92.
p. 34 "to completely flip around" their relationship with IBM,
   Rick Crandall quoted in *ADAPSO 2002 Reunion Transcript*, p 239.
p. 34 "There was a picture of a computer box with the top opened up"
   Rick Crandall quoted in *ADAPSO 2002 Reunion Transcript*, p 239.
p. 34 "opened the way for many more articles"
   Rick Crandall quoted in *ADAPSO 2002 Reunion Transcript*, p 239.

The Age of Information

p. 47 "The process of preparing ..."
   Knuth, Donald, *The Art of Computer Programming*, vol 1, Reading, MA, Addison Wesley,
      1973, p v.

Coming of Age

p. 51 "Widespread acceptance of computer word processing has begun"
   Stillman, Richard, "Microcomputers and the university computer center," *Proceedings of
      the 7th annual ACM SIGUCCS*, 1979, p 75–78.
p. 51 "We actually shipped it in June 1979"
   Interview of Seymour Rubinstein with Jeff Yost, May 7, 2004, Charles Babbage
      Institute.
p. 51 "handled letters and simple images well ..."
   Perry, T.S. "PostScript prints anything: a case history," *IEEE Spectrum*, May 1988, vol 25,
      no 5, p 42–46.
p. 51 "Their system could do simple things fast"
   Quoted in Perry, *op. cit.*
p. 52 The origins of the World Wide Web are often connected
   Bush, Vannevar, "As We May Think," *Atlantic Monthly*, July 1945, vol 176, no 1,
      p 101–108.

p. 52 "The Bush [machine] is a powerful microfilm instrument"
Nelson, T.H. "A File Structure for the Complex, the Changing and the Indeterminate," *Proceedings of the ACM Conference*, 1965, section 4.2.
p. 52 "The original idea"
Nelson, *op. cit.*
p. 52 "Let me introduce the word 'hypertext' "
Nelson, *op. cit.*
p. 52 "Rich returns can be expected from research on the most appropriate conceptual organization,"
Embley, David and Nagy, George, "Behavioral Aspects of Text Editors," *Computing Surveys*, March 1981, vol 13, no 1, p 33–70.
p. 52 "Hypertext systems are the next generation"
Marchionini, Gary and Shneiderman, Ben, "Finding facts vs. Browsing Knowledge in Hypertext Systems," *Computer*, Jan 1988, vol 21, no 1, p 70–80.
p. 52 "a multiply connected 'web' "
Berners-Lee, Tim, "Information Management: A Proposal," CERN, March 1989.
p. 52 "technical details of past projects"
Berners-Lee, *op. cit.*
p. 52 "The aim would be to allow a place"
Berners-Lee, *op. cit.*
p. 53 "early versions used the symbols ':' "
John Schlesinger, personal communication, May 1, 2006.
p. 53 "called appropriately the Standard Generalized Markup Language"
Khare, Rohit and Rifkin, Adam, *IEEE Internet Computing*, July–August 1997, p 78–87.
p. 53 "XML, the eXtensible Markup Language"
Adler, S., Cochrane, R., Morar, J.F. and Spector, A., "Technical context and cultural consequences of XML," *IBM Systems Journal*, 2006, vol 45, no 2; "Ishing: Four Myths about XML," Bosak, Jon, *Computer*, October 1998, Media-Independent Publishing, p 120–122.

The Language of Bad Love

p. 59 "It was typical of the unscholarly attitude"
Backus, John, "The History of FORTRAN I, II and III," in *History of Programming Language*, Richard Wexelblat, eds., New York, Academic Press, 1981, p 25–44; p 29.
p. 59 "They showed an early release of the code"
Backus, *op. cit.*, p 29.
p. 60 "so subtle that ALGOL translators"
Knuth, Donald and Merner, Jack, "ALGOL 60 Confidential," *Communications of the ACM*, 1961, vol 4, no 4, p 268–271.
p. 60 "English Language is not a panacea"
Sammet, Jean "The Early History of COBOL," in *History of Programming Language*, Richard Wexelblat, ed., New York, Academic Press, 1981, p 199–242; p 201.
p. 60 "major deficiencies which reduce its effectiveness"
Sammet, *op. cit.*, p 211.

p. 60 "At first it was maybe 20 e-mails a day"
Byous, Jon, "Java Technology, the Early Years," http://java.sun.com/features/1998/05/birthday.html.

p. 61 "Experience with real users and real compliers is separately"
Sammet, *op. cit.*, p 239.

Conflict-Free Memories

p. 67 "is to show *what* the Punched Card Method can do and *why* it can do it"
Baehne, George W., ed, *Practical Applications of the Punched Card Method in Colleges and Universities*, New York, Columbia, 1935, p vi.

p. 68 "It was more than just another debut or show"
_____, "Everyone talks about the Next Generation Computer," *The News* (Burroughs Corporation internal newsletter), June 10, 1963, p 3.

p. 68 "because we physically proved that [our machine] does what we said it would do"
ibid.

On the Right Side of the Road

p. 72 "the best year in history for Detroit's Big Three"
The Big Three sold 11.4 million cars in 1973, a mark that has not been repeated since.

p. 72 "Last year we sold a couple dozen cars"
David Fischer, Interview with author, October 1974.

p. 72 "Why don't we outlaw cancer?"
Alan Loofbourrow, Vice President Of Engineering for Chrysler, quoted in Wilson, George, "Mileage, Air Rules Linked," *Washington Post*, December 11, 1974, p E11.

p. 72 "relax a few of the safety standards"
ibid.

p. 72 "improve the gas mileage of their cars by 40 percent."
Anderson, J.W., "Detroit's Trend Toward Smaller Cars," *The Washington Post*, December 26, 1974, p A24.

p. 72 "processor chips that were being used in pocket calculators"
Russell, Ronald, and Frederikson, Thomas, "Automotive and Industrial Electronic Building Blocks," *IEEE Journal of Solid State Circuits*, December 1972, vol 7, no 6, p 446–454.

p. 72 "well understood by thousands of mechanics and car owners"
Sung, C.H. and Crocetti, M.F., "Air-fuel control in a microprocessor-based system for improving automobile fuel economy," *Proceedings of the 27th IEEE Vehicular Technology Conference*, 16–18 March 1977, p 83–85.

p. 73 "MISAR, a General Motors product that was installed on the 1977 Oldsmobile Toronado"
Evernham, Thomas W., "Misar-The Microprocessor Controlled Ignition System," SAE Report # 780666, Warrendale, PA, Society of Automobile Engineers, 1978.

p. 73 "MISAR system provides almost infinite [control] flexibility"
ibid.

p. 73 "The system converted this information into commands"
Sung C.H. and Crocetti, M.F., *op. cit.*

p. 73 "General Motors followed the MISAR project with a second, more sophisticated computer system"

Lockhart, Bruce D., "A Fuel Economy Development Vehicle with Electronic Programmed Engine Controls (Epec)," SAE Report # 790231, Warrendale, PA, Society of Automobile Engineers, 1979.

p. 73 "on the threshold of ending all auto pollution"

anonymous GM official quoted in Williams, Doug, "End of Auto Pollution is predicted soon by GM," *Washington Post,* January 13, 1978, p A1.

p. 73 "control-system engineers are bridging the gap"

Hagen, D.F., "Electronic Engine Controls at Ford Motor Company," SAE Report # 780842, Warrendale, PA, Society of Automobile Engineers, 1978.

p. 73 "It's a worldwide supply situation"

Harry Lyon quoted in Schuyten, Peter, "Detroit Seeks Semiconductors," *New York Times,* September 6, 1979, p D1.

p. 73 "General Motors turned to European suppliers ..."

p. 73 "Ford purchased integrated processors ..."

Schuyten, Peter, "Detroit Seeks Semiconductors," *New York Times,* September 6, 1979, p D1.

p. 73 Cars "are getting more complicated"

James Vorhes quoted in Skwira, Gregory, "Growing Increasingly Complex, Cars Pose New Repair Problems," *New York Times,* January 27, 1980, p Auto 1.

p. 74 "do-it-yourselver is being closed out"

George Trainor quoted in Skwira, *op. cit.*

p. 74 "biggest technological advance since the 1950s"

John Auman quoted in _____, "Automakers turn to Computers in Major Technological Advance," *New York Times,* February 10, 1978, p 67.

p. 74 "chips that controlled the brakes, door locks, and air-conditioning system"

Schuyten, *op. cit.*

Fork in the Path

p. 80 "was a relatively welcoming field for women"

Abbate, Janet, "How did you first get into computing?" *IEEE Annals of the History of Computing,* October-December 2003, vol 24, no 4, p 78–82.

p. 80 "I was able to work part time until my children were in school"

Koss, Adele Mildred, "Programming on the Univac I," *IEEE Annals of the History of Computing,* January–March 2003, vol 24, no 1, p 48–58.

The Best Deal in Town

p. 83 "supercomputers"

Grier, Peter, "In the works: a supercomputer," *The Christian Science Monitor;* Sept 13, 1978; p 19.

p. 84 "super-duper electronic brain"

Gould, Jack, "Radio and Television," *New York Times,* November 7, 1952, p 31.

p. 84 The first organizations to purchase a Cray-1

Russell, Richard, "The Cray-1 Computer System," *Communications of the ACM,* vol 21, no 1, January 1978, p 63–72.

p. 85 "rethink and reorganize their programs"
Petersen, W.P. "Vector FORTRAN for Numerical Problems on CRAY-1," *Communications of the ACM*, vol 26, p 1008–1021.

p. 85 "Originally, Seymour Cray had set out just to build 'the fastest computer in the world'"
Boeilie Elzen, Donald MacKenzie, "The Social Limits of Speed," *IEEE Annals of the History of Computing*, 1994, vol 16, no 1, p 46–61.

p. 85 "is the worry that American basic research and engineering science"
Dallaire, Gene, "American Universities Need Greater Access to Supercomputers," *Communications of the ACM*, 1984, vol 27, no 2, p 292–298.

p. 85 "the number of installed supercomputers increased sevenfold to 409 machines"
Markoff, John, "U.S. Gain in Computer Speed Race," *New York Times*, October 4, 1988, p D1.

p. 85 "they emerged envious and more than a little scared"
Sanger, David, "A High Tech lead in Danger," *New York Times*, December 18, 1988, p F1.

p. 86 "It is a matter of national pride and national identity"
Sanger, *op. cit.*

p. 86 "Japan took a different point of view and rejected this demand"
Markoff, John, "Export Restrictions Fail to Halt Spread of Supercomputers," *New York Times*, Aug 21, 1990, p A1.

p. 86 "see all the contracts that we are excluded from"
Sanger, David "Supercomputer Accord with Japan Advances," *New York Times*, March 2, 1990.

Crossing the Divide

p. 90 "It was a time of recovery, development and growth"
Diebold, William, "From the ITO to GATT and Back," in *The Bretton Woods-GATT System*, Orin Kirshner, ed, New York, M.E. Sharp, 1996, p 152–173.

p. 90 "Anyone who has sought to understand the shifts"
Vernon, Raymond, "International Investment and International Trade in the Product Cycle," *The Quarterly Journal of Economics*, vol 80, no 2. May, 1966, p 190–207.

p. 91 "He took a few bags of cores, rolls of wire"
Pugh, Emerson, *Memories that Shaped an Industry*, Cambridge, MA, 1984, p 250–251.

Auditions

p. 96 Benchmark Symbol
The one given is technically the one for altitudes above sea level. For those below sea level, the arrow points downward.

p. 96 "even as more people have become seriously concerned with computer economics"
Ford, C.A., "On calibrating a computer system," *ACM SIGCSIM Installation Management Review*, Proceedings of the 4th annual symposium on SIGCOSIM: management and evaluation of computer technology, October 1973, vol 2, issue 2.

p. 97 "get a measure that agrees fairly well with the others by using the cost of the system as an indicator of largeness"
Sid Fernbach quoted in Stokes, Gordon, "Evaluation of scientific computer systems," Proceedings of the 1970 25th annual conference on Computers, January 1970.

p. 98 "a young explorer standing on the threshold of a new age"
> Florman, Samuel, "The Hardy Boys and the Microkids Make a Computer," *New York Times*, August 23, 1981, p BR 1.

p. 98 "the triumph and glory,"
> *ibid.*

Annie and the Boys

p. 100 "They were young, immature and not disciplined"
p. 100 "I reluctantly concluded"
p. 100 "I was shocked at how successful it was ..."
> Oral History of Mitch Kapor with William Aspray, November 19, 2004, Computer History Museum, X3006.2005.

p. 102 "look and feel"
> Samuelson, Pamela, "Updating the Copyright Look and Feel Lawsuits," *Communications of the ACM*, vol 35, no 9, September 1992, p 25–31.

p. 103 "Lotus 1-2-3 was always 90% of the revenue"
> Oral History of Mitch Kapor with William Aspray, *op. cit.*

p. 103 "While some other courts appear to have touched on it briefly in dicta"
> BORLAND INTERNATIONAL, INC., Petitioner, LOTUS DEVELOPMENT, Plaintiff, Appellee, v. BORLAND INTERNATIONAL, INC., Defendant, Appellant, No. 95-1793, No. 95-1885, UNITED STATES COURT OF APPEALS FOR THE FIRST CIRCUIT, 1995 U.S. App. LEXIS 37394, December 28, 1995, Decided.

p. 103 "One justice,"
> Greenhouse, Linda, "Supreme Court Deadlocks in Key Case on Software," *New York Times*, January 17, 1996, p D2.

p. 104 "intellectual property laws are fundamentally ill-suited to software"
> Davis, Randall; Samuelson, Pamela; Kapor, Mitchell; and Reichman, Jerome, "A New View of Intellectual Property and Software," *Communications of the ACM*, March 1996, vol 39, no 3, p 21–30.

p. 104 "we will have unpredictability in computer software copyright law, which in turn will impede full throttle progress in the development of computer software. That result is bad for the economy, bad for consumers, and contrary to the directive of the Constitution's Copyright Clause."
> Hamilton, Marci, and Sabety, Ted, "Computer Science Concepts in Copyright Cases: The Path to a Coherent Law," *Harvard Journal of Law & Technology*, Winter, 1997, 239. (Lexis-Nexis).

p. 104 "ending one approach to protecting software"
> Samuelson, Pamela, "Good News and Bad News on the Intellectual Property Front," *Communications of the ACM*, March 1999, vol 42, no 3, p 19–24.

Mergers and Divestitures

p. 108 "In 1961, IBM had demonstrated Katakana characters"
> Hensch, K, "IBM history of far Eastern languages in computing. Part 1. Requirements and initial phonetic product solutions in the 1960s," *IEEE Annals of the History of Computing*, Jan–Mar 2005, vol 27, issue 1, p 17–26.

p. 108 "the Asahi Shimbun, to typeset its daily editions"
Hensch, K, Igi, Toshiaki, Iwao, Masumi and Takeshita, Toru, "IBM history of far Eastern languages in computing. Part 2. Initial Efforts for Full Kanji Solutions, Early 1970s," *IEEE Annals of the History of Computing*, Jan–Mar 2005, vol 27, issue 1, p 17–26.

p. 108 "It's kind of hard to see the synergy here"
Francis R. Gens, quoted in Berg, Eric, "Burroughs and Sperry in Talks; Big Computer Makers Weigh Merger Plan," *New York Times*, June 14, 1985. p. D1.

p. 109 "10,000 jobs might be lost"
Berg, Eric, "Burroughs and Sperry End Talks; Layoff Threat Called Factor; Sperry off 4 1/8 Burroughs and Sperry Call off Merger Talks," *New York Times*, June 18, 1985. p D1.

p. 109 "make clear to Burroughs"
quoted in Crudele, John, "Persistence Pays off in Burroughs Deal; Sperry Agrees to Higher Bid," *New York Times*, May 28, 1986, p D1.

p. 109 "unified entity"
Sims, Calvin, "Burroughs Announces New Company Name," *New York Times*, Nov 11, 1986, p D1.

Old Bottles

p. 111 "What today goes by the name of home computer"
Schuyten, Peter, "Technology—Home Computer Demand Lags," *New York Times*, June 7, 1979, p D2.

p. 112 "If you want to give a dinner party"
Slesin, Suzzane, "Kitchen Chic: Status Appliances," *New York Times*, December 27, 1979, p C1.

p. 112 "Compiling endless computerized lists"
Schuyten, *op. cit.*

p. 112 "Playing Star Trek and other computer games"
Langer, Richard, "Computers Find a Home—Yours," *New York Times*, August 25, 1977, p 48.

p. 113 "It took a year to put the thing together"

p. 113 "Nothing was included"

p. 113 "I got it working and a little over a year"
Wayne Ratliff Interview with Susan Lammers, undated, http://www.foxprohistory.org/ interview_wayne_ratliff.htm.

p. 113 "distribution and marketing efforts"
Evans, Philip, "Software Publishing and the Software Author," *Proceedings of the International Conference on APL: APL and the Future APL '85*, May 1985, vol 15, issue 4.

p. 113 "From the conditions of frontier life"
Turner, Frederick Jackson, "Significance of the Frontier in American History," *Report of the American Historical Association for 1893*, p 199–227.

The Days of Cyberspace

p. 115 "The network has engendered …"
Orenstein, S.M., Heart, F.E., Crowther, W.R., Rising, H.K., Russell, S.B., and Michel, A., "The Terminal IMP for the ARPA Computer network," AFIPS Conference, Spring 1972, p 243–254.

Alley Life

p. 117 "a period near the beginning of every man's life"
 White, E.B., "Years of Wonder," In *Points of My Compass*, New York, Harper Row, 1962, p 205.
p. 118 "Resourceful people lived for years in attractive residences on the avenues"
 Charles Weller quoted in Borchert, James, *Alley Life in Washington*, Champaign, IL, University of Illinois Press, 1982, p 2.
p. 118 "a brief role in a sex scandal"
 Dickenson, James, "Hart Weekend: Conflicting Stories," *Washington Post*, May 5, 1987, p A10.
p. 119 "Computer networks have spread to larger and smaller machines"
p. 119 "is as yet no universally accepted network addressing convention"
p. 121 "The moral of all this is that there is no magic formula"
 Quaterman, John and Hoskins, Josiah, "Notable Computer Networks," *Communications of the ACM*, October 1986, vol 29, no 10, p 932–971.
p. 121 "My spice route to nowhere was behind me"
 White, *op. cit.*

On the Camino Real

p. 124 "deviating very little from the North American pattern"
 Barquin, Ramon, "Computation in Latin America," *Latin American Research Review*, 1976, vol 11, no 1, p 75–102.
p. 124 "No computers, aside from tabulating equipment"
 Finerman, Aaron, "Computing Capabilities at Argentine and Chilean Universities," *Communications of the ACM*, August 1969, vol 12, no 8, p 425–431.
p. 124 "persistent internal economic and social problems"
 Muroyama, Janet and Stever, H. Guyford, Editors, Globalization of Technology International Perspectives, Proceedings of the Sixth Convocation of the Council of Academies of Engineering and Technological Sciences, Washington, D.C., National Academy Press, 1988, p 151.
p. 124 "Whereas it used to be that there were 30, 40, even 50 years of difference"
 Larsen, Mark, "The Emergence of Microcomputing in Latin American", *Hispania*, December 1985, vol 68, no 4, p 873–876.
p. 125 They had learned how to circumvent the tariffs
 Dedrick, J.L., Soogman, S.E., and Kraemer, K.L., "Little Engines that Could: Computing in Small Energetic Countries," *Communications of the ACM*, March 1995, vol 38, no 5, p 21–26.
p. 126 "My pocketbook is empty and my heart is filled with pain"
 "Waiting for a Train," Copyright 1929, Jimmie Rogers and Elsie McWilliams.
p. 126 "When any nation, whatever its motivation"
 Quoted in *Bitnews*, December 15, 1987.
p. 127 special opportunities to Spanish speaking engineers
 See _____, "Global Software Services Industry 2006," Cygnus Business Consulting and Research, Pub ID: CYG1422238, April 8, 2006.

Dirty Electricity

p. 131 "find bugs"

Kidwell, Peggy Aldrich, "Stalking the Elusive Computer Bug," *Annals of the History of Computing*, 1998, vol 20, no 4, p 5–9.

p. 131 "first actually case of a bug being found."

Hopper, Grace, "The First Bug," *Annals of the History of Computing*, 1981, vol 3, no 4, p 285–286. See also Shapiro, F.R., "The first 'Bug' Examined," *Annals of the History of Computing*, 1984, vol 6, no 2, p 164, Palmer, J.H., "The first Bug-Discussion," *Annals of the History of Computing*, 1991, vol 13, no 4, p 360–361, and Eklund, J., "The final Word on 'The Bug'," *Annals of the History of Computing*, 1992, vol 14, no 3, p 6–7.

p. 131 "Bugs ... show themselves and months of anxious watching,"

Quoted by John Lord, "Whence the 'Bug'," *Annals of the History of Computing*, 1988, vol 10, no 4, p 341–342.

p. 131 "Students and teachers are encouraged to minimize errors"

Mathis, Robert, "Teaching Debugging," *ACM SIGCSE Bulletin*, 1974, p 59–63.

p. 131 "Debugging is said to be the least established area in software development"

Araki, Keijiro, Furukawa, Zengo and Cheng, Jimgde, "Framework for Debugging," *IEEE Software*, May 1991, p 14–20.

p. 132 "It appears that many programmers of large scale computers today"

Ferguson, H. Earl and Berner, Elizabeth, "Debugging Systems at the Source Language Level," *Communications of the ACM*, August 1963, vol 6, no 8, p 430–432.

p. 132 "It appears that many programmers of large scale computers today"

Wu, Le-Chun, et al., "A New Framework for Debugging Globally Optimized Code," *ACM SIGPLAN*, 1999, p 181–191.

p. 132 "Debugging ... as labor-intensive and painful as it was five decades ago"

Zeller, Andreas, "Automated Debugging: Are We Close," *Computer*, November 2001, p 26–31.

Because We Were Different

p. 135 "A virus has been detected on media-lab"

p. 136 "The media was uniformly disappointed that the virus did nothing even remotely visual"

Quoted in Rochlis, Jon and Eichin, Mark, "With Microscope and Tweezers: The Worm from MIT's Perspective," *Communications of the ACM*, June 1989, p 689–698.

p. 137 "bored graduate student"

Philip Pomes quoted in Hilts, Philip, " 'Virus' Hits Vast Computer Network," *Washington Post*, November 4, 1988, p A1.

p. 137 "all gasped"

Quoted in Rochlis and Eichin, *op. cit.*

p. 137 "almost exclusively by peer pressure"

John Kelso quoted in Gellman, Barton, "The Computer Heard 'Round the Nation'," *Washington Post*, November 20, 1988, p A1.

p. 137 "I don't know of too many who want to see this kid rot away"

Burgess, John, "Hacker's Case May Shape Computer Security Law," *Washington Post*, January 9, 1990, p A4.

p. 137 "He was playing with fire"

Burgess, John, "No Jail Time Imposed in Hacker Case," *Washington Post*, May 5, 1990, p A1.

p. 137 "Industry was counting on a tough sentence for Morris"
Dreier, David, and Herger, Wally "No Harmless Hacker He," *Washington Post*, May 19, 1990, p A23.

p. 138 "The types of machines and operating systems"
Carr, C. Stephen, Crocker, Stephen, and Cerf, Vinton, "Host-Host Communication Protocol in the ARPA network," AFIPS Conference, Spring 1970, p 589–590.

p. 138 "They're either trying to look like a teenager or they are a teenager"
Richard M. Smith quoted in Markoff, John "A Disruptive Virus Invades Computers Around the World," *New York Times*, May 5, 2000, p A1.

p. 139 "de Guzman had shown talent in computer programming at a local computer school"
"Virus Suspect to Be Charged," *New York Times*, June 15, 2000, p C2.

p. 139 "A panel of prosecutors dismissed the charges"
"Computer Virus Charges Sought," *New York Times*, Sept 6, 2000, p C5.

A Winter of Hope and A Spring of Despair

p. 142 "Like a great business corporation"
Robinson, Claude, *Straw Votes*, New York, Columbia University, 1932, p 1.

p. 142 "administration is not to break down of its own size and complexity",
Wallace, Henry and McCamy, James, "Straw Polls and Public Administration," *Public Opinion Quarterly*, 1940, vol 4, no 2, p 221–223.

p. 143 "EMERGENCY!!! BLOODSHEDDING IN BEIJING NOW !!!"
Bo Xiong, *China News Digest*, June 3, 1989.

p. 144 "not affiliated with any political organization"
Interview of D. Tang, June 1993.

p. 144 "Many students seem to be very panic now"
Huang Yuan-geng, *China News Digest*, October 31, 1989.

p. 144 "Some times, there are things we can not post"
Zhao Haiching, *China News Digest*, November 2, 1989.

p. 144 "are good and they know exactly what they are doing"
Alan Simpson, *Congressional Record*, January 25, 1990.

Coming into the Country

p. 148 "Many jobs lost during this global downturn"
Keaton, John, "Layoffs in the Computer Industry," *Computer*, March 1993, vol 13, no 3, p 66–71.

p. 148 "Advances in computer science and technology are vital"

p. 148 "the technological feasibility of allowing commercial information service providers to use the Network and other federally funded research networks."
S272, High Performance Computing Act of 1991.

p. 148 "the technological feasibility of allowing commercial"

p. 148 "Cyberspace remains a frontier region,"
Barlow, John P., "Coming into the Country," *Communications of the ACM*, 1991, vol 34, no 3, p 19–21.

p. 149 "transcontinental railroad was sponsored by the federal government"
Pacfic Railroad Bill of 1862, "AN ACT to aid in the construction of a railroad and telegraph line from the Missouri river to the Pacific ocean, and to secure to the government the use of the same for postal, military, and other purposes."

p. 149 "Everything needed had to be brought into that barren country"
Billington, Ray Allen, *Westward Expansion*, 5th edition, New York, Macmillan, 1982, p 583.

p. 149 "Sovereignty over this new world is not well defined"

p. 149 "well suited to the task of civilizing Cyberspace"
Barlow, *op. cit.*

p. 149 "Advances in computer science and technology are vital"
S272, *op. cit.*

Outposts

p. 152 Holden Caufield
The moderator of this group actually used a different literary pseudonym and asked me to protect his false identity. A few literary references have been adjusted to keep his story consistent.

p. 152 "Do or should the organizations running the networks have policies"
Goodman, Sy, "Inside Risks," *Communications of the ACM*, February 1992, vol 35, no 2, p 174.

p. 152 "It would be a major blow to freedom of speech"
Sosic, Roc, "ACM FORUM," *Communications of the ACM*, March 1992, vol 35, no 3, p 16–17.

p. 155 "12 million bloggers"
Lehmann, Nicholas, "Amateur Hour," *New Yorker*, August 7, 2006.

The Captured Imagination

p. 157 "killer app for multimedia"
Nolan Bushnell interview with Joyce Gemperlein, *San Jose Mercury News*. www.thetech. org/revolutionaries/bushell

p. 157 "Although perhaps of no practical importance"

p. 158 "further experimental and theoretical work"
Shannon, Claude, "Programming a Computer for Playing Chess," Proceedings of the National IRE Convention, March 9, 1949.

p. 158 "power of the stored program idea was so great"

p. 158 "To avoid the admission that the machine could never play chess"
Sprague, Richard, "A Western View of Computer History," *Communications of the ACM*, July 1972, vol 15, no 7, p 686–692.

p. 158 "was not then and is not now part of the mainstream"
Goode, Harry and True, Wendell, "Simulation and Display of Four Inter-Related Vehicular Traffic Intersections," *Proceedings of the ACM*, 1959, p 65-1–65-2.

p. 159 "Any employee who can't see the day when we will have 1,000 planes"
C.R. Smith quoted in Copeland, Duncan et al., "Sabre: The Development of Information-Based Competence and Execution of Information-Based Competition," *IEEE Annals of the History of Computing*, 1995, vol 17, no 3, p 30–56.

p. 159 "beyond the state of the art in the late 1950s"
Reitman, Julian, "How the Hardware and Software World of 1967 Conspired (interacted?) to Produce the First in the Series of Winter Simulation Conferences," Proceedings of the 1992 Winter Simulation Conference.

p. 159 "corresponding to those of cars within the computer model"
Goode and True, *op. cit.*
p. 160 "The computer is a playing field"
Weisenbaum, Joseph, *Computer Power and Human Reason*, New York, Freeman, 1976, p 113.

Shutdown

p. 162 "This technology replaced minicomputers,"
Casey, Chris, *The Hill on the Net*, Boston, AP Professional, 1996, p 15.
p. 163 "quick look at the constituent history"
ibid., p 14.
p. 163 "did not allow for dialing out to any phone number"
ibid., p 18.
p. 163 a policy of requiring all potential correspondents to register
ibid., p 41 and 48.
p. 163 "Thank you for sending an email message to my office"
ibid., p 41 and 48.
p. 163 "had much stronger technical credentials than I did"
ibid., p 15.
p. 163 "Our posted guidelines made it clear that we would not be responding"
ibid., p 23.
p. 163 "soon as it became apparent that my experiment"
ibid., p 25.
p. 163 with the help of a researcher at MIT
ibid., p 33–34.
p. 163 Senate file server that ran the Gopher protocol
ibid., p 62.
p. 164 "7 Senators and 36 Representatives"
p. 164 "You could take a shower while you wait for some of this to come in over a regular line"
Andrews, Edmund, "Mr. Smith Goes to Cyberspace," *New York Times*, January 6, 1995, p A22.
p. 164 the White House had started its own server
Casey, *op. cit.*, p 30, 87.
p. 164 "800,000 employees"
Hershey, Robert D., "As Crisis Looms, Essential Services Are Assessed," *New York Times*, November 11, 1995, p 10.
p. 164 "the standoff in Washington"
Bennet, James, "In Michigan, Some G.O.P. Allies Are Soured by Tactics," *New York Times*, November 16, 1995, p B 13.
p. 164 "Lawmakers in both parties"
Toner, Robin, "Atmosphere in the House Becomes Personal and Mean and Nasty," *New York Times*, November 19, 1995, p 20.
p. 165 "On December 15, they shut the government a second time"
Kosar, Kevin, "Shutdown of the Federal Government: Causes, Effects, and Process," Congressional Research Service Document 98-844, September 20, 2004.
p. 165 "We wanted to help these poor people"
Allen, Mike, "On the Internet: Complaint Central about the Federal Shutdown," *New York Times*, December 31, 1995, p 19.

Force of Nature

p. 170 "Engineering is a scientific profession"

Layton, Edwin, *The Revolt of the Engineers*, Baltimore, MD, Johns Hopkins University Press, 1986, p vii.

p. 170 "What can be automated?"

Denning, Peter, et al., "Computing as a Discipline," *Communications of the ACM*, vol 32, no 1, January 1989, p 9–23.

p. 171 "As a result, in those cases where there is a business school or related department,"

Austing, Richard et al., editors, "Curriculum '78," *Communications of the ACM*, vol 22, no 3, March 1979, p 147–165.

p. 171 "communications, teamwork, self-confidence"

_____, "Computing Curricula 2001," www.acm.org

p. 171 "doubly important that the man of science should mix with the world"

Babbage, Charles, *On the Economy of Machinery and Manufactures*, London, Charles, Knight, 1835, p 458.

Ever Onward! Thanks for Asking!

p. 174 "Tis advertised in Boston"

"Blow ye winds in the morning," in *Best Loved American Folksongs,* Alan Lomax editor, New York, Grossett and Dunlap, 1947.

p. 174 "Ever Onward! Ever Onward!"

IBM Songbook, New York, IBM Corporation, 1958.

p. 175 "We tabulate statistics the new electric way"

"The IBM Workers and Service," Song 75, *IBM Songbook*, New York, IBM Corporation, 1958

p. 175 "We're co-workers in IBM, one big family"

"The IBM Family," Song 67, *IBM Songbook*, New York, IBM Corporation, 1958.

p. 176 "Meet the boss, Meet the wife," "Palo Alto," from Radiohead, *Airbag/How Am I Driving?*, Warner Chapell, 1998.

Emailing from Armenia

p. 178 "second only to the IBM 360/370 series in the number of installed mainframes"

Davis, N.C. and Goodman, S.E., "The Soviet Bloc's Unified System of Computers," *Computing Surveys*, June 1978, vol 10, no 2, p 93–122.

p. 178 "SM series was based on the DEC PDP-11"

Prokhorov, Sergei, "Computers in Russia: Science, Education and Industry," *IEEE Annals of the History of Computing*, summer 1999, vol 21, no 3, p 4–15.

p. 178 "Even computerizing simple accounting can be perceived as a threat"

McHenry, William and Goodman, Seymour, "MIS in Soviet Industrial Enterprises: the Limits of Reform from Above," *Communications of the ACM*, November 1986, vol 29, no 11, p 1034–1043.

p. 179 "The engineers did a heroic deed in designing these computers"

Interview with editorial staff Open Systems Journal in Russia, March 15, 2007.

p. 179 "Essentially nothing from before the early 1990s has survived"

Prokhorov, *op. cit.*; see also McHenry, William and Goodman, Seymour, "The Soviet Computer Industry: A Tale of Two Sectors," *Communications of the ACM*, June 1991, vol 34, no 6, p 25–39.

The Boundaries of Time

p. 184 "which could hardly be attempted"

Goldstein, H.H. and Goldstein, Adele, "The Electronic Numerical Integrator and Computer," *Mathematical Tables and Other Aids to Computation*, 1946, vol 2, no 15, p 97–110.

p. 184 "Each Sage machine had a vacuum tube clock"

Sage Manual, *Theory of Programming for AN/FSQ-7 Combat Direction Central*, IBM, Military Products Division, November 15, 1956, p 35–36.

p. 186 "the problem will still affect everyone, including us"

Smith, Howard, "What's ahead for 2000 A.D.?" *ACM SIGAPL APL Quote Quad*, Conference proceedings on APL 90: for the future APL '90, May 1990, vol 20 issue 4.

p. 186 no more than 5% of all computer centers

"The Millennium Bug," *New York Times*, May 28, 1998, p A28.

p. 186 "Although the price tag for making systems Year 2000 ready"

p. 186 "It seems odd"

"Facts about IBM and the year 2000," IBM Press Release, December 16, 1996.

p. 186 "avoid the countless genocides"

Letter to the Editor, *New York Times*, April 16, 1998, p G10.

p. 186 "should not be used beyond December 1999"

p. 187 "control their own cooling systems properly"

Wald, Matthew, "Warning Issued on Air Traffic Computers," *New York Times*, January 13, 1998, p A16.

p. 187 "many decided that they would be better served by replacing old systems with new"

Wyner, Peter, "Wanted: a fix with finesse for Year 2000 Problem," *New York Times*, April 23, 1998, p G11.

p. 187 "to merge with or buy a company"

Martin, Robert, "Dealing with Dates: Solutions for the Year 2000," *Computer*, March 1997, vol x, no 3, p 44–51.

p. 187 "now has both a baseline and systematic methodology"

Brown, Garland, et al., "Using the Lessons of Y2K to Improve Information Systems Architecture," *Communications of the ACM*, vol 43, no 10, October 2000, p 90–97.

Counting Beans

p. 189 "dropping a bean in a pot"

Gross, Charles, "The Early History of the Ballot in England," *The Ameridcan Historical Review*, April 1898, vol 3, no 3, p 456–463.

p. 190 "One of the first challenges facing the new Congress"

_____, "Updating the Way We Vote," *New York Times*, November 24, 2000, p A46.

p. 190 "Stop using punched cards"
Alvarez, Michael, et al., "Residual Votes Attributable to Technology," The Caltech/MIT
Voting Technology Project, Version 2, March 30, 2001.

p. 190 "new claims of voting irregularities and an official challenge to the result"
Holt, Rush, "Legal Issues, Policy Issues, and the Future of Democracy," *The Bridge*,
Summer 2007, vol 36, no 2, p 24–27.

p. 190 "A considerable amount of technical investigation has been done"
Jefferson, David, "What Happened Sarasota County?" *The Bridge*, Summer 2007, vol 36,
no 2, p 17–23.

p. 190 "often conflicting requirements of our democracy"
Epstein, Jeremy, "Electronic Voting," *Computer*, August 2007, vol 40, no 8, p 92–95.

p. 191 "New Yorkers tried to limit the influence of Tammany Hall"
Dana, Richard, "The Practical Working of the Australian System of Voting in Massachusetts,"
Annals of the American Academy of Political and Social Science, May 1892, vol 2,
p 1–18.

p. 191 "the Australian ballot"

p. 191 "four features that distinguished it from the balloting systems of the time"
Bernheim, Abram, "The Ballot in New York," *Political Science Quarterly*, March 1889,
vol 4, no 1, p 130–152.

p. 191 "Bribery is very greatly diminished, almost altogether ceasing,"
Dana, *op. cit.*

p. 191 "Oh, we're on to the new law!"
_____, "The Ring Boast Loudly," *New York Times*, October 19, 1890, p 13.

p. 192 "The Australian system is spreading over the country like a wave"
John Wigmore quoted in _____, "Secret Ballot Systems," *New York Times*, February
4, 1889, p 8.

p. 192 "The fittings in Boston cost $35 for each precinct"
Dana, *op. cit.*

p. 192 "My present invention"
Myers, Jacob, Patent No 415,549, "Voting Machine," 19 November, 1889.

p. 192 "is great economy in the use of voting machines"
A.C. Richardson quoted in _____, "Notes on Municipal Government," *Annals of
the American Academy of Political and Social Science*, vol 15, January 1900,
p 118–130.

p. 193 "It is generally not possible to exactly duplicate a count"

p. 193 "which the correctness of the reported results may be verified"
Saltman, Roy, "Accuracy, Integrity, and Security in Computerized Vote-Tallying,"
Washington, D.C., National Bureau of Standards (now National Institute for Standards
and Technology, NBS Special Publication 500-158, 1988.

p. 193 "often conflicting requirements of our democracy"
Epstein, Jeremy, "Electronic Voting," *Computer*, August 2007, vol 40, no 8, p 92–95.

The Eyes of the World

p. 196 "it calls the entire field of computer security into question"
Peisert, Sean and Bishop, Matt, "I am a scientist, not a philosopher!" *IEEE Security and
Privacy*, July August 2007, p 48–51.

p. 198 "The subject of Estonia"
p. 198 "Some experts had noted that the attack might have been arranged for as little as US $100,000."
  Lesk, Michael, "The New Front Line," *IEEE Security and Privacy*, July/August 2007, p 76–79.

The Lay of the Land

p. 200 "the creation of environments"
  Satyanarayanan, Mahadev, "A Catalyst for Mobile and Ubiquitous Computing," *IEEE Pervasive*, January 2002, vol 1, no 1, p 2–4.
p. 200 "the U.S. Air Force used several elements of pervasive computing in its Sage system"
  Edwards, Paul, *The Close World*, Cambridge, MIT Press, 1999.
p. 200 "freight tracking system of Herman Hollerith"
  Kistermann, Fritz, "The Invention and Development of the Hollerith Punched Card," *IEEE Annals of the History of Computing*, 1991, vol 13, no 3, p 245–259.
p. 200 "The most profound technologies are those that disappear"
p. 200 "the computer screen into a demanding focus of attention"
p. 200 "we are freed to use them without thinking"
  Weiser, Mark, "The Computer for the 21st Century," *Scientific American*, September, 1991, p 94–104.
p. 201 "By building pervasive computing into the [eldercare] environment"
  Stanford, Vince, "Using Pervasive Computing to Deliver Elder Care," *IEEE Pervasive*, 2002, vol 1, no 1, p 10–13; Consolvo, Sunny, et al., "Technology for Care Networks of Elders," *IEEE Pervasive*, 2004, vol 2, no 2, p 22–29.

Circle of Light

p. 204 "Dance me to the end of love"
  Cohen, Leonard, "Dance me to the end of love."

Beyond the Horizon

p. 207 "These fears were realized"
  Wolcott, Peter and Dorojevets, Mikhail, "The Institute of Precision Mechanics and Computer Technology and the El'brus Family of High-Speed Computers," *IEEE Annals of the History of Computing*, 1998, vol 20, no 1, p 4–14.

Indicator Lamps

p. 210 "one microprocessor for each person on earth"
  _____, "Embeded Microprocessors," *Computerworld*, August 28, 2000.

Index

Too Soon to Tell: Essays for the End of the Computer Revolution, by David Alan Grier
Copyright © 2009 IEEE Computer Society